GRAHAM BARNETT

GRAHAM BARNETT

A DANGEROUS MAN

James L. Coffey
Russell M. Drake
John T. Barnett

Denton, Texas

10 9 8 7 6 5 4 3 2 1

Permissions:
University of North Texas Press
1155 Union Circle #311336
Denton, TX 76203-5017

The paper used in this book meets the minimum requirements of the
American National Standard for Permanence of Paper for Printed Library
Materials, z39.48.1984. Binding materials have been chosen for durability.

Library of Congress Cataloging-in-Publication Data

Names: Coffey, James L., author. | Drake, Russell M., 1926- author. |
Barnett, John T., 1953- author.
Title: Graham Barnett : a dangerous man / James L. Coffey, Russell M. Drake,
John T. Barnett.
Description: Denton, TX : University of North Texas Press, [2017] |

Includes bibliographical references.
Identifiers: LCCN 2016056836 | ISBN 9781574416671 (cloth : alk. paper)
Subjects: LCSH: Barnett, Graham, 1890-1931. | Frontier and pioneer
life--Texas--Big Bend Region. | Gunfighters--Texas--Big Bend
Region--Biography. | Cowboys--Texas--Big Bend Region--Biography. |
Ranchers--Texas--Big Bend Region--Biography. | Big Bend Region
(Tex.)--Biography.
Classification: LCC F392.B54 C59 2017 | DDC 976.4/9306092 [B] --dc23

LC record available at https://lccn.loc.gov/2016056836

The electronic edition of this book was made possible
by the support of the Vick Family Foundation.

TABLE OF CONTENTS

List of Illustrations vii

Introduction ix

Overview: "...it was him or me" 1

Chapter 1: "He shot dove...with a rifle" 13

Chapter 2: "a Fair Man but he expected my brothers and me to
live by his strict rules" 23

Chapter 3: "When I put my hand in my pocket, he knew it was all
over" 43

Chapter 4: "I was shot all to pieces" 67

Chapter 5: "I knew Graham was in some kind of trouble" 81

Chapter 6: "To faithfully and impartially discharge and perform
all the duties incumbent on me as an officer in the
Ranger force" 89

Chapter 7: "Wild West—Wont do" 121

Chapter 8: "Come on in, you're as welcome as a corpse" 145

Chapter 9: "No, he isn't going to kill me. He hasn't nerve
enough" 177

Chapter 10: "I want you to send him a telegram and tell him
that I am the biggest damn liar...in the state of
Texas" 189

Chapter 11: "as frequently occurs, jealousy and enmity between
rival gangs developed" 205

Chapter 12: "He would kill you in a holy second" 225

Chapter 13: "I wasn't surprised when they told me"................... 245

Chapter 14: "It was all too true"... 273

Post Script: "Death steals everything except our stories"............. 291

Acknowledgments... 297

Endnotes... 301

Bibliography... 355

Index... 363

LIST OF ILLUSTRATIONS

Illustration 1: Taken somewhere in Mexico—Graham Barnett on left, and Pecos rancher Charlie Oates on right xiv

Illustration 2: Graham Barnett's West Texas xv

Illustration 3: Chicora Caroline Graham, circa 1884 15

Illustration 4: Graham and his brother, Dewitt "Boog" Barnett, circa 1890 16

Illustration 5: Graham Barnett, circa 1906 22

Illustration 6: Dodd Store Langtry, Texas. Site of the fight with Bill Ike Babb 65

Illustration 7: Annie Laura, Maude Carolyn, Graham Barnett, circa 1917 88

Illustration 8: Rangers of the Big Bend 109

Illustration 9: Zoom of Graham. Note the early Colt automatic pistol on his left side 110

Illustration 10: Annie and Graham on left, unknown location, and others on right, circa 1925 203

Illustration 11: Rock House in Alpine where Ann and Jerry were born 244

Illustration 12: Graham guiding a hunt, November 1931 248

Illustration 13: The courthouse and jail in Rankin, Texas, circa
1930 256

Illustration 14: Yoacham Filling Station, Rankin, Texas, circa
1930 264

Illustration 15: Elm Grove Cemetery in Alpine. Grave sites of
Graham and Boog Barnett 272

Illustration 16: WPA Seamstress Group, San Diego, 1933. Annie
Barnett, fifth from right, seated front row 285

Illustration 17: Bud (Joe Graham Barnett Jr.) on left, Bill on the
right, in San Diego, circa 1957 286

Illustration 18: Left to right: Maude, Bill, Jerry, and Ann after
Bud's funeral, circa1993 289

Illustration 19: Bill Barnett holding the machine gun that killed
his father 295

INTRODUCTION

In the 1920s and 30s, a time and place when old legends were being forgotten and new ones were being created, Graham Barnett, a cowboy and hired gunman, became a near mythic character as a result of the life that he led. He was admired by people who knew him, and many who did not. At the same time, he was feared because of his reputation as a killer and a man with an explosive temper made worse when he drank, and he drank whenever he chose to. He stood by his friends, even as that number dwindled, and he sought out his enemies wherever they were. He epitomized the description: no greater friend, no worst enemy.

The Texans of that period (and maybe later) seemed drawn to people who bent the rules of society. Every family seemed to have at least one outlaw and that outlaw might be disapproved of at the family reunion, but he or she was admired in private by many of the same people who disapproved in public. In the West Texas of the 1920s, there were a number of men who fit that model. Graham Barnett was one.

Orland Sims, a West Texas sheriff and judge, contended that Graham had the "sneaking admiration and respect of so many of our 'good people' for the criminal and the open hero worship of the gun-slinger..."[1] This admiration was well placed because at one time or another Graham had fit into both categories. He was a legendary character for many people, including some who still remember him with affection, and some who refuse to talk about him at all. In a world that was changing at a brisk pace, Graham Barnett clung to the frontier standards of a previous generation even as he watched those standards change.

During the first thirty years of the twentieth century, Texas reeled under the impact of several economic and social waves: the Mexican Revolution, Prohibition, the oil boom, and the Depression. During this time, the state moved from being an isolated backwater to becoming a critical player on the world stage. Surviving in this changing world meant that many of the old traditions and behaviors had to change. One of these was the acceptance of the frontier mentality and a reliance on a simplified method of problem solving. The idea that problems could be dealt with the way grandpa had, with buckshot and the justification of "he just needed killing," were giving way to different ideas brought by different people. The changes brought about by the impact of the new century caused the frontier mentality to slowly lose favor, and while still present it did not drive society the way that it had. But during that time the outlaw, the risk taker, remained a formidable figure in the collective mind.

Graham Barnett was a risk taker in a new world that seemed dominated by risk. He was a rancher and that vocation alone meant that a man was willing to take risks. The rancher was dependent on the economics of a market that was shaped hundreds of miles away, the weather, and the vagaries of disease and theft. When he wasn't ranching, Graham was involved on both sides of law enforcement. Early in his career he served as a stock detective for his uncle, enforcing an anti-rustling policy at the beginning of the Mexican Revolution. In the Big Bend he argued over grazing and access to water with other ranchers, and eventually killed one in an outgrowth of that struggle. That incident led to a lifelong vendetta with the dead man's family who were known as people who didn't forgive and didn't forget. He chased bootleggers as a deputy sheriff, and then became a bootlegger when he was no longer a lawman. There were indications that he continued to conduct raids on gamblers and bootleggers when he was no longer in law enforcement, taking a cut of their profits. He carried a huge reputation for violence, and he didn't do much to deny the stories told about him. That reputation served as a buffer between Graham and many of the beer joint brawlers who might want to take him on. No one wanted to mess with a man who had done some of the things Graham was supposed to have done. Oddly enough, the stories that protected him increased the risk that someone, someday, might want to see if he was really as tough as the legends seemed to say. His friend James Weatherby told him, "Graham, someday a sixteen-year-old kid is going to shoot you with a shotgun,"[2] and Graham would laugh at the idea that anyone could take him down.

His reputation was based on both his ability and his readiness to fight. The people who observed either of those activities swore that he was a master with weapons, and the truth was he was frighteningly good. He practiced and demonstrated his speed and accuracy with both the Colt Single Action Army revolver and the later Colt 1911 Automatic. His abilities seemed almost superhuman, and became more so with the retelling of informal plinking sessions, hunting adventures, and real and imagined shootings. He seemed almost too good to be beaten by anyone, and when he was killed in 1931, it happened because of his pride and the fact that he had underestimated his opponent.

He became a legend because for many people in West Texas, he was what they imagined that they were: a tough man with an explosive temper, competent with weapons, and someone who did not back down from a fight. The people were not all like that, but they wanted to think they were.

A note about writing this book: I became interested in Graham Barnett in 1983 when I read a series of columns by Rick Smith in the *San Angelo Standard Times*. Over the next several years, I continued to run across small bits of information about Graham, which I squirreled away with the idea of eventually writing something. Finally, I contacted John Barnett of San Diego, Graham's grandson, and we put together a short piece, which was published by Sul Ross University in their *Journal of the Big Bend*.[3] I thought we had said all there was to say about Graham when John was contacted by Russell Drake.

Russell had a lifelong interest in Graham, and had amassed a huge collection of data, including interviews and letters with many of the people, now deceased, who knew Graham. He had begun to interview people in the early 1950s and continued that process up into the 1990s. His material enhanced what we had written, and then went far beyond anything John or I had. He had three critical pieces of information that were available nowhere else. One was a long letter from Jeff Graham, Graham's cousin, describing how Graham and his brother grew up with their uncle Joe Graham. The second was a twelve-page document from Brian Montague, one of the lawyers who had worked with Graham over the years. Brian served both as a counselor for Graham and someone who knew the man and the legend. These documents provided personal insight concerning Graham that had not previously been published. The last piece of information was a series of letters and taped interviews with Tony Hess, one of two men who had accompanied Graham on his last trip to Rankin, Texas, in 1931. Hess was in the street within a few feet of Graham when he was killed and was perhaps the last living eyewitness to the shooting. Tony Hess provided what he said was the real reason that Graham took off on the Rankin trip, and what those last three days were like. Russell provided all of this material and over several years, this book was put together. Without Russell's research, and John's pictures and support, the story still would not have been told.

There are some other people whose expertise and input were critical to the writing of this book. Ron Chrisman, director of the University of North Texas Press, was supportive of the project throughout a number of ups and downs in its development. Anita Gregg read and reread and corrected grammar until I am sure she thought she was back in the classroom. Barbara McSpadden and Donna Bell of Rankin put up with phone calls and provided access to photographs. Celia Hooker of the Rankin Library likewise provided a necessary photo as well as assistance with locations. Suzanne Campbell and Shannon Sturm, both of Angelo State University's West Texas Collection, provided feedback, technical assistance, and sympathy during the lengthy period of development. Amelia Mueller, assistant editor at the University of North Texas Press, edited, asked questions, and improved the manuscript considerably. Finally, my wife, Carla, listened and provided input based on her lifetime spent in West Texas and on the border. My sons Joshua and Ethan both put up with me telling the stories over and over again, and for that I am grateful.

----------------JC

Illustration 1. Taken somewhere in Mexico—Graham Barnett on left, and Pecos rancher Charlie Oates on right.

(Courtesy Russell M. Drake)

Barnett had been hired to protect Oates while he traded livestock in war-torn Mexico in 1914. A holstered Colt .45 automatic pistol rests on the toe of Barnett's boot. The .45 was his weapon of choice, which he preferred to stuff at his belt line on his left side.

Illustration 2. Graham Barnett's West Texas

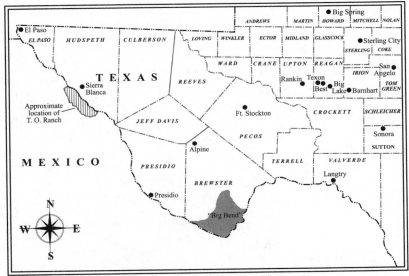

Graham Barnett's West Texas

(Courtesy James L Coffey)
Map by Alex Mendoza

GRAHAM BARNETT

OVERVIEW

"...IT WAS HIM OR ME"

GRAHAM BARNETT 1890-1931[1]

The headlines that topped the front page of the *San Angelo Standard* on the afternoon of December 7, 1931, said it all: "Sheriff slays Graham Barnett with machine gun."[2] It was unusual that the man who was killed was identified by name and the killer identified only as "Sheriff." People knew who Graham Barnett was, or thought they did. If they didn't know him personally, they knew him by reputation. In a part of Texas known for colorful characters, Graham Barnett held near celebrity status. For some of the people who knew him, that status was based on his law enforcement career. Others would remember him for some of his more shadowy activities: man hunter, stock detective, bootlegger, and body guard. He was a legend and now he was dead.

The headline added to the unreality of it all: he was killed with a "machine gun." Thompson submachine guns had captured the imagination of the public because of their appearances in movies and radio broadcasts. Now this mythic weapon had found its way into West Texas. The Thompson was special, but then it had to be something special to bring down a legend. Nothing ordinary would have worked. No one could have stood up against him in a pistol fight; everyone knew that.

When the surprised readers dove into the article, they found that the details of the death of a legend, killed by a fellow officer in a shootout, sounded like something they would have seen in a Friday night movie.

The article declared that he was "the most dangerous man with a gun in Texas."[3] That statement put him in pretty rarefied company because there were a number of men who were known to be impressive in their use of a gun. *Pistoleros* such as Tom Threepersons, Captain Will Wright, Charles Askins, and Jess Sweeten, while hardly remembered today, were men who were feared and respected because of their abilities. Hyperbole aside, the murder of Graham Barnett put the finishing touches on the short and violent life of a man who was remembered by some with fear and others with admiration. His friends remembered shootings, fistfights, and monumental drinking bouts that characterized his life. His enemies remembered the same events, but from a slightly different perspective. Either way, Graham Barnett had lived a life a little more intense and colorful than that of the people around him. Graham Barnett was a legend.

As with all good legends, the stories were based on facts, but as the stories were retold Graham moved from reality into the world of mythology. Men swore they had seen him practice his quick draw, and it was so fast that one second his hand was empty, the next the gun was there. He seemed to be without fear; he threatened Texas Rangers and backed down mobs. This reputation seemed to get away from him at times. Once when he was working a day job in an oil field, he listened as the roustabouts told a story about a recent fracas in which he was supposed to have been thrown through a plate glass window. Graham just listened. His cousin Otto asked him later why he didn't try to correct the story. Graham smiled and said, "I just wanted to catch up on what I had been doing."[4] He may have encouraged the stories, after all a big reputation could only help a man in the business of solving problems for others, especially when that problem solving involved violence.

The stories sounded like something that had come out of the old Texas frontier days. One of the most often heard claims was that no one knew exactly how many men Graham had killed. With each retelling of the stories, the numbers increased. From the time he was an unofficial stock detective for his uncle, Joe M. Graham, to the time he spent with the Texas Rangers, to his time as a deputy sheriff and private investigator, one thing people agreed on was that the number of people who had departed this life as a result of gun play with Graham Barnett was huge. Everyone was wrong. It was a case of a reputation going wild. The man who lived the reputation was carried on by it like a passenger on a runaway train. There is no doubt that he did kill a number of men, but nothing like the numbers mentioned in the tales. In both story and fact, he was able to survive because he was uncannily skillful with both pistol and rifle. He had recognized this talent early and practiced shooting skills constantly. He claimed to have worn the rifling out of the barrels of pistols because of his practice, and he had a trunk full of guns that allowed him to pick the right one for each occasion. Witnesses, who ranged from policemen to professors at Sul Ross University, told how he had killed deer at incredible distances with a .30-'06 and picked doves out of the air with a .45 automatic.[5]

Stories claimed that he was a successful but troubled law officer who had a tendency to slip over the line between law enforcer and law breaker and could not be completely trusted by his brother officers. When he died, newspapers claimed that sheriffs all over West Texas slept easier that night.[6] His trustworthiness was a major factor for many officers because Graham tended to drink and when he did, it was difficult to predict what he would do. When he drank, old memories and old insults came back to gnaw at him. He remembered other men's shortcomings and previous slights. When he was working up into one of his rages, he made plans to pay them back for what they had done or what he thought they had done. When he was this furious, he promised that someone would die. His threats were enough that many believed him and would have nothing to do with him until he calmed down or sobered up. Many believed it was this tendency to threaten people and to mean it that caused on old friend, Bill Fowler, to become one of the few men who faced him in the street in a shootout that would have fit into a James Cagney-Humphrey Bogart film. Bill Fowler described the shooting with, "I had to do it, it was him or me."[7] It was the same explanation and defense that Graham had used in two murder trials. It was something people could identify with and something most had grown up hearing. It was the "him or me" thinking that put a bunch of volunteers at the Alamo. "Him or me" justified the long and bloody wars against the Comanche. It was "him or me" that described the desperate struggle of farmers and ranchers who wrestled daily against the combined elements of drought, blizzard, and greedy bankers. "Him or me" described the attitude that had brought people to Texas and had allowed only the strong to stay. It was the code by which the old line Texan fought his wars.

Graham Barnett became a legend because he lived a life that was recognizable by people based on a code from the previous century. His world was still dominated by the frontier, and frontier mentality was very much in evidence during the first half of the new twentieth century. Understanding the impact of that code on the social history of the new decade helps to understand Graham Barnett.

This frontier mentality spawned a code of behavior based on conflict and expectations of conflict. That world was much different than the modern one, and it centered on some hard-held core beliefs about what a man's role was, how it was influenced by his race, and an expectation of how other people ought to behave. While few people would have been able to sit down and write out a code of conduct based on the frontier, most of them would be able to recognize that code in action when they saw it. A man was defined by how well he lived his life based on this unwritten code. If anything, it was an ideal that many people tried to live up to. Some did, many did not.

Part of the code was based on the concept that eventually a man would have to deal with some kind of violence. People on the Texas frontier spent much of their lives expecting they would encounter some kind of violence. From Indians raiding the countryside, or Mexicans fighting to return the land to their home country, or outlaw Anglos who were as predatory as any of the other groups, violence was expected. Whether a settler actually encountered these forces, or only thought that they might, the threat caused people to develop some strong ideas about how life was going to have to be conducted.

In order to survive on the frontier, a man had to be prepared to deal individually with problems. In the old days, men settled their own accounts and in rural Texas that was still expected. If it became necessary, a man had to be able to defend, by hand or weapon, himself, his property, and those people for whom he was responsible. Men on the frontier had to be prepared to address difficulties and to deal with them personally.

In order to do this, a man had to be armed, and be prepared to use that weapon at any time and any place. An armed man was a free man; an unarmed man was a slave. A man protected his own property, and if he could not protect what was his, maybe he should not have it.

Formal law enforcement existed to support the man's role in society. On the frontier the law was spotty and not always to be trusted to come up with the correct solutions to social problems. Law enforcement bodies existed to maintain the status quo, to support the market place, to reduce social disruptions, and to maintain order. The role of law enforcement from the frontier viewpoint was plain: it should be seen and not heard. Lawmen were expected to catch the bad people, and leave alone the good ones, who might occasionally break a small law here or there. The lawman learned to accommodate the people he served, providing them with the kind of law they wanted, not always what the law required.

At the state level, the law was provided by the Texas Rangers, the only state law enforcement body with arrest authority across the entire state. The Texas Rangers had existed as a largely volunteer ranging force before the Civil War, afterwards Texas had flirted with a State Police force but that idea was rejected along with others of the Reconstructionist era. After Reconstruction the Texas Rangers returned to service, but they were a miniscule force controlled by the governor. They were subject to his political whims as well as the financial restraints of the legislature. The Rangers were respected for the most part, but they were made up of people who might not be from the geographic area in which they served. Because of this, they could not always be trusted; they were "not from here." The law that was most trusted was the law that was closest to the people, and that would have been the county sheriff.

The sheriff was the highest elected official in a county, and when the sheriff's office was combined with that of the tax assessor collector, he became especially important. Because the county sheriff was an elected official, the degree to which he dealt with crime was influenced, on occasion, by reelection concerns. The successful sheriff was the man who could handle people easily and still deal with problems effectively. People expected the sheriff might fire off a shot on occasion, or fight a man on the weekend, but they also expected that he would make adjustments from time to time for the people he served. Some of this thinking didn't end with the beginning of the twentieth century. During the 1950s and 60s, one West Texas sheriff known to the author would call some of the people he had warrants for. The message was always the same, "I've got some paper on you, why don't you come on in and let's get this mess straightened out. I know you're busy."[8] It should be noted that he didn't use this technique on everyone. There were an ample number of people that he had to go and see concerning problems they had created for themselves and others.

At the turn of the century some of these problems existed because there was a relaxed view of how a man should spend what little spare time he had. Two common recreational activities, drinking and gambling, caused a good many of the problems that were found on the frontier, and those activities and their results moved forward with the calendar into the twentieth century. Both activities could have been considered unofficial state sports. Every town had access to liquor and games of chance, whether legal or not, until the political progressives banned them during the reform movements of the 1890s through 1920s. The new laws were touted as common sense reforms that would improve society, protect women and children, and make men better men.

The results were far from what was hoped for and promised. Prohibition and the crackdown on gambling created problems that were unimagined by the political reformers of the time. The law ignored the subtle ways the frontier society had to deal with such issues. The frontier had rules in place that governed how the people viewed drinking and gambling. A man was expected to be able to drink and control his behavior. If he gambled, he was expected to pay his debts. That was part of the definition of being a man. If a man could not take care of his business, he had no business drinking and gambling. The social punishment ranged from loss of social status to shunning. Some people were just too sorry to drink with. There was also financial punishment. If a man lost his ranch because he could not control his behavior, perhaps it was time to start again somewhere else.

If Texas had a relaxed attitude toward vice, its attitudes toward minorities certainly were not. In the nineteenth century, the concept of Manifest Destiny had declared that it was God's will for the United States to control most of the North American continent. The philosophy that the white race was predisposed to conquer and control other races had come to Texas with the settlers from the expanding United States. The idea that minorities were not equal to the Anglo settlers was not held by everyone, but the effects of that attitude were felt by everyone. The prejudices that the Anglo settler brought applied not just to different races but also to different economic classes and religions. Texas in the 1890s was a world that seemed made for the Anglo Protestant who had money or was on his way up the economic ladder. It was a white man's world and the closer a person of color came to being white, the better off they were. The judgments made on race were not limited solely to the Texans.

In Mexico and the Texas border country, there was a differentiation made between Mexican and Spanish origins to indicate the degree of

European blood and, therefore, acceptance. The lighter the skin, the more European blood was present and, therefore, the more acceptability.

In Mexico, specific terminology was developed to describe the genetic makeup of the inhabitants. *Mestizo* (one Spanish parent and one Indian parent) and *criollo* (native born in the New World), as well as twelve to fifteen other terms, described the people of Spanish Mexico. Colorful charts were developed to illustrate what the families looked like to make identification easier. This *sistema de casta* that had existed in Mexico for centuries was generally done away with after 1830, but centuries of tradition were hard to shed and blood still mattered.

When the *haciendado* system of huge ranches developed, the concept of peonage developed with it. People born onto a ranch tended to stay there for the rest of their lives. A system of involuntary servitude developed and continued for centuries. The peon became a class similar to the Russian serf, a person tied to the land with little hope of change. In some cases the peon moved to Texas and found life similar in some ways and better in others. His pay might be higher, and on some ranches he was treated better. Despite this step up economically, Mexicans were still a second-class group because of the jobs they held, the conditions they lived in, and the religion that they supported. Mexicans were viewed in the border country as a semi-skilled group of people who could provide some services to the Anglos, but people who would never attain equality because they were not white. The supremacy of the white race was expected, and the law came perilously close to guaranteeing that supremacy. It made for some unusual social arrangements. Anglos and Hispanics might work closely together at jobs on the ranch, but class kept them separated dramatically. That separation was illustrated most easily in the numerous "Little Mexico's," or Mexican barrios, that grew up as separate communities on the outskirts of many West Texas towns. They had their own schools, grocery stores, and, sometimes, general stores and cafes, but they remained a place for Mexicans, not Anglos, just as the town remained a place for Anglos.

Attitudes toward women were as complicated as those toward minorities. On the frontier, the family was the smallest basic unit of civilization, and that unit centered on the woman. She filled the mother role, and most mothers remained an influential figure in the lives of their children. The woman's success, in most cases, was linked to the success of her family.

They were loved, respected, protected, and elevated to as high a standard as the man's status, economy, and attitude would allow. In most financial and economic situations, the times would not allow her to be the equal of her husband. There were things he could do that she could not, among them voting and serving on a jury. Despite the inequities, women on the frontier were the cornerstone of the society. The frontier mentality demanded that a man take care of his wife and to protect and support his family. Without family, there were no hands to help out on the place, and no future for a man's name. Family extended beyond husband, wife, and children: it included sisters and brothers and any of the other extended family members who lived close enough to be expected to help with problems. The clan or tribe concept continued well into the twentieth century in parts of Texas and contributed to the power structures in many counties. For people on the frontier, there was no stronger tie than that of family, and when that tie was broken, the person who broke it was condemned.

On the frontier, women played as critical a role as situations required them to play. They might not vote, but they maintained a strong influence over the family and society. When there was a crisis, it was not unusual for a woman on the frontier to take on a different role than women in the cities. To assure that the family survived a crisis, a woman might work cattle, fill in around a ranch or farm, and do whatever she needed to protect assets and her family.[9] When the emergency was over, it was expected that she would return to her woman's duties.

Mothers were the focus of the family, but for many men on the frontier, prostitutes were frequently the other women in their lives. When the frontier closed, many of those attitudes didn't change. For cowboys, oilfield workers, and railroad men, the prostitute provided the only connection to women outside of the family. She became a transient partner in what was becoming a transient society. The workers followed the money, and the hookers followed the dollars. Oddly enough, while "decent" women were put on pedestals, prostitutes became an icon for many of the men on the frontier. While some of the prostitutes lived short and unhappy lives, others saved their money and moved up and out of the business. Some became fast friends with their clients, and others formed long lasting business and social connections.[10] Stories are told of prostitutes who married out of some of the parlor houses and eased into a town's society as easily as they moved across a dance floor. Those lucky few became stalwart members of the society, and many people forgot their original employment. Many forgot, but not all. [11]

Finally, swamps could be drained, bridges built, and water wells drilled, but some things could not be changed, and what could not be changed, had to be endured. If people risked greatly, they failed in spectacular fashion some of the time and they had to learn to live with failure. Men made mistakes, they sold the cattle at the wrong time, their children died in accidents, or wives ran off with the local preacher. The failures had to be lived with. The way people dealt with both success and failure was the mark of a man or a woman. Failure and tragedy were going to be found in everyone's lives, but how a person dealt with it established their character. A man's character was defined as much by how he dealt with failure, as how he dealt with success.

The world of Graham Barnett was colored by this social code, which explained, in part, some of his behavior. The attitudes of the frontier clashed in the new world he found himself in. Texas faced a number of major challenges in the first thirty years of the new century: the Mexican Revolution, the discovery of oil, the changes brought about by prohibition, the Depression, and economics. Life was not as simple as it had been, and suddenly things did not always fit as easily into the model as they had before.

Life was changing. Oil brought new wealth to poor families, and they began to expect change. Women worked outside of the home and were not looked down on. Mexicans wanted to vote, to go to school like everyone else, and to assume their role in society. How people dealt with violence was changing; the time when you could kill people who had created problems for you had passed. Graham had become a legend because he continued to live the old style life valued by Texans, but he was doing it in a new era. Like many legends he found that admiration is thin, and celebrity is dependent on continued activity. Since his reputation centered on violent behavior, people expected him to continue to carry on as he always had. Many people still accepted him as he always was, the rough talking, sometimes mean, fast gun from the border country. For other people, that Graham Barnett was an embarrassment now. He didn't fit in anymore. Times were changing, and he was "country come to town" and town didn't value all the tough old timers any more. At some point, he had quit making history and started watching it happen around him.

Everyone knew him, or thought they did. Most of them only knew the fiction about him. He was the man with the gun; the man you couldn't afford to make mad. He was a man with a bounty on his head, and he had spent nearly half his life watching for the people who would try to collect it. That made him sort of hard to live with. His reputation as the most dangerous man in Texas provided credibility for his jobs as deputy sheriff, private investigator, and Ranger. It was this reputation that protected him for years. After all, who would want to go up against the most dangerous man in Texas? In the end, that reputation played a huge role in getting him killed on a cold Sunday morning in an obscure West Texas town by a man who had been his friend, but also a man Graham had sworn to kill.

CHAPTER 1

"HE SHOT DOVE...WITH A RIFLE"

1890-1908[1]

Nearly twenty years after Graham's death, a family friend, James Weatherby, was asked if he knew anything about Graham's family. "Graham came from an eye-for-an-eye kind of people," said Weatherby.[2] The Barnetts were survivors of every war fought from the Revolution to the Border Wars of the early 1900s. Barnett's great-great-grandfather, Captain John Files, was a militia leader who led his company, including his sons, against the British at the Battle of Cowpens in 1781. Later that year, Captain Files was captured, and he, along with some other prisoners, were turned over to the Tories and their Indian allies to be tortured and killed. When his sons found him, they were able to identify him only by his teeth. The sons tended to be a little less forgiving of their enemies after that encounter.[3]

The family moved west, each generation pushing the border a little further than the previous one. By the 1830s, they had heard of a land of opportunity called Texas, and in 1837 David Sidney Files had journeyed to the northeast corner of Hill County. Hill County was not on the frontier but was so close that the threat of Comanche raids was still common. David Files built a house in the county and rode with the ranging companies that tried to keep it safe. He homesteaded near a small community called Eureka Valley, and that site became known as Files Valley. The Files had nine children, one of whom, Caroline, had her own adventures.

Caroline's life was typical of one on the Texas frontier. Children married early and families were large because life was short and people needed all the help they could get. She married in 1855 at age 16 to James Smith and had four children with him. She was widowed by the time she was 23. In 1864 she married Joseph E. Graham who had served in the Confederate Army. Joe Graham was captured by federal troops and interned in a prisoner of war camp. He told his family that the only way he survived was because of food smuggled to him by an Indian woman named Chicora. He had promised her that if he had a daughter, he would name her for his benefactor. When their first daughter was born in June of 1866, he kept the promise and named her Chicora Caroline. Each succeeding generation preserved that tradition by ensuring that one daughter inherited the name Chicora. The Grahams had four children before Joseph died in 1874, and Caroline married one more time, this time to a carpenter and farmer named John Lane with whom she had three more children.

John and Caroline moved to a farm owned by the Lane family. They referred to this farm as "The Mountain" and began the task of raising a large family. All of the children were close, but Chicora was especially close to her twin brothers, Joe and Will. She and Joe would remain nearly inseparable for the rest of their lives. Even Chicora's marriage didn't break the bond.

In 1887, Chicora Graham married Frank Barnett and the new couple settled in on their farm. The family must have loved formal names; they named their first born Dewitt Talmadge Barnett, born on August 3, 1888. That got shortened quickly to "Boog," pronounced "Bug."

Illustration 3. Chicora Caroline Graham, circa 1884

(Courtesy John T. Barnett)

Illustration 4. Graham and his brother, Dewitt "Boog" Barnett, circa 1890

(Courtesy John T. Barnett)

Boog Barnett was destined to become a Texas Ranger and a strong supporter of his younger brother, Graham, who was born August 28, 1890. The younger brother was officially named Joseph Graham Barnett after his grandfather, the late Civil War captain. Graham's Uncle Joe, with whom he also shared a name, felt unusually close to his nephew. Joe and his twin brother Will were 18 years old when Graham was born and, despite the difference in their ages, the two shared a strong bond. The family continued to grow after Graham's birth with three girls: Francis Marion, called Frankie, born in 1892; Anna Lee, called Polly, born in 1894; and Sidney, born in 1896. They made a handsome group, but life on a crowded family farm became difficult. While there were enough people to do the work, there were also a large number of people to feed, clothe, and care for.

In 1896 Frank Barnett decided that there must be something else out in the larger world beyond Hill County. His brother was in New Mexico, and Frank saddled up and headed west. There are indications that he intended the family to join him once he got settled, but settling took a long time. He worked as a miner for a while and then moved to his brother's ranch and contacted Chicora. He asked her to join him in New Mexico, and according to some accounts, sent money to pay for the trip. She and the family sat down and talked. The family maintained that New Mexico had a reputation for being wild country, and they worried about "Chic," as she was known to the family, living there. In the end, she decided to remain with the family. That decision had a lasting impact on Graham.

Even though it was Chicora who decided not to make the move, Graham believed that his father had abandoned the family. As he grew older, he told anyone who would listen that he hated his father, and that he would kill him if he ever found him. Graham's cousin, Jeff Graham, remembered years later that he thought the threat was a little emotional: "A young person might say something like that whether he meant it or not."[4] Others were not so sure. The betting odds were that Graham said it and he meant it. Graham saw his father's abandonment as an affront to the entire family and an insult that could only be answered with blood. It was the first of a long list of potential killings the young man would talk about.

With Frank gone, the family struggled with the everyday problems of life on a farm. They constantly pulled up stakes for some kind of better place just a little further west. In 1896 they sold the farm and moved to a place four miles east of Hillsboro. The rest of the family was on the move too.

Joe Graham, Chicora's favorite brother, had begun to work sheep for his uncles as early as 1887. By 1902 he had established himself as a man who had a way with stock and he also had a plan for achieving some success in the world of ranching. Joe Graham was developing a name as a smart cattle buyer, and he did most of it on borrowed money. He was a "commission man." He would take a contract with a beef supplying company to supply so many head of cattle at a particular price or at the market price at the time of the sale. He would borrow money from his family or a bank, and buy the cattle cheap. He could lease a place (or run them on open range), feed the cattle, and then sell them to complete his contract. The key to success in the business was buying cattle cheap, feeding them equally cheap, and selling at the contract price to make money. Part of the time he would simply buy the cattle from a rancher and sell to a supplier at a higher price. He could then pay off the bank and start all over again.[5] Cattle or sheep, it made no difference. He would contract for wool or beef. He partnered with bankers, used their money as much as he could and made a profit for both the bank and himself. His uncle, Frank Files, was president of the Itasca State Bank, and Joe made friends with bank presidents all over Central and West Texas. He seemed to turn a profit with every venture.

To be successful he had to know the cattle market, read trends, understand what was on the horizon internationally, and have friends who would sell or lease to him. It was a business of juggling information and stock. Many men went broke trying to do what Joe Graham did.

One project nearly ended in disaster but did provide him with a new opportunity. He had put a herd on a ranch near San Saba. Without a lot of fanfare the ranch was sold and he was left holding a herd of cattle with no pasture. Charley Crowley ran the Hat Ranch near Ozona, a distance of nearly two hundred miles. With the Hats he found both a pasture and a new job. "I had to move them [cattle] to the Hat Ranch, west of Ozona in Crockett County... I went to work for the Hats and Charlie Crowley was boss."[6] Joe ran his cattle in with the stock on the Hat Ranch. Actually, they were the bank's cattle but that didn't make much difference. Joe Graham dealt with ideas first and then property. "We moved into the house with the Crowleys and another man and his wife that was working there the old Rock House was a good big house so three families lived there for a while."[7]

While Joe lived the life of an itinerant cattle buyer the Barnett family was having their own adventures in farming and travel. Boog recalled: "From the time of Graham's birth 'til 1905 the family was living in Hill and Bosque Counties. We were farming all this time. Graham and I went to school in Hill and Bosque Counties. In 1905 we moved to Coke County, stayed one year and moved to Sterling County."[8]

John Lane had family in Sterling County, about forty-three miles northwest of San Angelo. This last move brought them some kind of stability. The family was looking for an end to the constant moving, and the move to Sterling City seemed to promise that. The moving did have one consolation: it provided unending adventures for Boog and Graham. Sterling City was in the middle of a huge tract of sparsely settled land full of small game up to deer size. Someone found a rifle for the two, likely a .22 rim fire, and Graham quickly excelled with it. In a world where boys were expected to be good shots, Graham exceeded expectations. He got a reputation for being either a great shot or one of the luckiest juvenile hunters in the county. For years Boog proudly told about an early hunting experience: "It was in Bosque County when he [Graham] was eight years old. He shot two dove with a rifle."[9] That story was the first of many that would circulate about Graham's shooting ability. That first rifle created in Graham a fascination for firearms, which continued throughout his life. He was going to be good at something, and shooting might just be it.

When the Lanes moved to Sterling City, they found that the "City" part of the town's name was based on optimism. The town was founded in 1891 and struggled out of the West Texas dust to increase its population to 300 by 1895. The arrival of the railroad in 1910 made a great difference in population and growth. The town spawned a school, several stores, and homes all centered on the railroad. The new Barnett-Lane family fit into the society of Sterling City well. Graham grew up living the kind of life that most of the other kids lived. He joked, played tricks, and was fondly remembered as just another kid. "Graham was a well-behaved, likeable kid," remembered Vern Davis, a friend who grew up to be county sheriff.[10] Maybe "well-behaved" to the future sheriff was different than well-behaved to his family and friends.

When the local school girls decided to beat the Texas heat with a swim in a stock tank, Graham was there. "He liked to tie their shoes and socks together and throw 'em in the tank. He was a tease. He would kid you a lot,"[11] his cousin R. P. Brown remembered. "He was as full of mischief as a young cat. He was full of pranks and liked to fight with his fists."[12] Graham may have been a tease, but the fighting was a little more serious. Neither Graham nor Boog walked away from a fight. Even though Boog was older, he was shorter and thinner than his brother. As boys they developed a talent for backing the other up in fights on the school yard or on the way home. Usually if you saw one of the Barnett boys, the other was close at hand.

For Graham the teasing and kidding would continue for the rest of his life, but education was coming to an end. By 1906 most of the family realized that the boys had all the reading and ciphering they could stand and besides, the family needed money. Since jobs in Sterling County were pretty well limited to ranching, the boys began training for a lifelong career as cowboys. They did day work for anyone who needed help, and they worked for their Uncle Joe. Joe was finding success in the livestock business. He had leased a place in Sterling County, and it became one more stop on a long trail of Graham enterprises that ranged from the Hats Ranch in Ozona, north to Sterling, and then further north to Oklahoma. In Oklahoma his brother, Omar Lane, had secured land that could be used to hold stock or to grow hay. As Joe Graham began to flirt with success, he seemed to draw the entire family along with him. It was an exciting time, and Graham was about to become a bigger part of the whole activity.

Illustration 5. Graham Barnett, circa 1906

(Courtesy John T. Barnett)

Chapter 2

"A Fair Man but he expected my brothers and me to live by his strict rules"

1908-1913

The Graham Barnett legend began with stories told within the family. The first story that established who Graham was dates back to about 1906. Eighteen-year-old Boog and sixteen-year-old Graham drifted north toward the New Mexico line and took jobs with a prominent rancher in the area. The job they took was with a cowman who spent a lot of time out on the ranch with his men. The rancher was a detailed person who knew what he wanted done and exactly how he wanted it to happen. There may have been problems from the beginning with the boss closely managing everything that was done and correcting it with a good cussing. It seems to be a typical experience on a ranch that no one can do a job exactly the way the boss wants it done and he will generously share his views on a hand's incompetence.[1] On this occasion, either the cook got sick or the boss was a little more eccentric than anyone knew because the men rotated the job of cooking for the crew. The job of cook was critical on a ranch. If the cook was good, the hands were happy; if he was bad, people didn't stay with the place. There were apparently a number of different levels of competence with the amateur cooks and they were closely watched.

When it became Boog's turn to cook, he found that they were far enough out on the prairie that there was no firewood, and the cook fire was fueled by an inexhaustible supply of dried cow manure or cow patties. Boog started the fire and began his experience with Dutch oven cooking. Biscuits were on the menu, and the dough was mixed on the tailgate of the chuck wagon, placed in one of the Dutch ovens and covered with a lid. Cow patties are transferred to the top to bake the biscuits. The problem was the fire; cow dung gives off a lot of heat and also a fair amount of ash. When burned patties are disturbed the ash goes off into the air, and everywhere else that the wind will take it. Unfortunately, the wind took a lot of it onto the cooking biscuits when Boog lifted the lid to check them. The cattle boss saw it, walked over, commenting on Boog's lack of ability and cleanliness in general, turned the mess over into the fire and told him to start again. Boog did, but under protest. Later he told his younger brother about the cooking situation and warned Graham that he would face the problem the next day. He also added that the cook kept a pistol in the chuck wagon, and he had been tempted to pull it when the cursing and threats of getting a whipping began.

Graham was no better cook than his brother, but he did have a direct plan for dealing with criticism. The biscuits were made, the fire was started, the lid was lifted, and when the ash found its way into the dough, Graham was ready. The range boss made his comments and dumped the biscuit dough into the fire. One thing Graham had managed to locate along with the flour and salt was the previous cook's pistol. Graham reached up into the cupboard, pulled the old pistol out, and the cursing stopped immediately. No one knew if the pistol was loaded, or if it would work, but the boss wasn't going to press the question. Graham took his silence as an acknowledgement that now the boy was in charge of the man.

Graham cursed the range boss like he heard the boss do previously. In the shocked silence that followed, Graham turned the tables again. He ordered the boss to mix the biscuits and start them cooking. While the boss began cooking, it occurred to Graham that every good act needs an equally good exit and Graham decided that he needed to find the road back to Sterling City pretty quick. He suggested that the boss ride out and bring in the other hands while the biscuits slowly browned. Under the threat of the pistol, the boss drifted out looking for his hands. When he had moved far enough away, Graham and Boog loaded their gear and headed home. Boog always claimed that they did so in a hail of bullets from the range boss, but he was no better a shot than he was a cooking supervisor. Both boys made it back home safely to Sterling City and the family.

The ride back to Sterling was long enough that the boys evaluated what had happened and both were able to identify some lessons learned from it. First, a gun was a useful tool and a man should not be far from one. If you were going to have to defend yourself you needed the method to do so, and the gun tended to provide that method. In this case, the gun had a way of calming a situation down. Graham didn't want a cussing or whipping and the gun kept both from happening. It was lesson he never forgot. He also never forgot that the man who prepared for the fight was going to be the man who walked off from it. Those lessons remained with the brothers for the rest of their lives.

The story of the near gunfight, as narrated by his brother Boog, was the beginning of the Graham Barnett legend. Since he and Boog were the only known witnesses who were telling the story, it went the way they wanted it to. It was their first big adventure in risk taking, and they had emerged from the adventure intact. Graham had faced down a man who had more experience than he, and had come away from the encounter with an understanding that if he intended to survive in this rough world, he had to be a little rougher. The strong language and the reliance on the gun became part of the Barnett persona and it remained with him for the rest of his life.[2]

The family continued to live in Sterling City, but kept close ties with Joe Graham. Joe was expanding his business. He had moved a few miles south from the Hat Ranch, and bought two sections of school land, and leased another section along with a lot in Ozona where he intended to build a house.[3] Before that could happen, the Graham's lived in a tent, and it was there that Chicora helped with the delivery of Joe's son, Billie, in 1905 during a snowstorm. It is likely that by 1908, the family, or at least Boog and Graham, had moved onto the ranch and were working as cowboys for him.

The move to live with Joe Graham, his wife Mollie, and the Graham family, was the single most important move the family would make. While Joe had been important to the Barnett's before, this move solidified his role in the family. If he was not seen as a surrogate father to the Barnett children, he was certainly seen as the patriarch of the clan and a man with influence both in the family and out of it. While making the move might have been seen as a simple job choice, continuing to work there assured the Barnetts a degree of permanence in their lives. With that decision, the Barnetts and the Grahams welded their families together and the two groups, brothers, sisters and cousins, would be joined together in good times and bad until death parted them.

From the time that the Grahams and the Barnetts began to share jobs and futures, Graham Barnett was directly impacted by the character and personality of Joe Graham.[4] Joe was eighteen years older than Graham and was the most significant man in the boy's life. Joe Graham was everything that an unsettled young man might need in a world that hadn't treated him too well. He was a successful, engaging individual who had dreams for the future. In a society that valued power, money, and land, Joe Graham was on his way to acquiring all of them. He became the man who provided jobs, connections, and lawyers for Graham, and in doing so, became one of his fiercest defenders. He welcomed his nephews into his family, and treated them nearly like long lost sons. He also began to provide rules and a character model for the Barnetts.[5]

Brian Montague, a friend and lawyer who handled legal matters for both families, considered Joe Graham one of the "best men I knew."[6] With that kind of reputation, the expectation might have been that Graham Barnett would follow in the footprints of his uncle. Growing up with the Joe Graham family meant a different kind of life than the Barnett boys had lead. That, combined with the fact that they were older than their cousins, meant that Boog and Graham had to relearn some things about life in a family from their new employer and mentor. They might not have been Joe's direct family, but they were expected to behave like it. Boog and Graham had rules now, not suggestions, and the rules covered everything from stock management to saying grace at meals. Joe's son Jeff Graham thought the Barnetts benefitted greatly from the deal but still remembered some resentment. "Working for their Uncle Joe was probably the best arrangement that could be made for the two boys, but it would not be like working for their own father and they may have had some resentment at their lot. [Joe was] a fair man but he expected my brothers and me to live by his strict rules and moral code. Boog and Graham probably found that pretty hard to tolerate as it may be that my father seemed to treat (his sons) Frank and Stanley and Bill differently (better) than he did Boog and Graham."[7] Whether Joe treated Graham and Boog less well would be an issue that could be debated, he took better care of Graham than many people would have expected.

If Joe established strict rules for behavior, he also provided Graham with some ideas about money and life. Joe was successful because he bought and speculated in land, and he knew ranching. He had connections in banking which allowed him to buy cattle and land on credit. He expanded his finances, and, as often as not, sold the stock he was feeding and paid off the bank before anything came due. Graham was witness to this kind of financial management, and although it eventually led to Joe's undoing, the model was a sound one if the market held, rains came on time, and disease didn't thin the herd. Graham bought land and cattle when he could, sold when he had to, and generally attempted to duplicate some of Joe's success.

If he had a goal in life it was to be a rancher, not just a cowboy. There is a difference: a cowboy works for someone, the rancher is the man he works for. Graham wanted to be the man in charge. His entire life seemed to fit into a model of trying to make enough money in order to buy a place big enough that he could be like Joe Graham. The geographic focus for both men centered on the southwestern corner of the state, the vast, open country of the Big Bend, and the mountains and valleys that defined that huge expanse of land. It was wild country, and seemed to be created for men who were willing to risk much in order to accomplish everything. It had the tremendous potential to fulfill dreams and break hearts.

If there was one common characteristic of both men, it was that they were risk-takers: Joe in real estate and ranching, Graham with cards, dice, and the law. It seemed obvious to both men that if they intended to break out of the "just another cowboy" mold, they would have to risk a great deal. Complicating the decision was the understanding that they had to take care of their family at the same time. In a situation such as this, neither could afford to fail. Their lives became a balance of how to test serious financial or legal boundaries and at the same time protect those people who depended on them. It was the nineteenth century jerked into the modern world of 1910.

One thing that Graham apparently learned from watching Joe was that he needed to be prepared for things not to work out as planned, and to have some alternatives to back up the original plan. As Graham got older he began to be troubled by what would happen to the family if something happened to him. Like a good gambler, he hedged some bets. Late in life, he took a strange step for a gunfighter; he took out some life insurance.

Joe continued with his speculating and in 1905 leased land in Val Verde County near Langtry. "I stayed around Langtry with my sheep and goats all that winter and in the spring of 1907 and after shering [sic]

I sold my sheep at a good profit and kept my goats...I kept one hearder [sic] with goats, establish a permant [sic] camp at Rattlesnake Springs and where later I built a house and corrals and moved my family out there in a wild country."[8]

The camp at Rattlesnake Springs was going to be the center of the Graham project in the Langtry area. Joe built a house from railroad crossties that had been condemned by the railroad.

It is not clear if Graham and the rest of the Barnetts moved to Langtry immediately. They probably remained at the ranch near Ozona until 1908. Joe had problems that may have brought them to the border: "My health got bad in the early part of the spring [1908] I could not ride a horse in trot [sic]."[9] It would make sense that if Joe needed more help, the Barnetts could provide it.

When the Graham and Barnett clans moved to the Langtry area, they were moving into a part of the country that was still considered frontier. It was sparsely populated, law enforcement was spotty, medical support was almost nonexistent, and the area was a pistol shot from Mexico, the site of one of the first major revolutions of the twentieth century. Although the revolution didn't formally begin until 1910, the border was alive with revolutionists and federal troops from both countries who were trying to close the border to smugglers and rustlers. The instability in Mexico was a constant topic of discussion, especially after July of 1908, when a large quantity of ammunition was discovered in houses in Del Rio, and customs officers received information concerning revolutionists in the hills west of Las Vacas (now known as Ciudad Acuna).[10] Those hills would have put the revolutionary activity just about half way between Del Rio and Langtry but on the Mexican side. If the problems in Mexico caused worry among the new comers to Langtry, it wasn't recorded. The families began to settle in and to get used to the new territory that was somewhat different from where they had lived previously.

The area around Langtry was part of the Chihuahuan Desert. It is a typical high desert county framed by the Chisos, Guadalupe, and Davis

Mountains in the United States and the Sierra Madre in Mexico. For much of the year the land is uniformly beige broken by vivid splashes of green from the succulents. When the rains come the gray-green sage plants erupt with purple flowers that change the landscape into an explosion of color. The country is dominated by creosote bushes, a low gnarled growth that gives up its space grudgingly. Bright green splotches of yucca and lechagilla are found dotted with prickly pear cactus. The yearly average of ten inches of rain a year produces wispy blue gramma grass that struggles out of the clay like caliche earth. Near Langtry, the area is defined by steep bluffs and rugged defiles that produce sparse grazing. Cattle could find grazing in the meadows or *vegas,* and sheep and goats worked well in the rough country.

The town of Langtry grew up near the Eagle's Nest crossing of the Rio Grande, so named for an enormous nest that perched on the edge of a cavern and overlooked both the ford and the town. It was a grading camp for the Southern Pacific Railroad and became more important as the Galveston, Harrisburg, and San Antonio rail tracks crawled across the desert from the east. The two railroads finally met near the site of the town. By 1882 the town began to take shape around a tent saloon created by Roy Bean, an itinerant saloon keeper who had moved there from New Mexico. An early source of revenue for the town was the business of providing liquor and entertainment for the railroad workers. For years the area was strewn with broken opium pipes and bottles that marked the temporary sites for the Chinese workers. Its strong points and weaker ones were described: "Eagles Nest is one of the most peculiar places in the state...The only wood building being the store of Max Meyer, who has a good stock and does a good business. There are, at the lowest estimates, twenty saloons and gambling tents, two tents of ill fame, and a dance hall, which is on full run every Sunday and two or three times a week."[11]

As the town began to gather steam it needed a name and the residents had selected Langtry for George Langtry, who had been in charge of one of the Chinese work camps. Among the most prominent of the early entrepreneurs was Jesus Torres, who owned much of the land originally, Roy Bean, who became justice of the peace, and W. H. Dodds, who established a store and eventually owned parts of the town itself. While there was not exactly a growth boom, the coming of the railroad opened the area up to farming and ranching interests. The attraction was cheap land, and a lot of it.

The land was, for the most part, railroad land, school land, and some privately owned tracts. Texas had a lot of land and used it to accomplish a series of priorities. The railroads had originally been given sixteen sections of land for every mile of track laid to encourage them to connect Central Texas with the west coast. With the railroads completed, the companies sold off the land to cover expenses and increase their capitol. Land had been appropriated to support a school system in Texas. By 1900, these school lands began to be sold with the money going into the permanent school fund. When the land was public land, the state leased some of it for grazing, and some of it was simply grazed on in a first come, first served basis. By 1900 changes brought about by the legislature opened much of the land to private buyers. The newcomers were drawn by the promise of cheap land and few fences. The lack of fences meant lot of room to graze stock even though some of that grazing might technically be found on other peoples land. Joe recalled, "There were no fences for one hundred miles in any direction. We could run stock for one hundred miles up and down the Rio Grande and Pecos Rivers."[12] It seemed like a rancher's version of a no limit poker game and like a poker game there was competition from the first deal, only this time the competition was for grass and water.

Joe Graham was optimistic about a land that had just come out of a drought. The new rains promised grass and the water holes slowly filled and grass began to sprout, as did ranches populated by new settlers. Land ownership that accessed the Pecos and Rio Grande rivers had been sewn up early by families who had moved in years before. Late comers to the area sought out land that held a few water holes and springs and seeps that might provide the single commodity that meant the difference between success and failure. Water wells were drilled wherever water was suspected and windmills began to sprout in the area. Despite people seeking their own water, there continued to be competition for the water holes that were not on fenced land.

It wasn't unusual for the herds of water-starved sheep to drink a waterhole dry, leaving behind little but mud. The same pattern was followed with grass. Sheep would graze an area and move on after browsing the grass close to the ground. With enough water the grass would spring back, but in a drought situation grass became as scarce as the precious water.

Joe Graham had already set up his system for ranching in the area. He bought cattle from Mexico, sheep and goats where ever he could find them, and ran them all in the parts of the country that worked best for the stock. Goats worked well in the hilly, rough country. Sheep and cattle did better in the smoother valleys. It kept him and his herders busy. Cattle were fattened and traded quickly. Because of the time involved in raising sheep for wool, the time table was a bit more complicated.

The sheep man's year was predictable but subject to interruption based on changes in the weather and the ever-changing market. October to May was primarily a time for grazing and taking care of the ewes during their gestation period. Lambing needed to be done in the late spring, after the last norther and before the summer heat grew too much. Along the border, weather tended to be less of a problem than further north, but it remained a factor. Shearing generally took place after lambing. If the sheep were sheared too early they had no protection from a late norther blowing through. If they were sheared too late in the summer they carried too much wool and the heat could make them hard to work.

The sheep had been sheared by shearing crews from Mexico. By 1910 local crews were beginning to take over the job. The need for skilled shearers made it critical for the rancher to schedule the shearing crew as early as possible. Often the crews were made up of a number of family members who worked the same ranches year after year. The crew, headed by a *capitan*, would arrive by wagon, set up shop, and using hand clippers snip off the wool and mohair. Often they would work in sheds especially built for the purpose and shared by several ranchers. Joe Graham built a special shearing "plant" at his headquarters place in October of 1913. It was shared by the Billings brothers and W. Rathbone.[13] The men on the shearing crew would shear, boys would tie up the fleece, or "clip" as it was known, and it would be stuffed in burlap bags that might weigh 300 pounds before they were closed up. An individual shearer might shear a hundred sheep a day. In the early days a *capitan* might note the numbers by tying a knot in a string or rope. Tokens or washers were used to document the number of sheep sheared later.

The ranchers or their hands would work the sheep after they were sheared in chutes where cuts would be doctored, medicine would be administered, and ears marked with the ranchers mark. The end of the ear might be cut straight, the right ear might be cut on an angle or "sloped" or some other variation. Records were kept of earmarks. Most of the male lambs would be castrated, and sometimes the sheep might be marked with a number in paint on their sides. The clip was hauled to market or taken to a wool and mohair warehouse where it would be stored until the market made a profitable sale possible.

The ranchers of the area had to deal with a number of challenges: the market, the lack of rain, problems with diseases and predators, but all of that seemed to shrink by another factor in 1910. At that time, they began to realize that they had to deal with the day-to-day reality of a revolution going on just across the river.

The trouble in Mexico refused to go away. When the Revolution finally exploded in both the north and south of Mexico in 1911, it threatened both Mexico and the American borderlands with social and economic instability. Mexico, like so many large state controlled economies, was based on a large, rural population. Although by 1910, there was a small middle class emerging, the majority of the people lived on land that made up the *hacienda* system. Ninety-five percent of the land was owned by five percent of the people. Most of the population lived in rural poverty with no chance of ever leaving the *hacienda* they were born on. The unrest in the society was based on this unwieldy system of land ownership and control over the population by a tiny fraction of the power elite.

Power had been in the hands of the president, Don Porfirio Diaz, for nearly thirty-five years. As an army officer and later president, he had promised reforms but they were slow coming. The old soldier opened the country up to foreign investment and promised that he would rule using a "scientific approach" to both managing the economy and the society. The presidential advisors, or *cientificos*, made more decisions, the rich made more money, and nothing changed for the people. Progress was slow in coming and Don Porfirio explained the country was still too unsettled and that there must be order before there was progress and he would define what constituted both order and progress.

The rural-based economy that supported Mexico was dependent on a permanent class of rural workers who knew their jobs and performed them well. That system promised no future for the workers other than being tied for life to the hacienda. For years, land reforms had been discussed and dreamed about by many of the workers. In their plans, the large estates would be broken up and private ownership of land would be guaranteed. The reforms were dreamed about but were not happening.

By 1911 dissatisfaction had grown to the point that revolution exploded in the southern state of Chiapas and in the northern border states of Coahuila and Chihuahua. In the north the revolution was dominated by a rancher-politico named Francisco Madero and a cowboy turned revolutionist named Doroteo Arango, better known to his followers as Pancho Villa.

The Mexican Revolution was gaining strength and by 1912 it washed over the Texas border and international problems complicated life for the ranchers who lived along the river. Joe Graham moved his family to Del Rio, the Val Verde county seat, at the insistence of his wife, Mollie.

She wanted their children to attend the best schools available. What was left unmentioned was that it was a little safer in Del Rio. Joe spent a lot of time in Del Rio as well, setting up cattle deals with Mexican ranchers anxious to sell before they lost their investments to the Revolution.

With Joe away, he relied on Chicora, Graham, and Boog more than any other time. His son, Jeff, recalled his "Aunt Chic" was "a small, black-eyed lady who was said to be beautiful when she was a young lady. I knew her as a kindly, witty, elderly lady with a fiery temper when aroused... and there were times when Aunt Chic really gave my father fits when they didn't agree on something... she was fiery!"[14]

What they might not have agreed on may have been how her children and Joe's children benefitted from being on the ranch. Her children were older and were able to take on a more active role around the place, but they didn't benefit the way Joe's children did. They weren't treated exactly like family; Joe paid them standard cowboy wages, twenty-five dollars per month, and provided food. He also went beyond that by providing some additional benefits. He gave them an unknown, but thought to be small, percentage of the increase in his cow herd. Their brand, the Lazy B, was recorded in the county brand book and with the Texas and Southwestern Cattle Raisers Association. Several years later, he allowed the brothers to graze their own herd of goats on his Rosillos Ranch. With these benefits Graham made some efforts to expand on his own.

The El Paso Herald noted that on June 26, 1911, he bought O. L. Fisher's interest in the Fisher and McDowell Cattle Company and moved the cattle to Rattlesnake and G. F. Canyons.[15] Perhaps he borrowed the money either from the bank or from his Uncle Joe but he was in the cattle business. The move to Rattlesnake Canyon put him directly in the middle of the property that Joe had purchased when he first bought land in the area. Letting Graham run stock on Joe's land may have come as a way to allow the Barnetts a little more access to the success that Joe seemed to be having. Jeff Graham noted some problems when he thought about the family arrangements later in life. "It is my own opinion when I say that in all likelihood there was some jealousy between the Barnett cousins and my older brothers. They had so little and my brothers had so much more there must have been some hidden resentment on Boog's and Graham's part. I can recall no overt actions or words, however, about this."[16]

The resentment that Jeff Graham mentioned may have had to do with the impression that the Barnetts were neither complete family nor complete partners. They existed in some kind of social borderland between the two. When there was friction, it was usually over Joe Graham's rules. Joe knew how he wanted things done and he required his children and the Barnetts to follow those rules. There were rules for everything and they were enforced across the board, it made no difference which part of the family people were from. Horses weren't run without reason, cattle were looked after, sheep were moved when necessary, food was not eaten until it was blessed, and a high moral tone was expected of the children. Jeff recalled..."although Papa was very human and outgoing with people, when it came to his religious beliefs and practices and [when the] 'chips were down, he could be very stern and rather unbending. Mollie [mother], while she did not hold a tight rein on us...reared no rowdies or alcoholics."[17]

Mollie may not have raised any rowdies or alcoholics but that didn't hold for the Barnetts. Graham and Boog appeared to be just about as rowdy as they wanted to be. They did, however, toe the line around Uncle Joe and they did it out of respect for the man who had become a patriarch for the two. The place that Graham seemed to break most of the rules dealt with alcohol. Drinking was a major activity for many Texans of the time and Graham attempted to excel at it. Jeff Graham noted two things, first Graham fell into the swing of things with a careful enthusiasm, and second, he recalled the sharp difference in behavior between Graham when he drank and when he was sober. "They say, and I've always heard, that Graham was a heavy drinker, and got pretty rough and rowdy when he drank to excess. [He] was really a quiet person around the home or ranch. He took things seriously (my father's influence I think). Graham had a healthy respect for my father, his 'Uncle Joe.' I feel sure he loved my father, and would have done anything for him."[18]

Joe must have known he was dealing with the inconsistencies of an apprentice alcoholic. "Graham was alright when he stayed sober, he would give you the shirt off his back, but he might take it back tomorrow," Joe would remark later.[19] Boog, always one to take his brother's side, excused some of Graham's behavior. "He was a good cowboy, you couldn't beat him. You couldn't find a better guy. He would get drunk and raise a little hell but any ordinary guy does that!"[20]

Raising hell included gambling. He liked to gamble and preferred poker. That preference became the beginning of a life-long addiction to gambling. He had a good memory for the cards and that combined with some minor grade card marking gave him an edge. He liked to show off by dealing a deck of cards one-handed, with blinding speed, and he would gamble for almost anything.

He was not only known for the drinking and gambling, he was recognizable because of his appearance. When he was working stock and away from the house for periods of time he would not shave and also let his hair grow long. People began to call him "Bush" Barnett when he came to town. If they remembered the scruffy appearance they also remembered the remarkable gray eyes and a few other particulars. Most of the time he was quiet, he avoided trouble but the stories followed him. Some people called him "Grim" Barnett because of obscure stories told about him taking a shot at people from time to time.

Even with all the stories, people liked him. He seemed to represent the wild cowboy of all the songs: drinking, gambling, shooting, and destined to become a legend, if he could stay out of jail long enough. He was the guy people told stories about. Jeff Graham recalled, "He also was said to be very witty when he was out with a group of men who were his friends. I can recall his wit as I grew older and got to know and like him. I spent many pleasant summer months on our ranch and farm in lower Brewster County with Boog, Graham, and my older brothers. During those times I was fortunate to be able to really observe and get to know these cousins, and to love to be with them. This was a time when I grew to admire and love both Boog and Graham. They were always good to me although sometimes they teased me a great deal. I grew to know and love Graham as a young boy."[21] When he needed to, it seemed that Graham could get along with everyone.

The person Graham really had to get along with was Joe Graham. Joe was the steadiest individual in Graham's life. They were two dramatically different men. Joe Graham mixed ethical behavior based on conservative Christian principles with the rough and tumble world of cattle trading. Graham mixed alcohol, gambling, and general rowdiness in the same world that Joe traveled in. Joe continued to hold out hope that his nephew would settle down and become a credit to the family. Graham gave the older man a lot to hope for. It was as if Joe played the forgiving father to Graham's prodigal son. Neither man gave up his characteristic behavior for as long as he was alive. Despite the differences they might have had on some aspects of behavior, the two men relied on one another for different kinds of support over the years. Graham took care of problems for Joe, while Joe provided jobs, money, and direction for his nephew, as well as lawyers when they were needed.

Graham was making a name for himself as a tough man in the tough country along the Mexican border. Graham herded and looked after Joe Graham's stock and property, and he dealt with most of the day-to-day problems that could be found on a ranch that was only a pistol shot from a revolution. Predators, both human and animal, proved to be a challenge for the entire community. Eagles, coyotes, bobcat, and what local ranchers called panthers (probably mountain lions out of Mexico), were drawn by the flocks of sheep, especially during lambing season. In October of 1913, coyotes were so numerous that government trappers were brought in. John and Ike Babb, along with E. Billings, were putting together packs of dogs to run panthers in the area.[22] Since everyone was faced with the problems of predators and an emerging rustling problem, most of the men were armed and Graham began to develop a reputation as someone who was good with both rifle and a pistol.

Several people recall Graham carrying a single action Colt .44 with pearl grips.[23] It was showy but it went along with the gal legged spurs and Angelo stitching on his boots. Cowboys liked to show off and Graham was a cowboy. He had skills to match the outfit. He shot coins out of the air, held a silver dollar on his hand at shoulder height and drew and fired before it hit the ground. He was as good with a rifle as he was a pistol.[24] Part of the show was just to compete with whoever he was shooting against, but there was a more serious reason for improving his weapons skills.

The competition for grass and water was getting intense, and it wasn't something that was handled with kid gloves. When people counted on finding water for their animals in a certain place, and upon getting there finding the water hole drunk dry, it was more than a small irritant. Since the majority of men in the area carried a rifle on their saddle and frequently a pistol on their belt, disputes had the potential of becoming deadly if they escalated. Suddenly, being able to shoot well became more than a game, and Graham needed a teacher. He found that mentor in one of the men who worked for his uncle.

George Coots, the son of an Irish immigrant, was in his late thirties. He had drifted to the border and cowboyed for a number of ranches near Langtry.[25] He worked for Joe Graham for an extended time and made friends with Graham Barnett. The two ran trap lines together to raise cash, and raced horses when they could find one to run. Along with the horses and hunting he and Graham shared a common interest: the pistol.[26] It is likely that Coots and Graham both carried the most commonly encountered weapon of the time, the single action Colt revolver, but they experimented with anything that would shoot.

George Coots brought some practical thoughts about the science of gun handling. Coots' ideas centered on practice that involved not just standing and shooting at a mark but practicing with the shooter moving and the target as well. It is thought that he suggested that Graham practice shooting from the back of a horse by riding down a fence line and shooting at the fence posts as he passed. This was a common practice technique and one that Graham carried forward with him, although he later substituted telephone poles for the fence posts and an automobile for the horse.[27] Coots taught that speed was good, but accuracy was forever, and taught him to practice a technique that has become known as point shooting. He told Graham to look at what he wanted to hit and then point his pistol like he would a finger.

Graham practiced until he could literally shoot from the hip almost as quickly as the gun came on target. For longer range shots Coots told him to bring the gun to shoulder height and snap off the shot when he centered the target. It was a technique that required practice, and he continued the practice for the rest of his life. Graham later told a friend that he literally shot up cases of ammunition practicing.[28]

Practice was only going to work if you had a gun with you. Carrying a weapon wasn't so much a problem in the country, but when he came to town Graham had to adapt to state laws that did not allow open carry. It really wasn't much of a problem in Langtry, but sixty miles down the road in Del Rio carrying a pistol could get you in trouble. Graham, along with many other men, carried concealed even though it was against the law. Many cowboys on the way to town left their gun belts at home, and simply tucked the pistol into their belt under their coat. Graham carried his pistol on his left side with the grips angled forward for a cross draw. This method for carrying small, easily concealed weapons was fairly common on the border up into the 1960s.[29] Graham usually wore a coat that covered the pistol and he developed a method of drawing the gun that contributed to his speed. He would put his hand in the coat pocket, reach through the lining and push the gun upward, allowing it to fall forward, and then reach across with his right hand and complete the draw.[30] During the warmer weather he was known to tuck the pistol into his waistband and blouse his shirt out over the grips. Other times he tucked the pistol inside his shirt and left a button undone so he could reach it. As with any weapon-based exercise, it was the practice that contributed to his success more than anything else. He practiced until he was faster than anyone had a right to expect.[31]

Modern movies and television have led many viewers to believe that all cowboys carried a heavy revolver in a belt and holster. For many cowboys it was easier to carry a small revolver or semi-automatic in coat pockets or tucked into the pockets of chaps, or leggings, as they are frequently referred to in West Texas. Having the pistol in a pocket allowed quick access, and the ability to carry it without attracting a lot of attention from law enforcement or other concerned citizens provided another benefit. Most of the men who worked in the heavy brush in the area around Langtry wore short denim or canvas "ducking" jackets to protect against the mesquite and other thorny plant life. Besides providing protection from the brush, the ducking jacket pockets provided a ready built concealed holster for a small pistol.

Graham found that he could carry a short Model 1907 Savage .32 caliber semi-automatic in his pocket, and it became a constant companion that he used for practice as he moved sheep and goats or as he ran his trap line. The Savage was a trendy, well-advertised firearm made famous for such taglines as "Ten shots quick" and "Aims as easy as pointing your finger." It fit Graham's style and provided a reliable piece of equipment that Graham could have with him most of the time. It had another advantage; it was similar in operation to several of the newer Colt semi-automatic pistols that were finding their way to the border. Graham could use the Savage for practice and that would carry over to the larger frame Colt. The newer technology represented by the Colt semi autos had found their way to the border and were attracting attention of the *pistoleros* in the area.

The Mexican government had purchased several thousand of the Colt Military Model of 1902 for selected troops. Undoubtedly stray examples of the pistol were found on both sides of the border. It was followed quickly by a storm of newer models. The Colt Model of 1911 began to be sold on the civilian market as early as 1913 and quickly found a place on the belts of men on the border. A later picture of Graham in the Rangers in 1915 shows him with an early Colt automatic pistol using the cross draw carry. One thing was certain: Graham had a gun with him almost all of the time. The question of being armed or not became a serious issue for two reasons. The first was that unrest beginning in Mexico had contributed to an increase in rustling of stock. The other focused on not only threats from outside the area, but from within. Conflicts over water and grazing were beginning to mushroom.

CHAPTER 3

"WHEN I PUT MY HAND IN MY POCKET, HE KNEW IT WAS ALL OVER"

1912-1913[1]

While everyone was in a struggle for resources, one family seemed to stand out both in their opposition to other ranchers and in their single-mindedness that justified their own struggle. They were the family headed by William Ike Babb, universally known as "Bill Ike." The Babb family had come to Langtry as a result of a long and sometimes painful journey that took them across West Texas, just ahead of a court warrant in many cases. The family had a mixed reputation with their neighbors. Attorney Brian Montague recalled the Babbs had a "general reputation with respect to being peaceable and law abiding citizens, but that reputation masked activities...distinctly otherwise than in conformity with legal standards of conduct. The Babbs were of a mind to conduct themselves as they saw fit, and not according to the rules of others."[2] They were a family that could not or would not forget an insult, whether it was real or imagined, and tended to act as they pleased. Their actions in Val Verde County carried on a long family tradition.

Bill Ike's father, commonly called "Cherokee Bill" Babb, was born in Cape Girardeau, Missouri, in 1835 and was in the mercantile business. By 1860, he had moved to Texas and settled in Coryell County west of Waco. There the family owned and operated a store that was a center of activity in the community and described as the largest store west of Waco.[3] Despite their successes in business they were involved in some extra-legal activities that attracted the attention of the law in the area. In May of 1878, a man named Vaughan was robbed and killed, and the blame was directed toward the Babbs. John Stull, a deputy U.S. Marshall, arrested Cherokee Bill and several of his sons including Bill Ike. The Babbs were released on bond, and shortly afterwards Stull ended up dead, killed in an ambush by night riders who set his house on fire and killed him and a neighbor when they rushed outside. The Babbs were suspected of being involved, and a Coryell County grand jury summoned them to testify in compliance with the obligation of their bail bonds in the Vaughan case. To their amazement, Cherokee Bill, the family patriarch, made a brazen quid pro quo: if they would not indict him in the Stull case, he would leave the county, taking all of his family and friends.

Brian Montague described the grand jury as so "stupefied" by Cherokee Bill's request that they ignored their civic duty.[4] The more the court thought about it, the more it seemed to be a good deal. They could get rid of the Babbs and the rascals who were running with them for good, without the uncertainty of a trial since one never could tell how something like a trial might turn out. The grand jury accepted the offer. Cherokee Bill, in turn, returned home and gave the deal a little thought. He decided that perhaps he had been a bit too hasty, and the "Baron of Coryell County" decided he wanted to stay. He made that announcement to anyone who would listen. That was a mistake.[5]

The county was full of men who had, in the vernacular of the times, "seen the elephant." They had fought Comanche, Yankees, each other, and now decided they would take on the Babbs in order to calm things down. According to J. B. Cranfill, four hundred of them met on the full of the moon and made a decision. They sent a five-man committee to visit with Cherokee Bill. Their message was brief: unless the Babbs left the county as promised, they would "...swoop down among them and exterminate them root and branch. It was their purpose to kill every man of them, at whatever cost, and to wipe them off the face of the earth."[6]

Things had never been explained to Cherokee Bill quite that plainly before. He gathered his family, his followers, and all his stock and left. The Babbs then began a trek across the Texas landscape, making appearances in Bosque, Hamilton, Coleman, Sutton, and Pecos counties, leaving in their wake a list of alleged offenses ranging from theft of livestock to murder.

Cherokee Bill's son, known to family and others as Bill Ike, continued his father's impressive social ways of living life the way he wanted. That activity continued to cause the family problems, which drew more attention as they moved west. The long march almost ended in Sonora, Texas, in February 1898. Bill Ike was a constable in the town but still had brushes with the law. One indictment was brought forward on February 23, 1898: an assault with intent to murder. Two days after that indictment, February 25, 1898, he was tried for the murder of a child known only as C. Banty in the court records. Brian Montague's recollections do not connect the two events, but they may have referred to the same case. The Banty case was a particularly gruesome case of abuse in which an underage child suffered extreme neglect and eventually died, apparently while in the care of the Babbs. With continuances and delays, that case was not settled until March of 1901, when Bill Ike was convicted and fined fifty dollars. The jury pronounced Bill Ike "not guilty of the offense of murder," but "guilty of aggravated assault" and fixed his punishment at "two months in the County Jail and a fine of one hundred fifty dollars."[7] James Cornell, a judge and lawyer privy to details of the case, told Montague that while no one doubted that Bill Ike was guilty of murder, the state was unable to produce enough evidence to establish his guilt.[8] The Babbs moved out of Sonora and off to New Mexico for a while, and then returned to Texas to take up residence in Val Verde County in 1900 where they pitched into the rough business of finding land and holding it.

Bill Ike amassed 105 sections of rock-strewn hills between Pandale and Langtry.[9] He built a two-story wooden house atop a mesa rising 150 feet above the surrounding terrain, which gave him a commanding view of the water holes on Harkell and Little Fielder draws. Even with all their moves, the family grew; eventually ten children were born to Bill Ike and Sarah Babb. The boys, from eldest to youngest, were Willie Lewis, John, Boye, Coleman (Buster), Dillard, and Walter. The girls were Maudie, Laura, Rosa, and Myrtle. Myrtle's twin, May, died in infancy. Bill Ike had land, family, and a place in the community. The problem was that the community was about to grow.

When the newcomers began to flood into the area around Langtry in the 1908-1910 period, the Babbs and others who had been there for several years found that there were inevitable clashes. Many of the disputes grew out of the use and ownership of the land and water. In a country with few fences, the problem faced by everyone was whose property was it, who had a right to it, and how could you tell where one piece of land ended and the next began?

Much of the land had been deeded to railroads or designated as school land but the grazing rights were leased to a number of ranchers. While it remained unfenced, many of the ranchers considered the land theirs because they had used it over time. Even after the land began to be sold to individuals, fences came slowly, and herds of sheep didn't recognize property lines. After the fencing of an area took place, fences had a tendency to slightly shift depending on whether or not rains washed them out or animals pushed them down. When a plot was being fenced, often the property lines were vague and typically were not surveyed using the most modern methods. Property lines were designated by natural features of the land such as a large tree or a prominent rock, and measurement in many areas was still given in *varas*, an archaic Spanish measurement subject to different interpretations in different states. In

Texas there was general agreement that it was a measurement of 33 1/3 inches. The upshot of all of this meant that when a man fenced six sections of land, a slight variation might mean a gain or loss of a number of acres and that might change with the shifting of fences or a challenge from a neighbor about a property line.[10]

Problems with boundaries were complicated further by attitudes held by many people at the beginning of the twentieth century. There was a tendency for people who lived in a rural area to maintain an attitude that whatever they did on their own land was their business and no one else's. That included the use of resources and the collection of stock that might be unmarked or that had wandered into another herd. When other people tried to intrude, whether by grazing or by pointing out a perceived mistake, it usually wasn't accepted very well. Feuds grew out of differences of opinion and those feuds continued for years. The Babb family was already famous for the feuds they had been involved in. By this time, Bill Ike and his family had lived on the place that they owned for ten years and had cemented a relationship with the land and their neighbors. Newcomers to the area would have to stand in line for water and other resources, and they would have to line up behind the Babb outfit. Longevity in a place and money meant power, and the Babbs had power.

Joe Graham and the newcomers faced this with a common understanding of the situation. Many of them had been in that position where they had come from. As powerful families and families seeking power brushed against one another, sparks would fly, and those sparks were usually created over the issues of water and grazing.

Joe Graham understood that access to the rivers was a prize, and he struggled to expand his "33 Ranch" to include access to the Pecos River which would guarantee a steady water supply. Until then he would have to drill wells and set up windmills to pump water into earthen tanks to supply his animals. This approach provided water at the headquarters ranch and selected locations. Away from these sites, there was a reliance on natural water holes that were on both public and private lands. In a few places, there were slow seeps that filled after being depleted by the stock. The seeps and water holes could be quickly emptied by the thirsty stock and that meant that latecomers went without water. Stock going without water could cause a serious economic impact. Dead sheep don't produce wool. So the Babbs, who had grazed the land exclusively, now could expect Graham, Boog, or other cowboys to be watering livestock at places like Harkell Draw, G-4 Canyon, and Little Fielder Draw.

To be fair, the newcomers were probably as much to blame as the established ranchers for the conflicts. Joe Graham allegedly told his herders to water their stock at any place that was not privately owned. That meant railroad land and school land was fair game.[11] Ownership of these plots remained in dispute, with the Babbs maintaining partial control of several hundred acres of the Val Verde County school and railroad land that they claimed in addition to what they owned. This claim was seriously challenged by the arrival of Joe Graham and others like him and another newcomer, Victor Tippett.

Victor Tippett ran sheep with his brothers Homer and John and had ranched from Sheffield down to Langtry, mostly on public land and sometimes on land not so public.[12] According to Mildred Babb Adams, Victor and his brothers Homer and John "grazed their sheep all over West Texas, many times on other people's land."[13] In a land with no fences that was easy to do. On the day he met Bill Ike Babb Tippett insisted, "I didn't know where I was."[14] His Mexican sheepherders, he said, were grazing his sheep in the hills near Fielder Draw when the sheep smelled water and broke for the water hole. In the middle of the dash for water, Bill Ike appeared on his horse. "He got raunchy. He said, 'I've got my gun. You get yours. Let's fight.'"[15] Tippett, who probably had been in this situation before replied, "I don't have a gun and if I did I wouldn't kill you."[16]

Tippett's attitude seemed to put Bill Ike off guard. "We talked for a while," Tippett recalled, and then Babb said, "Come on down, let's get something to eat."[17] Tippett accepted and the two families began a conversation that had an unlikely sequel. His brother, Homer, eloped with Bill Ike's second-born daughter, Laura Babb. From then on, when the Tippetts showed up on Babb range, they were family.

The Babbs sensed more trouble when they found that land they thought they had leased was suddenly leased to other ranchers. The Babbs claimed that some of the newcomers were using contacts at the Land Office in Austin to pick up some of the public land as it came on the market. After years of being the top dogs, they began to believe that the tables were slowly turning, and they were becoming victims in the war for water. As the conflicts continued in Austin, skirmishes began to occur near Langtry.[18]

All of the competition wasn't violent. Joe Graham, the Tippett brothers, and the Babb family engaged in a constant round of buying, selling, and leasing land. They all watched market trends and Joe Graham had an eye on the future. In June of 1911, he began to sport around town in a new Ford touring car complete with a powerful twenty-two horsepower engine. Considering the condition of the roads in the area, "sport around" may be too strong a term to use. He immediately announced that "conditions in the cattle business had so changed that an auto is now a necessity and that cowboys must now add to their qualifications as cow hands that of understanding gasoline motors and the ability to drive a motor car."[19] Victor Tippett bought one shortly afterwards. The twentieth century had arrived. As if in support of his uncle, Graham began a lifelong love affair with cars and speed. As he grew older he was seldom without a car and it was usually one that allowed him to run as fast he wanted. Technology intervened in the sheep business in other ways also; it began to be applied to the water business in a big way.

There was a rush to drill water wells and to build earthen tanks to hold the drilled water and the anticipated rain. The Tippets built a water tank that would hold 8,000,000 gallons, an optimistic projection at best. The well-digging business was brisk enough that well diggers, such as the Strickland Well Digging outfit, moved into the area to drill multiple wells beginning with several for Joe in October of 1911.[20]

In March of 1912, the biggest crop of mohair seen in the area had just been sheared. Joe bought 2000 head of sheep from his neighbor and competitor, Bill Ike Babb, and additionally bought eight sections of land, bordering on the Pecos six miles from town.[21] By September both men were trading again. Babb bought the Jaboncillo section complete with two tanks and a pumping plant. Joe also sold Will Babb, Will Ike's oldest son, the Aaron Billings place on the Pecos east of town. It was a place that Will had wanted for some time because of the access to the Pecos River. Will moved his family into Langtry and began to work on the ranch during the week and visit in town on weekends. The sale brought him water, but also led to more encounters with members of the Graham and Barnett families.[22]

As often as not, Graham Barnett seemed to be the man they had the most run-ins with and the disputes were getting more abrasive. People were aware of what was becoming bad blood between the two families and especially between Graham Barnett and Will Babb. Success over grazing and water rights were based on who could be driven off the prize. It was a case of who could make the other man back up. Opinion was about evenly divided between who came out the winner most of the time. The Grahams were adamant about one thing: "Graham wasn't afraid. The boy wasn't afraid," said Joe Graham. "Will didn't like Graham because Graham wasn't afraid of him."[23] Not everyone saw it that way. Years later, Vern Davis, Sheriff of Sterling County, had the opinion that Graham was probably intimidated by Will Babb. Babb was older, more of a fixture in the country and enjoyed the support of a large family. Davis used the language of the cow camp when he described the encounters between Will and Graham. Babb "choused" Graham, the term meant to push or herd cattle in a rough way. He also recalled Will Babb as being overbearing.[24]

For the Babb family, Will was anything but overbearing. For the family, he was the heroic older brother who seemed dogged by bad luck. When he was fifteen, he set out on a planned trip to New Mexico and supported himself by working along the way. When he reached Menard, he was chopping wood in exchange for bread when a chip flew up and hit him in the eye. He lost the eye, but gained an attitude that he would do as much with one eye as other men could with two. Victor Tippett remembered him as a "small and dried up" man who had lived a life full of the kinds of daily tragedy found on the border.[25] His niece, Ruth Babb Sprott of Alpine, described Will as "a short, slender man who could wear a woman's slipper."[26] To his adoring daughter Mildred, who was three when Will died, "Will was about the best race horse rider in the whole country, of small frame and weighing in at 125 pounds when a race was coming up...Will was an acrobat on a horse, half the time riding standing up in the saddle."[27] Will rode Babb racehorses, and he also rode for Sutton County rancher Jess Mayfield, who had some of the finest race horses in West Texas. Within the family he was a hero, but not everyone saw him like his family saw him.

He reacted strongly to people grazing stock on his land or drinking from his water holes. He wasn't going to take very much off of anyone. He was a Babb and that meant something, or ought to. His family maintained that he was even-tempered, but others thought he got angry easily. That strong anger was directed toward people who crossed him. When he was angry, he tended to get loud. He had a habit of blinking his eyes rapidly and when that happened, people knew that something was going to follow.[28] Will and the rest of his family stood up for themselves in the best frontier tradition and worked steadily at intimidating people they had problems with, and he had problems with Graham Barnett.

It wasn't just the Babb family that the Grahams and Barnetts had to look out for. The Mexican Revolution had exploded into full bloom, and all of the residents of the Langtry area were aware that the Texas border country had become a source for much needed horses for all sides in the war. The Texas ranches also provided a source for cattle to be rustled and sold to fund activities on both sides of the river. There was little protection extended from the sheriff's office or the Texas Rangers, and the ranchers had to protect themselves as well as they could. The Grahams were hit several times, and Boog and Graham, officially or not, took on the responsibility to recover the lost stock.

One of the first incidents happened when the brothers were at the crosstie house that had been built on Rattlesnake Draw. Boog told the story years later: there were no pens for the horses, and they had been hobbled to keep them from wandering too far off. Boog began to cook bread for breakfast and Graham went to get up the horses, but he came back quickly and announced, "Well, they put us afoot last night." The brothers knew something had to be done so they prepared for a raid. "We put some jerky and bread in a *morral*,[29] filled our canteens with water and took a can of coffee. When we hit the river, we took the border with us. Trailed 'em about 20 miles south of the border. Finally located our horses at a big headquarters sheep camp, belonged to Don Lorenzo Trevino. We backed off in a canyon where there was some water, camped until the moon came up, cooked supper, and then we eased down and unhobbled our horses and everything they had too, so they couldn't come after us. Graham took the lead and I brought up the rear and we headed for the river. We brought 'em across the river, and threw 'em up the river to the mouth of Lozier Canyon. I went into Langtry that evening and reported to the customs officers, invited 'em out, told 'em I'd found some wet stock. We helped customs bring the horses back to Langtry and the government sold 'em. 'Course, we had our horses cut out before we threw the others up the river."[30]

The brothers went into Mexico sporadically over the next few years, sometimes forming a raiding party with other ranchers to retrieve stolen livestock, other times by themselves. The men they were chasing were not amateurs. Many of them were seasoned by years of cowboying and refined in the furnace of the Revolution. When they stole stock, they protected it from the previous owners; some of the men pushed the stolen animals as fast as they could, leaving sharpshooters back to pick off the pursuers. Running gunfights were not unusual on both sides of the river and became somewhat expected in many situations.

On one occasion Graham, Boog, and George Coots were riding across the river looking for some strays when they saw a big troop of Mexicans. Boog remembered the fight well: "We didn't know if they were friendly so we decided to get the hell out. Just before we hit the river, Graham's hat fell off. We bull frogged into the river but George Coots stopped to get Graham's hat. The Mexicans started popping at George with their 7 mm. Mausers. We swam on across the river. All you could see was our horses' noses, our heads and our rifles we were holding above the water. When we got across we smoked the Mexicans off Coots. Several of 'em were hit."[31]

Skirmishes such as these were fairly common, and probably led to later stories about Graham being what his Uncle Joe called an "unofficial stock detective."[32] The term stock detective was applied to men who usually worked for a stockman's association and who reduced the number of cattle thefts by reducing the number of thieves. The burden of proof was a light one for many of these stock detectives, and they frequently dealt with the thieves they found on the range and never mentioned it to anyone. With the unrest in Mexico, it was a bad time to be caught in someone else's pasture with no plausible reason to be there.

Graham began to develop a reputation as someone who actively pursued his role as a stock detective for his uncle. From an economic standpoint, Joe Graham did not want to lose any stock to support the Mexican Revolution. Part of Graham's job seems to have been to see that that didn't happen. On the border at that time, there was very little talk and a lot of action when a suspected cattle thief was found.

The Mexican Rurales had implemented what they called "*la ley de fuga*," the law of flight. *La ley* was brutally simple. The suspected man was allowed access to a horse or an open door. If you ran, you must be guilty of something, and in Mexico, an attempted escape assured that the next few minutes were going to be active ones for both parties, especially if the thief had a slow horse.[33] The technique found its way across the Rio Grande and became an explanation for a number of shootings. Graham quickly adopted the Texas version of *la ley* and applied it to anyone who was found without a reason on the ranch property. There is no evidence this was directed toward Mexicans exclusively; instead, it was directed toward anyone who stole from his uncle or intended to interrupt the flow of commerce on the Graham ranches.

The stories that began to grow up around him and his protection work fueled the Graham Barnett legend, and Graham did little to deny it. When it came to building a reputation, talking about it was as good as doing it if no one can check on it. There were very few witnesses to anything Graham did. Several of Graham's contemporaries quoted numbers of people he was supposed to have killed, secretly buried, dumped in the Rio Grande, or otherwise disposed of. His cousin Jeff Graham said, "My brother told me that he saw Graham kill a Mexican and throw him in the river, and I have no reason to doubt my brother. The Mexicans that worked on our ranch were scared to death of him and stayed away from him if they could."[34]

Graham apparently learned early that fear was a useful tool in motivating people and his job had become one of motivating thieves to leave the 33 Ranch alone. One of the best ways to keep people off the ranch was with the threat of being found dead and stories of people disappearing continued to grow. Most of the stories were repeated with little or no proof. As with many other men on the border, the truth about what Graham did, didn't always make the story better; in fact truth might ruin it for everyone. Brian Montague swore that he had heard stories that Graham sat on the bluffs on the Texas side of the river and took shots at Mexicans on the other side. Montague went on to say that he had not heard of Graham actually hitting anyone but expressed concern over the indiscriminate shooting.[35] Others repeated the stories with whatever additions were necessary to make it better.

Whether he wanted it or not, Graham began to be seen as a man who handled problems for his uncle and did so quietly and forcefully. Perhaps because he began to see himself as a troubleshooter for his uncle, a role that none of Joe's children filled, Graham began to expect to be treated more like a son than a nephew. That expectation was not fulfilled, but son or nephew, Graham had become the embodiment of the man who fixed things. Many people began to call him "Grim" Barnett, perhaps reflecting the serious nature of how he carried his work for his uncle. Even the family was divided on how Graham was seen by people. Was he the protector or was he a predator?

In a 1958 interview in National City, California, two of Graham Barnett's children insisted that Joe Graham used Boog and Graham to handle the dangerous work of protecting his livestock from Mexican raiders. To the Grahams it was work that Joe himself was reluctant to do, and from which he sheltered his sons. Bud Barnett, Graham's eldest son, said of Joe's sons, "Frank, Stanley, Bill and Jeff...they herded goats and plowed cotton on Joe's river farm. From the time he was eighteen until he was killed it was always go get Graham to do the hard work."[36] For the family, the term "hard work" invariably meant that Graham was going to be involved in something dangerous.

The view of Graham as an enforcer wasn't entirely shared by Joe Graham's family. Joe's youngest son Jeff Graham hadn't been born when the Revolution was spilling over into his family's lives, but he contended that the picture of the Barnett brothers roaming Coahuila in search of bad men and lost stock was a myth. He scoffed at the notion that "my father expected Boog and Graham to be his emissaries in Mexico."[37] Jeff did concede that Graham and Boog may have "participated in recovering strayed or stolen livestock, but it was the practice of the ranchers in the Langtry to Del Rio area to band together to do this sort of work."[38] In either case, the foundation for the legendary activities of Graham

Barnett as a man hunter on the border was created by the impact of the revolution and Graham's tendency to let the stories grow as they might.

The stories that grew about Graham around Langtry didn't impress the Babb family very much. The Babbs didn't seem eager to take him on, even when they outnumbered and outgunned him, but they didn't back down from him. The face-offs at the waterholes began to get more serious, and they seemed to focus more and more on Graham. Joe continued to see the encounters as generated by the Babbs and done to intimidate both he and Graham. While Joe continued to wonder "why didn't they [Babbs] leave that boy [Graham] alone?"[39] The position of the Babbs was that they couldn't afford to leave him alone. Mildred Babb remembered what members of her family had told her: "Other people were always trying to run their stock in on Will's water hole and he had much hardship trying to keep water for his goats. The water was his own; it was on his own land. He put Graham Barnett on the run from there several times."[40]

While there was tension between the families, it did not stop both social and financial deals from being conducted. Graham had a date for the 1913 Christmas Dance with Myrtle Babb, Will's sister.[41] Both families continued to trade sheep and goats, and the sale of the Pecos River ranch to Will Babb seemed to reduce some of the conflicts over water holes. Will began to work the Pecos river ranch but the country was rough enough that he could not move his pregnant wife and their three-year-old daughter on to the place. He did move them to Langtry and put them up in the old Judge Roy Bean Opera House, which Bill Ike now owned. He worked at the ranch during the week and came to town on the weekends to visit his family. On the weekend of December 6-7, 1913, he headed into town to see his wife and new baby. He was not the only person coming to Langtry that weekend.

W. H. Dodd's store proved to be an attraction for people on both sides of the border, and the weekends brought all kinds of people to town to buy or trade. A group of Mexican horse traders eased into town and prepared to sell horses and mules that had just been brought up from Mexico. A particular bay mule in their herd had attracted a lot of attention, and several people made a point of trying to trade for it.

Graham and a cowboying friend named Reid House were in town. They had taken a job with Buck Billings, a friend of Joe Graham and the son of an early settler in the area. Joe had purchased his 33 Ranch from Billings' father. Billings' wife Beulah recalled the weekend: "Buck was working cattle at Eight Mile [crossing] on the Pecos, and he hired these boys [Graham and Reid House] to help him."[42] Since it was late, Billings asked Graham and Reid to spend the night with him and told them he would write a check and pay them in the morning. Graham had expected to see his brother Boog who was doing day work for cowman Ab Blocker, and Boog turned up with the Blocker cowboys later. A large number of people, including the Barnett brothers, drifted down to the Mexican camp and began to inspect the stock that had come from across the river.

Will Babb had seen the fabled mule and decided to buy it, but the Mexicans wouldn't budge from their $40 asking price, which was the going rate for a good saddle horse. Will chose to let the Mexicans sleep on his $30 offer, and joined his family at the Opera House.

Exactly what happened after he left the horse traders still isn't clear. What is most likely is that both Graham and Boog wandered down to the horse trading and began to negotiate for stock. Boog mentioned there was drinking and dealing going on, and it seems unlikely that Graham would have walked off from a party as long as a bottle was involved. What both brothers maintained is that they did not know Will Babb had tried to buy the mule. During the evening, one of the brothers made a deal for the mule. Boog said he did, others said that Graham made the deal, but by the end of the evening the ownership had transferred. Monday morning, Will Babb, accompanied by his brother John, went to the Mexican camp to resume dickering over the price of the mule, only to discover to his considerable consternation that it had been sold. It is said that when Will asked who bought the mule, the Mexicans replied only "Senor Barnett."[43] Exactly which Barnett wasn't specified. Boog claimed that honor, but Will could only see his old rival from the water holes. He set about looking for Graham, and he didn't have far to look. Boog had tied the mule to a hitching post next to Victor Tippett's black Model T Ford in front of the W. H. Dodd General Store.

Dodd's Store was a one-story wooden building with a large overhang that provided shade for two low benches that flanked the double doors. Splashed across the top of the building on a false front was a sign stating "W. H. Dodd General Merchandise." The store formed the central location for the small town by handling most of the supplies and operating as the local post office. For years the only telephones in the town were in the store and in the Dodd's residence behind the store.[44] Whatever went on in town eventually went on at Dodd's.

Graham and Reid House had spent the night with Buck Billings and his wife Beulah. The next morning Buck found he didn't have a check so they all decided to walk over to the store so he could get one to pay Graham and Reid. The three left the Billings house and walked the short distance to the store. For some reason, Buck, who usually carried a pistol, left it under his pillow where Beulah found it, minutes after they left.[45] Graham, however, had dropped his familiar .32 Savage into the pocket of his ducking jacket.[46]

Inside Dodd's store, Eula Crist, the young clerk, was filling Victor Tippett's shopping list of beans, coffee, and other necessities for his Mexican sheepherders. Graham, Reid House, and Buck Billings ambled in. Graham slouched against the counter, leaning on his elbow and taking in all the action that could take place in a small border store and attempting to make light talk with Eula Crist as she passed back and forth. The store's owner, Englishman W. H. Dodd, was outside talking cattle prices and weather with a group of ranchers gathered in the shade of the porch overhang.

When they left the Mexican's camp, Will and John began to look for Graham. Dodd's store stood at the end of the main street. The two strode down the street and as Will neared the store, he must have noticed the mule, which Boog said he had saddled and brought to the store.[47] Will Babb's state of mind can only be imagined, but based on the events of the next few minutes, he could only be described as furious. Barnett had stolen his water, grazed his sheep on Babb land, and now had beaten him on a mule trade. The mule stood in the center of town, evidence to anyone who could see that Barnett had made the trade.

The fact that he might have the wrong man in mind would have done little to calm Will down. If he did know that Boog had made the deal, it didn't matter. It was a case of Graham having overstepped his boundaries once again; this time something would have to be done. Moments before Will reached the front porch, his brother John had found Graham, Reid House, and Buck Billings in the store. In the fashion of the border, he had given Graham an *abrazo*, a hug exchanged between men in lieu of a handshake. The gesture also had the added advantage of making it easier to check someone to see if they were carrying a weapon. In this case, John was looking for a pistol in a shoulder holster or on a belt. He made a critical mistake when he determined that Graham wasn't armed.

As Will stormed past the ranchers in front of the store, John Babb emerged from the group and muttered, "He ain't got a gun, Will!"[48] That may have been the factor that helped Will decide that the time had come to confront Graham again. He had run Graham off before, from water holes and disputed grass, and this was going to be one more time when the older man made the younger man run. Bursting into Dodd's store, in front of a startled Eula Crist, Victor Tippett, and a handful of witnesses, Will angrily accused Graham of interfering with the mule trade. Babb was furious. He got louder with his cussing, reached into his pocket, and jerked out a large folding knife.[49] Babb snapped the blade open and began to gesture with it and continued his cussing at Graham. Victor Tippett watched the exchange between the two men, and saw Babb reach out and swing at Graham, raking the knife across his vest.[50] Eyes batting furiously, Will waved the knife at Graham. Victor Tippett recalled, "Will was shaking that knife."[51]

Tippett witnessed the rest of the exchange between the two men. "Will said, 'Goddamn you, you butted in on that mule trade didn't you?' Graham had his head kinda ducked. He said he hadn't butted in on the mule trade intentionally."[52] The question of who really did the trade for the mule was no longer important. There was no question about which brother had walked off with the mule; the conversation had gone well beyond any point of rational discussion. Considering Will's state of mind as evidenced by his behavior, the talking was just about over. In the evidence that still exists, there is little or no record of Graham engaging in any kind of aggressive talk or action in the store. He is reported as being quiet, almost reticent, in the exchange. If it was true that he was intimidated by Will Babb at the water holes, this time he wouldn't back down. The next thing Babb said set the stage for the final phase.

Victor Tippett recalled the actions of both men. "Will said, 'You are a damn liar, come outside and we will settle it, then Graham came off the counter, he went for the gun."[53] It seems clear in light of the rest of the action that Graham put his hand in his jacket pocket, but didn't draw the gun. There was no mention of the gun being in sight in the store.

The two men walked out, Graham leading the way, the angry Will Babb following him, still talking. What happened next was observed by Buck Billings, and a number of other men. "Babb advanced with knife in hand. 'You're a goddamn liar if you say you didn't butt in,' and at the same time tried to cut Barnett. Then Barnett shot him."[54] Graham had turned, and pulled the Savage .32; he extended his arm and fired one time. He must have been looking Will in the face because the .32 caliber slug struck the older man in his eye. Babb went down without a sound.

In the store, Tippett said, "I heard a shot."[55] He rushed outside to join W. H. Dodd, ranchmen Henry Mills, French Ingram, Buck Billings, Ike Billings, Reid House, and a few Mexican section hands. The ranchmen gathered in a circle around Babb's body. "I'll be goddamned!" a stunned Buck Billings exclaimed. "Shot out his good eye."[56] John Babb was standing with them and Graham, expecting more trouble, turned and pointed the gun at him. Babb looked at him and said, "Why Graham, I'm ashamed of you."[57] The group of witnesses began to divide and decide what to do next. While some others gathered at the scene, some of the crowd began the process of telling the two factions their version of what had happened.

French Ingram ran up to the Opera House to tell Bessie Mae that Graham shot Will. "Is he dead?" she asked. "If not, I will take his gun to him." But French said, "Yes, he's dead."[58] Bessie Mae ran down across the railroad tracks to Dodd's store, Mildred scrambling behind her mother as fast as she could. There was nothing they could do.

Reid House was trying to saddle a horse in the Billings horse pen, perhaps to take word to the Babbs, perhaps to assist with an escape, when Beulah Billings asked him what was happening. "Reid turned toward us and said 'Graham shot Will Babb'. I said 'Reid, did he kill him?' Reid said 'He is very dead.'"[59]

Ike Billings was the Langtry City Constable and immediately knew something was going to have to be done. He took Graham's pistol but knew that wasn't going to be the end of it. There was no jail in Langtry; if Graham decided to leave, the only thing to stop him would be the crowd. If he stayed in town, there was no way to keep him safe from the Babbs who would be informed of the killing very soon. No one knew what the reaction might be from that family, but everyone agreed it wouldn't be good. The best plan that anyone could come up with was to take Graham to Del Rio, sixty miles away. The east-bound Southern Pacific train was due to steam into town at eleven o'clock. Ike Billings, Buck, and Joe Graham walked Graham over to the train station and waited there.[60]

Victor Tippett saddled a horse and rode it at a gallop until it dropped dead to carry the news to Bill Ike and Alice at their ranch fourteen miles north of Langtry. Mildred Babb Adams stated later that Will's mother talked to her widowed daughter-in-law. "Alice begged Bessie to take a gun and shoot Graham Barnett down, you would be vindicated, no law would touch you for doing it." Bessie was horrified and heartbroken, but kept her head. "I cannot do that, two wrongs would not make a right and I could not live with myself."[61] The rest of the Babbs didn't adopt such a Christian attitude. Talk began immediately about what should be done to even the score.

Graham, in the meantime, was safe from immediate reprisal by any member of the Babb family. In the custody of Ike Billings and accompanied by Joe Graham and the others from the train station, he was on a Southern Pacific train puffing south through the canyon and desert country across the Pecos River High Bridge to Del Rio, county seat of Val Verde, for delivery to the sheriff on charges of murder. He was placed in the Val Verde County jail, and Joe Graham began the bail process.

The shooting brought immediate controversy, much of it engendered by talk from people who were not involved in it either as witnesses or as members of either faction. The witnesses all saw Will behind Graham, saw the knife and had heard the invitation to go outside and had seen the mark on Graham's leather vest from the swipe that Will had made inside the store.

It seemed that everyone had a version of the truth whether they were there when it happened or not. Beulah Billings later maintained that Will had closed the knife and was putting it away when Graham shot him.[62] The problem with that was that she was in her house and not a witness. The people who were in the store saw part of it, those outside saw the end. Both groups agreed that there was a confrontation, that a threat was made against a man who seemed to be unarmed. That fact, confirmed by the announcement from John Babb to his brother, seemed to point to a desperate need on Graham's part to balance the weapons score card a little during the walk across the store's front porch. Had not two deadly weapons shown up at the same time, the situation might have been resolved by a fist fight, but Will had pulled his knife. Most of the men in the crowd were familiar with how quickly a determined man could get some cutting done if he were serious about it, and Will Babb was a determined man.

The decision Graham made to pull a gun previously unnoticed or not, was a typical one for the time and place. He was threatened, the talking was done, and the man behind him had a knife. Graham, the only person to witness the entire encounter, summed it up with one terse statement: "When I put my hand in my pocket, he knew it was all over."[63]

The Graham Barnett legend really finds its basis with this fight. While the Grahams and Barnetts remained quiet about the shooting, the Babbs talked about it long and hard. The more everyone talked, the more heinous the incident became, and the fight itself became greater. For the Babbs it was a treacherous murder and with the passage of years and with each retelling, the story got a bit more awful. If Will Babb had ever done anything mean in his life to the people around him, it was forgotten. His family remembered him as a loving father, a wonderful son, and a man who had struggled most of his life with circumstances that were beyond his control.

Mildred Babb Adams, who was three years old at the time of Will's death, told a different version of her father's death, which bears little resemblance to the public record or the recollections of eyewitnesses. Mrs. Adams agreed that Will and Graham had angry encounters on the range, but her construction of circumstances leading up to the killing, and the actual killing itself, is a story of conspiracy and planned murder. Her version spreads the guilt across a wider range than just Graham.

"Buck Billings was the one that had my daddy killed," said Mrs. Adams. "He had undercut Will on two separate land deals... Will was now at a location that interfered greatly with the enterprises of this man."[64] Further, Billings held a grudge because Will had beaten him in a horse race, Mildred said. She also claimed that Joe Graham was in on the killing. Buck Billings and Joe Graham planned the killing at the Dodd store, and they gave Graham one thousand dollars and Buck's pistol. They "told him to go practice for a while, then to induce Will into some kind of an argument and shoot him before he would even know what was happening. He had to be disposed of." Billings and Joe Graham "were in the store waiting to see it all take place," said Mildred. Lawyers had already been hired, she said, to defend Graham in the shooting.[65] If any of this material came out in the subsequent trials, little was made of it.

If there had been a conspiracy to kill Will Babb, the easiest thing to do would have been to kill him out of town and leave him to be discovered by his herders. This would have led people to suspect rustlers or smugglers and also would get away from the problem with an abundance of witnesses who seemed to be coming out of the adobe in Langtry. None of this kept the Babbs from continuing to see conspiracies.

The killing had some immediate consequences. The first involved Graham himself. Stories began to circulate that the Babbs had put a ten thousand dollar bounty on the heads of Graham and Buck Billings, payable upon proof of death. In a world where bread was .06 cents a loaf and a skilled brick layer made .75 cents an hour, money like that would have attracted a lot of attention and would have been hard to pass up. Whether it was true or not is a different story. The Babbs denied it at a later date although it became a central part of the Graham Barnett legend. The threat was taken seriously by Graham and the rest of the family.

Graham began to watch for people who might be out to collect the bounty. It was a constant threat that could be found anywhere. He began to prepare himself for the potential of having to face down one or more people intent on his death. Sterling County Sheriff Vern Davis observed how it changed his friend: "From that time on Graham started preparing himself for trouble. He told me that the Babb killing started him on his career as a gunman. In other words, the Babbs calculated to kill him, so Graham started practicing, learning how to shoot. In my opinion, Graham was more or less driven to the hard life he lived. I think he was a good boy gone wrong and would never have gone wrong except through fear of the people he first had trouble with, the Babbs."[66]

H. W. "Pat" Patterson, a keen observer of good men and bad on the border, began to collect stories about Graham as they emerged. "The killing of Will Babb conferred a reputation upon Graham Barnett that was more than equal to the killing of a dozen ordinary men. He had bought himself a package that most men would have held with regret. No one was quicker than Barnett himself to realize the gravity of his situation. He proceeded at once to make himself into a superman in the art of gun fighting"[67]

In the classic fashion of legends all over the world, the reputation of the man killed enhanced the reputation of the man who survived. It takes a superman to kill a superman. The killing, the story of the revenge promised by the Babbs, and the constant practice by Graham to prepare himself for what he thought was coming, all contributed to the legend and to a great deal of talk about the part-time stock detective and apprentice *pistolero* from the border. His actions over the next two years only helped the stories grow.

Illustration 6. Dodd Store Langtry, Texas. Site of the fight with Bill Ike Babb

(Photo used with permission of Dr. Douglas Braudaway, Southwest Texas Junior College, Del Rio, Texas)

CHAPTER 4

"I WAS SHOT ALL TO PIECES"

1914-1916[1]

If 1913 ended in tragedy for three families, 1914 did not promise much relief. Joe Graham put up the original five-thousand-dollar bond in the case and began a search for lawyers. That process proved to be both a lengthy and expensive one. The bond money was only the first installment on two years of costly legal skirmishing that would eventually require the services of four lawyers.

Lawyers didn't come cheap. It isn't clear if it was the aftermath of the shooting or just a desire to move, but by February 1914, Joe Graham was beginning to sell stock and property. The *El Paso Herald* reported that he sold five hundred head of sheep on February 2, and that "Del Rio parties are negotiating for the purchase of J. M. Graham's '33' Ranch."[2] Two weeks later he sold an additional three thousand one hundred head of sheep to three different parties and began to close out operations in Langtry.[3] There was no doubt that he and the family were getting out of the area. Joe bought a house in Del Rio and a ranch in Kinney County, about eighteen miles east of Del Rio. By the end of February 1914, he sent his wife and three girls to Del Rio by train. He and his sons followed in their car. They decided to cut the road trip by about one hundred miles by crossing the Pecos on the railroad tracks of the Pecos high bridge. They waited until the trains had passed and drove on the railroad tracks to cross the river.[4] The bridge stood about three hundred twenty feet above the river. Joe drove the car onto the tracks and maneuvered it across the open bridge. That crossing must have provided stories to be told for years as well as an ample opportunity for prayer.[5] By March 1914, they were out of Langtry and the family began to prepare to face the continued aftermath of the shooting.

Graham's lawyers, George Thurmond and Walter Gillis, both of Del Rio, had been aggressively seeking dismissal of murder charges against their client on the grounds that the grand jury had been tampered with. They asserted that District Attorney C. C. Belcher of Marfa and "certain persons not authorized by law were present when the grand jury was deliberating upon the accusation against Barnett and discussing presenting the bill of indictment."[6] Exactly who those persons were was not stated and the jury tampering charge was denied. In the middle of all the preparation, someone offered up the idea of a change of venue. It isn't clear which side proposed the change. The prosecution had the greater interest in getting the trial out of Val Verde County where Will's well-known temper and the bullying of Barnett were likely to influence the jury. The defense may not have opposed the move because Graham's reputation was about as strong as Will Babb's. Everyone may have recognized that both sides would benefit from a move to a site where both were less well-known.

The case was transferred from Val Verde County to Pecos County for trial in the September 1914 term of the 63rd District Court in Fort Stockton. To help the defense, Joe Graham hired two more lawyers, Joe Jones ("Walter" in some accounts) from Del Rio, and Pecos County Judge Howell Johnson.

As for the prosecution, the state was represented by C. C. Belcher, the new district attorney for Val Verde County, and J. J. Foster. Foster had represented the Babbs for years but had not assisted with a criminal prosecution in some time. Belcher was a relatively new district attorney, so the Babbs decided they should hire someone with more experience to assist with the prosecution. In their discussions Belcher suggested James Cornell of Sonora. Belcher commented that Cornell was a good lawyer and an honest man. Bill Ike Babb indicated he was more interested in a conviction: "...Cliff, we don't want him too damn honest."[7] Honest or not, the prosecution was ready.

The first trial was set for October 4, 1914, in Fort Stockton. The defense had an impressive list of witnesses including former Rangers Oscar Latta and Frank Hamer. Both had been Rangers in Del Rio as early as 1908, and knew something of the reputations of both men. Current Ranger E. A. Palmer and Graham's old pal Vern Davis of Sterling City were scheduled, presumably, to provide a more current view of events. It seemed as though everyone who had been in Dodd's store that morning were included as witnesses. The trial immediately ran into a couple of problems.

Because of the nature of the killing and the reputations of the people involved, one of the first issues anticipated was crowd control. Both the Babbs and the Grahams seemed to travel with an entourage, and a large group of angry, armed men was going to be hard to control. The man to handle most of the serious challenges was the county sheriff, Dudley Barker. A better man could not have been found. Dudley Barker was a former Texas Ranger who had dealt with feuds and outlaws for years. He was perhaps best known for a gunfight in Fort Stockton in 1912 when he took on nine drunk cowboys and killed four of them. The final total may have been higher, but those were the only bodies found in the city limits. Dud Barker had become something of a friend to Graham and had decided that the young man would get a fair trial in his county, and that it would not be interfered with by the Babbs. The Babb family might have carried a lot a weight on the border, but were just one more grieving, contrary family in Fort Stockton. On the afternoon of October 1, Bill Ike Babb, grief stricken and somewhat drunk, met Dudley Barker, high sheriff for Pecos County, in the yard of the county courthouse.

Bill Ike Babb had come to town to see justice done and he had not come alone. He brought his family and his reputation. The Fort Stockton Pioneer provided a description: "Bill Ike Babb, as he is familiarly known, is considered a very dangerous man and has the reputation of having killed more than one person."[8] That kind of reputation must have prepared Sheriff Dudley Barker for what was going to happen. While waiting for the trial to begin, Bill Ike and two of his supporters decided to have a drink. They must have had several drinks because they decided to move the drinking to the courthouse square. Once there Bill Ike began a speech about the expected court proceedings that attracted a lot of attention. The newspaper described it as "boisterous talk" and that brought Dudley Barker into the picture. He had watched the crowd and when he noticed that the Babbs had begun to drink and that Bill Ike was beginning to make speeches, he decided the time had come to put an end to it.

When Barker approached the Babbs, he didn't do it alone. He was backed by several friends who were acting as unofficial deputies. Barker told Babb he was going to jail, and as part of that process began to search him for weapons. Bill Ike was "heeled" with a pistol in a shoulder holster. He did not offer any resistance until Barker found the pistol. Barker reached for the pistol and Babb reacted as he "fiercely resented being searched." The old man must have reached for his gun, and when he did, Barker grasped his arms in a bear hug and tossed him to the ground where he could manage him a little better. Once on the ground, Barker relieved him of his pistol while Barker's backup kept the others at bay. Shortly afterwards Bill Ike was deposited in the Fort Stockton jail where he spent the evening and the next day, paid his bail and headed back out into the community. Boisterous talk was not the only problem.

Graham and his lawyers, George Thurmond and Walter Gillis, appeared before District Judge W. C. Douglas in the 63rd District Court in Fort Stockton to ask for a postponement of the trial. The reason was clear: no one could seem to find Buck Billings, who was a critically important witness. The legalese of the court records describes the mysterious disappearance of Mister Billings. "Buck Billings was served a subpoena May 22, 1914, by the sheriff of Val Verde County but went to Mexico to purchase and bring back livestock but he [Barnett] further believes that said witness has been prevented from returning to said State of Texas and being present at this trial by the disturbed and warlike conditions in said Republic of Mexico but that he does not know and is not informed as to what place in Mexico said witness is at the present time."[9]

The newspaper coverage got a little more colorful. According to the *Fort Stockton Pioneer*, "Billings at that time was a prisoner in the hands of the Mexican revolutionists."[10] Other members of the public clouded the issue even further, claiming that Boog Barnett was hiding Billings to keep the Babbs from killing him to keep him from testifying. Regardless of who was currently keeping Buck out of sight, the trial couldn't go on without him.

Judge Douglas granted a delay in the trial until the next term of the court, March, 1915. With the circus over, people began to drift out of town. There were a few repercussions however. Graham's son, Bud Barnett, claimed the Babbs openly declared that "they would kill Graham Barnett before, during, or after the trial."[11] Because of the danger from the Babbs, Bud claimed Sheriff Barker allowed Graham to carry a pistol at all stages of the trial, including inside the courtroom in the presence of the judge, jury, and spectators. Bud Barnett added, "The Babbs were a threat to Graham as long as he lived."[12] A whole new cycle of hero and villain stories about the Babbs and Barnetts began to evolve and they illustrate the extent of the hate and fear generated by both families. When the excitement was over, and the trial date reset, Graham headed back to work and tried to stay out of the Babbs's way.

To stay out of their way, he chose to spend time in the Dead Horse Mountains. The Dead Horse were a thirty-mile stretch of desolation formed by the Sierra del Carmen range that juts up out of Mexico through what is now the Big Bend National Park. The southern end forms part of Boquillas Canyon, and the range extends to Dagger Flats in the north.

It stands about four thousand feet above sea level with several peaks reaching higher. It is spectacular in its beauty and isolation, and provided an ideal location for a cowboy to find work on a secluded ranch or for a man on the run to stay out of the public eye. It is unknown if Graham had been in the area before, but for the rest of his life, the Big Bend became the place he returned to when he faced problems or needed to be out of sight.

He was likely working for one of several ranches in that area whose owners were friends of Joe Graham. When he was not working stock he was polishing gun skills. Later, he told one friend that he literally shot up cases of ammunition practicing during this time.[13] It paid to be prepared. While Graham worked and fretted in the Big Bend, Boog and Buck Billings were doing some fretting of their own in Mexico.

If Mildred Babb Adams was correct in her allegation that the Babb family believed that Buck Billings played a role in Will Babb's death Billings might have been seen as big a target for their hatred as Graham. Regardless of the truth of that allegation, Billings remained a critical witness for the defense. Billings had heard of the threats at the waterholes, and was ready to testify that Will started the fight at the Dodd store. While there were a number of people who had seen some aspect of the ongoing series of confrontations between the families, he had seen the beginning and the end of it. Therefore, it was in the best interests of the Barnett faction to protect Billings from Babb reprisal. Mexico seemed to be the ideal place to escape to for a short time. There was also the factor that cattle and sheep were cheap in Mexico, and a man could make some money if he bought and sold at the right time.

Setting up their own witness protection program, Boog and Buck decided to use their time to buy Mexican cattle from ranchers uprooted by the revolution. They bought livestock at bargain prices and shipped them to Texas border ports, sometimes on order of US buyers, sometimes on speculation, picking up what commissions and profits they could. While Boog roamed the interior, shopping for Mexican livestock bargains, Buck prowled the border scouting for likely buyers. Plunging into the middle of the Mexican Revolution to avoid the Babbs might have struck some people as stepping out of the frying pan onto the hot stove. They found out that such activity was not always without incident.

Boog bought Mexican sheep which he shipped to Las Vacas (now Ciudad Acuna), opposite Del Rio, Texas, and found such a favorable market that he returned at once to the interior for more. Afraid that the Babbs may have spotted him in Del Rio, Billings decamped to Piedras Negras, across the river from Eagle Pass, south of Del Rio, where he tried to attract as little attention as possible while plying his trade. At Catorce, a village in the state of San Luis Potosi, Boog loaded 3,200 sheep on railroad cars. Before he had gone very far the track was cut by Villistas, who also burned the bridge in front of the train, a common practice in Villa's campaign to deny his foes use of the railroads in northern Mexico. He and his sheep were detained by a group of federal cavalrymen and if he had not made friends with one of the local military commanders previously, it is doubtful that he would have made it back to the United States at all. As it worked out, he and the sheep arrived at the border late but intact.

While Boog and Buck Billings were in Mexico, Graham continued to look for a way to make money and stay relatively out of sight. He decided that Mexico might provide as good a refuge for him as it seemed to be for his brother and Buck Billings, so he headed south in 1914. If he was looking for a job that promised quiet and a lowered profile, he picked the wrong one. He went to work for the T. O. Ranch in Chihuahua, a place that was as big in legend as it was in size.

The T. O. (Texas and Old Mexico) was originally owned by Dr. W. S. Woods, a financier and bank president from Kansas City. It was called the Riverside Ranch when he owned it. It was typical of an American enterprise in Mexico: money from outside of the country was designed to produce more money to be moved outside of the country. Over the years, it seemed to devolve from an example of American entrepreneurism to the site of crime and revolution. The ranch was located seventy-five miles southeast from El Paso and across from Sierra Blanca, Texas. Sierra Blanca provided access to the railroad and a method of moving stock quickly and easily from the pasture to the packing plant. The ranch consisted of 2,250,000 acres. With a ranch of that size, something was always going on, and the T. O. Ranch developed a name synonymous with violence.

In January of 1905, there was a gunfight on the property resulting in the death of Walter Blunt and the arrest and subsequent trial of the accused killer, Jack Bendele. Bendele was found not guilty in Mexico, but in June was brought to Texas for a second opportunity to meet the hangman.[14] He avoided the meeting when the court decided one trial, even if it was in Mexico, was ample and he was freed. In 1906 reality met fiction when the model for Oliver Wister's novel The Virginian, John Hicks, married a schoolteacher and the two moved to the ranch. Hicks had been hired as manager, a role he filled for several years.[15] Management was not the biggest problem; the sheer size of the enterprise and growing unrest in Northern Mexico influenced Dr. Woods to get rid of the property.

On February 4, 1910, he sold the ranch to Edwin Morris of the Nelson Morris Packing Company for $700,000.00, in one of the largest sales of its kind in Northern Mexico at the time.[16] The Nelson Morris Company at one time owned over 100 different properties controlled from its corporate offices in Chicago. Nelson Morris had plans for the ranch, but the coming of the Revolution meant that it had became just one more part of Chihuahua that was raided and fought over. On July 28, 1911, the model that would be followed for the next several years was established; a fight would occur and the ranch would be raided. Two groups of rebels, supporters of Flores Magon, and another group supporting Francisco Madero, fought a skirmish near the headquarters of the ranch. When the Maderistas ran out of ammunition, they left and the Magonistas raided the ranch store and held two American cattle buyers hostage. Tom Kingsberry reported that the meeting was cordial. "I want to say we were treated as well as possible the whole time we were in their power. Our meals were specially cooked for us and we ate in the house while the officers and the men ate outside...Both sides fought splendidly."[17]

While their story ended well, it would not be long before both Mexicans and Americans at the T. O. would have a different story to tell.

For years the T. O. was reputed to have been an exchange point for stolen stock coming out of Mexico. Bandits would steal stock from a number of ranches, move them onto the T. O., and cross them into Texas for sale. The sale usually occurred at Sierra Blanca, Texas. The profit from the rustled stock sales funded weapons and contraband flowing back into the war-torn country, as well the ongoing activities of a number of outlaws on both sides of the river. Thieves were attracted to the ranch, not just for the cattle, but for horses which were in high demand by the fast moving Revolutionists as well as the Federals. On February 12, 1912, one of the foremen, A. B. Paschal, reported that they were moving surplus horses out of Mexico to reduce potential losses.[18] Perhaps to lessen the impact the story might have on trade and business overall, the general manager of the ranch, W. N. Pence, denied it. If the horses were moved they were moved back into Mexico shortly afterwards. The readership of the newspapers might have believed the story about no surplus horses at the ranch; unfortunately the Mexican forces didn't read the newspaper. On August 28, 1912, the ranch was looted, probably for horses, by what the *El Paso Herald* estimated was part of a 1,200 man force that was raiding east of Juarez.[19] Elements of a federal cavalry troop cut telephone lines connecting the ranch with Sierra Blanca on January 13, 1914, burned a number of the buildings, and stole horses and saddles. The ranch foreman escaped but was not able to determine what might have happened to a number of the cowboys who had remained at the ranch.[20] Based on the common practice of the time, it is likely they were jailed until a sizable bail was paid. The ranch was beginning to be seen as a dangerous place to be a drover.

In response to the raids, a force of about a hundred Villaistas moved onto the ranch in late January, ostensibly to provide protection for it and the men who worked there.[21] It was questionable how much protection they provided. Thefts began to be noted weekly and the cowboys realized that they might have been hired to move cattle but they were going to have to deal with both sides of a highly volatile revolution. The ranchmen were a little better prepared on September 13, 1913, when an armed group of Mexican horsemen approached the ranch. A sharp fight began and ended when the Mexicans identified themselves as Villaistas who were in pursuit of the bandits who had been raiding the ranch.[22] It became apparent that if the ranch was going to continue to operate, it was going to have to be able to protect its stock, and the men who worked there. Relying on the local bandits for security was not working out. The protection they provided was both expensive and dangerous. A major change was going to have to take place.

On September 4, 1914, H. L. "Hod" Roberson resigned for the Texas Rangers.[23] Roberson left the Rangers with a reputation as a tough man and, according to a number of accounts, a killer. He had been in the Rangers since 1911, and while he was a favorite of Captain John Hughes, he seemed to be dedicated to ending arrest attempts with shootings.[24] He went to work for the T. O. almost immediately and adopted a more aggressive policy toward the Revolution. He was soon joined by a number of men who were good cowboys but equally good with a gun.

It appears that Graham was a member of the T. O. protection group in late September or early October. He could have been with them earlier but the trials in Fort Stockton would have required him to be out of Mexico and back in Texas for the legal proceedings. While little is known about the activities of the new men, there remain strong feelings on the border as to what Roberson was up to. "As foreman he led some dozen or so gun men that ran roughshod over the huge border ranch. The T. O. men controlled a fair amount of the border north of Candelaria to El Paso on the Mexican side terrorizing anyone who got in their way."[25] Roberson's crew moved Mexican cattle, which were stolen in many cases, into Texas and sold them cheap in Sierra Blanca.[26] While Roberson seemed to be running wild, the Revolution intervened to put an end to much of the activity.

The ranch owners, the Nelson Morris Company, decided they needed to brand the stock they could find and began to sell what was there before it was lost to either bandits or the federal forces. Pancho Villa seemed to be in charge of the area so in October the company worked out an agreement to allow a group of cowboys to move onto the ranch to brand and roundup cattle. Along with that group the Villaistas agreed to allow thirty additional men to guard the working cowboys.[27] Based on later comments, Graham was probably part of the guard group. They arrived on Monday the 16th and prepared to head out to guard the branding crew. Almost immediately a force of about seventy-five Mexicans rode up to the men, drew their guns, and began to take them prisoner.

How that many armed men got close enough to arrest what was supposed to be a fairly competent group of killers remains unanswered. Stories from the time say that Roberson may have thought that the mounted men were part of a group of friendly Villaistas. As it turned out, they were far from friendly. Local lore claimed, "Graham Barnett asked if he [Roberson] thought they should fight. He had answered 'No, these men coming are friends. I recognize their horses'."[28] Roberson may have known the horses but he didn't know the men. The Mexicans were not Villaistas but were federal guerillas who didn't care what kind of deal Pancho Villa had made. He was on the other side and the Americans could be held hostage for a fair amount of money. The federals quickly surrounded the cowboys, and began the process of disarming them and stealing whatever valuables they had with them. There was a considerable amount of confusion as the groups moved through the swirls of dust stirred up in the brush by the cattle. Graham had the opportunity to watch what was happening and made a decision about the entire matter. He had come to Mexico to avoid jail, not get into one. The northern boundary of the ranch was the Rio Grande River and all Graham had to do was win a horse race.

"I was working for H. L. Roberson at the T. O. Ranch when he, and a lot of his men, were captured by the revolutionists and were looking down the barrel of a Mauser rifle. I managed to ride away just as they rode into camp."[29] It was a little more dramatic than riding out of camp. Graham kicked his horse into a run and headed for the border. The Villaistas responded with a hail of 7 mm. bullets and a fast pursuit. He later declared that "I was shot all to pieces," but he was probably describing the condition of his clothing and gear since members of Graham's family dispute the statement that he was wounded.[30] Whatever his condition, he made it to the border and managed to escape the short imprisonment of the other men who had been picked up in the sweep. The glamorous job of soldier of fortune had ended quickly for him.

What finally happened to the Roberson bunch was clear: they left Mexico. Exactly why is more confusing. "About 1914, some said General Villa personally ran Hod Roberson and his men out of Mexico outside Ojinaga. Another account states that the Roberson gang were arrested and deported by Mexican soldiers for branding stolen Terrazas cattle."[31] Either way, jobs in Mexico for American *pistoleros* were going to be scarce until there was a shift in power.

Life in Mexico was over for a while, but the self-exile was not. Graham went back to day work, moving stock and intercepting outlaws in the Big Bend area for his uncle and other people who needed someone to balance the books. What seems to emerge from this period is a large number of stories attributing a number of killings to Graham. Only in rare cases was there any kind of witness to the violence. It is equally important to note that no indictments were issued, and no angry families attempted to search him out for revenge. During this time, he was continuing with what Joe Graham had referred to as stock detective work. Stories were told in beer joints and Sunday school classes that he had become someone who shot rustlers, who assassinated people who were crossing fences at the wrong time, or killed just for the sake of killing. Few of the stories had witnesses or proof of any sort but on some occasions a witness turned up. One such was Walter Riggs, an ex T. O. cowboy who worked with Graham when they both worked for T. M. "Stormy" Leach.

According to Riggs, they came upon three Mexican riders cutting through the ranch. Graham and Riggs approached the men to determine who they were and what business they had on the property. They caught up to them in a rough mountainous area of the ranch and when they were approached, the Mexicans ran. Graham and Riggs headed up the side of the mountain and clattered along the rim parallel to the trail in the canyon below them. Then Graham made a decision. "While they were running along the bottom, we managed to get up a few feet above them on the side of the mountain. When we got close enough, Graham shot and killed all three of them. When he finished covering their bodies with some rocks, he said to me, 'You little -------------, if you ever tell that, I'll give you some of it.'"[32] Riggs never explained what made Graham decide to shoot. It could have been that the men were running and for him, that was all it took. Running meant guilt and the vaqueros were in the wrong pasture at the wrong time.

There is the further question of did the shooting actually happen at all, or was this another story told when someone bought the next round? It is impossible to know, too much time has passed, and too many bodies have been buried in unmarked graves, but the story does illustrate several points. First, Graham had a growing reputation as a killer, and the public expected that kind of behavior from a known gunman. It defined who he was. He had become a legendary figure who unsolved killings could be blamed on, and the people who told the stories in beer joints and around town would recall him as someone not to be trifled with. Second, the people who told the story became part of the legend. Whether Walter Riggs was an active participant or a shocked witness makes no difference, he was on site and was involved to a degree. He was ready to tell the story and by telling the story, he became part of it. Finally, the story reflected a grim reality of life on the border. Predators of any kind could not be tolerated. If they were in the pasture, they were going to be shot: eagles, coyotes, or bandits. Graham's job was to protect the property and he was going to do that. Bandits were predators and he thought no more of shooting them than he would have an animal. It was something he did to keep the place safe, and it was, as he observed later, "like shooting wolves in a field of sheep."[33] It was something he did because it had become his job.

CHAPTER 5

"I KNEW GRAHAM WAS IN SOME KIND OF TROUBLE"

1914-1915[1]

They must have known each other for some time before 1914. In a town as small as Sterling City, everyone knows everyone else, or thinks they do. The town gossip was that Graham Barnett worked at Joe Graham's place and traded horses and mules part-time. He had been away and then moved back to where he had grown up. He had been in some mysterious business down on the border but he seemed ready to settle down in Sterling now. She heard some of the gossip and believed little of it. And they had noticed each other.

She was Annie Laura Conger, born September 22, 1895, and was five years younger than Graham. W. T. Conger was her father, and she lived on the family ranch, about twenty miles from Sterling City. She was five feet tall, slender with dark brown hair piled up on her head. She lived the life of country girl, complete with the horses she loved and rode. She was about to become the most important person in Graham Barnett's world. The only thing that made the courtship a little difficult was the matter of the murder indictment hanging over the potential bridegroom. She remembered the courting as part of a storybook romance.

"He was awfully good looking and a real good dancer," she told her friends.[2] She recalled how they went to as many dances as they could find. One of their favorite destinations was the George McEntire ranch, fifty jolting Model T miles from Sterling City. At ranch dances of the time, frequently all the furniture was moved outside and the dancing took place in the house. Because of the distances involved, people might come and go, extending the dance into the morning hours of the next day when breakfast might be served. As with a lot of romances, some things changed after the wedding. "After we married, we went to very few dances."[3] Graham had a pet name for Annie; he called her "Noots." "Why?" she asked. "Because you're so little," he answered. No one seemed to know where the nickname came from but he called her that for the rest of his life.[4] The courtship phase of the relationship was a little rough. "At first, Graham and I didn't see much of each other. He was out of town a lot on business."[5] Part of the business involved horses and mules but some of it dealt with a more serious issue, the business of the Babbs.

"I knew Graham was in some kind of trouble," Annie continued, "but I didn't know that he had killed anybody."[6] As Graham struggled with the murder indictment, the Conger family struggled with the idea that their potential son-in-law might go to jail. "My brothers got along fine with Graham and my parents liked him, but they objected to Graham because of the Babb shooting."[7] While her parents might have been worried, the legal situation didn't make any difference to Annie then or later. The couple was in love, and it seemed that neither legal problems nor family objections would make a difference. The family's objections must have not been too great because on December 29, 1914, the couple applied for a marriage license at the courthouse and they were married on January 24, 1915.[8]

Although Graham seemed committed to her and to the marriage, he took a job out of town almost immediately. The couple lived in a tent for two months while he cowboyed on a Hudspeth County ranch between Sierra Blanca and the Rio Grande. The Conger family and Joe Graham must have decided that they needed to do something to keep the newlyweds out of a tent and decided to provide them some security.

W. T. Conger bought 1,000 sheep for Graham, gave his daughter 12 Hereford heifers, and leased a place to put them: the Eddins ranch in Sterling County.[9] On occasion, Joe Graham moved stock from his places in southwest Texas and fed them out at the Sterling City ranch. Graham had some responsibility for that outfit also.

Before Graham could settle into his new role as country squire, there was the matter of another trial, and on March 8, 1915, he was hauled into court again to answer the charge of murder. When he returned to court this time, he had his new bride at his side. Again the trial had to be postponed. Buck Billings had finished his business or captivity, depending on whose story one believed. But he was not so lucky on the roads of Texas. He was in a Del Rio hospital recovering from serious injuries in a car crash that killed the other occupant of the car, Crockett County cowman Dock Russell, *the Pioneer* reported.[10] Details of the crash, such as how it happened and who was driving, were not disclosed.

The *Fort Stockton Pioneer* took this occasion to state its policy on coverage of the Babb murder trial: "The *Pioneer* will not print anything concerning the merits of the case, or even an account of same, for fear of rendering it a difficult matter to secure a jury when the case comes on for trial."[11] Complete court records of the trial, including transcripts of the testimony, have been scattered over the years. However, using some surviving newspaper records and witness's statements, it is possible to put together an overview of what happened at the trial.

When the four-day trial finally got underway, Monday, October 4, 1915, *Pioneer* coverage, as promised, was thin. "The evidence of a large number of witnesses" was heard, the paper reported in its edition of October 8, without specifying who the witnesses were or what they said.[12] Why the paper did not report what happened at the trial after it was over when nothing printed could affect a juror's judgment is hard to understand by today's standards but the *Pioneer* had spoken.

The *Pioneer* might not have covered the trial as completely as it could have but one thing was clear: the plea was going to be not guilty by virtue of self-defense. For such a plea to be successful, Will Babb would have to be depicted as a man who made a threat and was capable of carrying it out. That kind of defense was something that people in Texas understood. A man had to defend himself. Sometimes you could not walk off from a situation. It was the classic "him or me" defense.

Texas case law defined self-defense as being justified if the subject "... reasonably believes the force is immediately necessary to protect himself against the other's use or attempted use of unlawful force."[13] The question of whether the force was immediately necessary could be answered quickly. Will Babb had threatened Graham with an open knife. He had motive and method, and was certainly angry enough to get the job done. Graham apparently being unarmed must have contributed to the urgency in the situation. A man with a knife behind a seemingly unarmed man was a deadly situation, and an unarmed man being threatened by an armed one justified him taking action. If the question of gun versus knife came up it was quickly disposed of. A man had the responsibility to use whatever tool he might have to terminate the threat.

Presumable Rangers Oscar Latta and Frank Hamer were brought back to discuss the Babbs' activities prior to 1913. Joe Graham was likely called to discuss the confrontations at the water holes. All of that was background. The question to be answered dealt with the action of the individuals between 10:30 and 11:00 on that Monday morning in December, 1913. Was it self-defense?

It must have been an eye-opener for the new bride to sit and listen to descriptions of the man she had married, and must have wondered, just who was this man? Was he the gunman who had chased rustlers in Mexico? Was he the cowboy who had been run off from another man's water hole? Was he the steely-eyed assassin who killed a man outside a country store over a mule? She must have wondered who Graham Barnett really was, and how she could separate all of these stories from the reality of the man she knew.

The jury may have had some problems trying to distinguish between truth as it happened and truth as it was remembered, but they got to the facts of the case. What was clear was that the two had argued, and started outside to finish the dispute. Will had threatened Graham with a knife and was behind Graham as they left the store. Graham walked out, down the two wooden steps and turned, drawing his pistol when he did. He had practiced the technique of pointing a pistol as he had pointed his finger. He pointed at Will Babb and pulled the trigger.

The jury was out forty minutes before it came back with a verdict. "The deceased Will Babb was in the very act of making an unlawful and deadly attack upon the defendant at the same time he shot and killed the deceased, and that the shooting was necessary self-defense. We, the jury, find the defendant Graham Barnett not guilty," announced the foreman E. E. Townsend.[14]

The trial put an official end to a great deal of speculation that had been tossed around about conspiracies and shooting in the back. Apparently the question of a conspiracy on the part of Joe Graham and Buck Billings never came up. Neither man was mentioned in any existing newspaper article or in any stories except from the family of the murdered man. The allegation that somehow Graham had gotten behind Will and shot him in the back, as was maintained by some of his relatives, was not mentioned either.

Once the finding came in from the jury, many people tried to explain it away or ignore the facts of the case. People who supported Graham and those who supported the late Mr. Babb both seemed to be searching for explanations for the verdict. The change of venue certainly played a role, but it could have favored either party since the reputation of both men would have been in the minds of a Val Verde County jury. Since the Babbs had a reputation as a family that was pretty tough, the change of venue could have worked in their favor. The Graham family was not as well-known as the Babbs but enough people knew Joe that his reputation, and that of the family, probably convinced some of Barnett's innocence before the trial began. Beula Billings, who was married to Buck Billings and had more than a passing interest in the whole affair, also could not get away from the family factor. She attributed the acquittal to the prominence of the Grahams. "They moved the trial to Fort Stockton and Graham Barnett came clear as a whistle, because of his and his family's reputation of being good citizens," she said.[15] By implication, the Babbs were considered not quite as good a set of citizens.

The Babbs believed that the verdict represented a prejudiced view against them as a family. Following a familiar pattern of the times, Mildred blamed the secretive society of Masons for Graham's acquittal, claiming that the outcome of the trial was "a foregone conclusion because Joe Graham [a Mason] had contacted Masons of highest rank. His lawyers were careful to get Masons on the jury."[16] The Babbs, at least the patriarch, Bill Ike, were not Masons. The family continued to claim that Bill Ike finally found a lawyer to help prosecute Graham for the killing of his son. The lawyer turned out to be a Mason. Based on the popularity of the organization at that time, it would be hard to find many prominent men who were not members of the Masons, although the idea of them packing a jury and using the affiliation to free a defendant seems to be difficult to imagine.

Both families were immediately and permanently impacted by the decision. The grief of the Babbs was easily seen when Graham's mother, Chicora, introduced herself to Bessie Mae on the train that was taking both of them to the trial and offered to shake hands. Bessie Mae answered, "I am fully aware that you are Mrs. Barnett and I am not about to shake hands with you."[17] There was not going to be any forgive and forget. The verdict seemed to crush Will's wife Bessie. "He [Will] was her life. She never remarried," said her son Bennie in a 1990 interview. "My mother was real bitter all her life." Bessie Mae wore black for three years and made black dresses for Mildred until one day Bennie wondered plaintively why they did not wear pretty clothes as other people did? Only then did Bessie Mae quit wearing black. She bought a 160-acre farm near Medina in Bandera County with proceeds from the sale of Will's goats and tried to make a living for her children. "We nearly starved to death," Bennie chuckled.[18]

For the people who knew Graham, the verdict seemed to validate their views of him. He was not the grim killer, but the local boy who had run into a terrible problem and had been forced to deal with it. The *Sterling City Record* of October 15, 1915, summed up many people's attitudes: "The quiet, peaceful bearing of young Barnett in his past life led his many friends to believe that his provocation and danger when he shot Babb must have been extreme and the verdict of the jury which tried him undoubtedly confirmed this belief."[19]

The trial ended the suspense regarding what the state of Texas would do about Graham but it didn't do anything to end the suspense about what the Babbs would do. For the rest of his life, Graham lived looking over his shoulder, waiting for the sound of a rifle shot or the few quick steps that preceded a knife attack. Graham and Boog both believed the Babbs had a $10,000 bounty on them and Graham was never far from a gun after that. Guns became part of his every day routine. "Guns to us were like having a coffee pot around the house," his son Bud recalled. When Graham went to sleep, his .45 was on a chair beside the bed, and when he went out to the privy, the .45 went along as well.[20] When he returned to Sterling City and the life of a sheep man, it was clear that he was a man who could not afford to take a chance by going somewhere unarmed.

Life in Sterling City must have seemed like a dream after Mexico and the uncertainties of the trial. He adjusted to the life of a rancher and Annie adjusted to creating a new life for both of them. For Annie Laura, the young woman from Sterling City who had married into a legendary life, the verdict must have seemed to mark an end to the strange new life she had started. Now things could get back to normal, whatever that was. Both Graham and Annie looked forward to letting life unfold around them at the new place in Sterling County. Their daughter, Maude Caroline, was born there in February 1916. The family was happy, the sheep market was good, the baby was healthy, and Graham was restless. He had almost a month before history invaded his life.

Illustration 7. Annie Laura, Maude Carolyn, Graham Barnett, circa 1917

(Courtesy John T. Barnett)

CHAPTER 6

"To faithfully and impartially discharge and perform all the duties incumbent on me as an officer in the Ranger force"

1915-1917[1]

Graham's world changed again in 1915; this time it was an international situation that intruded into his life and still haunts the border county. The revolution in Mexico set into play a number of events that placed Graham in a position to join the Texas Rangers. That move linked his name and the title "Texas Ranger" for the rest of his life. For a career that seemed to be defined by being a member of the Rangers, his time with them was brief and relatively undistinguished. However, it was dominated by international and state politics, the most critical of which was the ongoing guerilla war along the border.

The Mexican Revolution impacted Texas in several ways. There was a flood of refugees that no one knew what to do with that created unrest throughout the state. A series of cross border raids which became known as the Bandit War lead to expanded and sometimes repressive law enforcement. An increase in vigilantism in response to the raids swept through South Texas and contributed to years of distrust on the part of Mexican, Tejano, and Anglo populations. There was a perceived increase in crime as a result of the refugees and the Border raids, which unnerved the Anglo population, and contributed further to crimes against Mexicans in Texas. Each of these factors led to a highly unsettled situation in the state.

Waves of refugees fleeing the fighting poured out of Mexico into Texas and other border states, none of which were prepared to deal with the onslaught. Between 1910 and 1914, 82,588 Mexicans were processed officially by the Immigration Service as compared with 21,732 between 1905 and 1909.[2] The actual figure of emigrants, legal and non-legal, vary considerably, but estimates for between 250,000 and 300,000 seem plausible.[3] The border was open, and people had crossed for years; now they crossed with less intention of going back. The move to Texas promised relief from the warfare that seemed to be constant, and there was the added benefit of jobs. A man could work for $1.00 or $1.25 per day in the United States and make as much money in three months as he could in a year in Mexico.[4] The refugees desperately sought a roof, a meal, a job, and a future in a new land, at least until the old country had calmed down. A few refugee camps were set up to deal with them in the Rio Grande Valley and at Fort Bliss in El Paso. Basically no one knew what to do with the problem of refugees since no one had ever dealt with the situation at this level before. In some cases, the newcomers were absorbed into the *colonias,* Mexican communities that had existed previously near Anglo communities. Other refugees moved into the larger cities. Many were left to fend for themselves and find work, or the lack of it on their own. It was years before the refugee question began to be addressed on an organized basis.

It wasn't just the refugee question. By 1915, the numbers of cross border raids were increasing as the Revolution washed over into Texas. While both Mexicans and Texans had raided back and forth across the river for years, this time the level of violence had intensified. What became known as the Bandit Wars began to develop in South Texas and extended up the Rio Grande into the Big Bend area. Mexican and Anglo residents north of the Rio Grande began to be plagued by a series of raids for supplies, cattle, and weapons. People who lived along the border and in the areas targeted by the raiders bombarded Austin and Washington with demands for protection. In response, the army moved troops into the Valley in South Texas and began to station cavalry detachments at isolated locations in West Texas.

Reaction from the Anglo community was brisk and generally misdirected toward Mexicans. For some of the Anglos, the unrest provided an opportunity to seize property of Tejanos, or Mexican Texans, the ownership of which had been in dispute for years. A period of lynchings and murders carried out by night riders shook the border and crept as far north as Central Texas. Anglos contended that they were responding to continued Mexican raiding, but many times the response was not directed toward the raiders, but toward any Mexican they could find. A period of fear and distrust descended, and both Anglo and Mexicans began to withdraw as much as possible from formal contact with each other.

Most of this violence was centered on the Rio Grande Valley, which was beginning to bring in both investors and their money from northern states. Texas was in an awkward position of encouraging land investment and then appearing to not be able to control crime in the area. In an attempt to crack down on the violence, Governor Ferguson decided to expand the Rangers by one company. The decision might have been a popular one, but the implementation was faulty. The company was led by the recently appointed Captain Harry Ransom.

Ransom had seen service with the army in the Philippines where he had observed war against both the *insurrectos* and the civilian population.

After that, he had served several enlistments with the Rangers. Most recently he had been a special officer with the Houston Police Department where he had been involved in two questionable shootings.[5] Ransom received blunt instructions; he was told to pacify the Valley. E. A. Sterling told of a conversation between Governor Ferguson, Captain Ransom, and several other men. "He [the governor] had given Ransom instructions to go down there and clean up that nest, that thing had been going on long enough, and to clean it up if he had to kill every damned man connected with it."[6] Ransom built the new Company D and manned it with prison guards and cronies of his. He introduced to South Texas a version of the total war he had seen in the Philippines. The Rangers arrested people on weak charges, searched property without warrants, and cracked down on ownership and transportation of weapons. Prisoners were shot while in Ranger custody or passed off to civilians who carried out the execution. The actions of the company were a blot on the Ranger reputation that was slowly evolving from the old Frontier Battalion. These excesses contributed to long-standing distrust of the Rangers on the part of many Mexicans and Anglos, and eventually to a Legislative investigation conducted by Representative J. T. Canales.

At what might be considered the worst possible time for it, several revolutionists and Texas Mexicans decided that it was time to develop a plan to take back not only Texas, but the entire Southwest, which had been seized from Mexico during the period 1836-1850. What they developed was called the Plan of San Diego after the Texas town in which it was allegedly developed. The plan was actually written in a jail cell in Monterrey, Nuevo Leon, and had been transported north. In a monumentally optimistic, but incredibly foolish move, the developers printed the plan and decided to distribute it in order to whip up support for their planned revolution.

The Plan had as a goal to kill all American males over the age of 15, and then form a "Liberating Army of Races and Peoples" consisting of Mexicans, African Americans, and Japanese that would go on a march of liberation to take back the Southwest. Subsequent plans included moving into Oklahoma and Mississippi. The blood bath was scheduled to begin early in the morning of February 20, 1915. One of the authors, Basilio Ramos, had a copy of the plan with him when he had the misfortune to be arrested while trying to raise funds to support the Plan in South Texas, the very area he expected to turn into a charnel house. He and nine others were arrested and charged in federal court in Laredo, Texas, with "conspiring to steal certain property of the United States of America, contrary to the authority thereof, to wit, the states of Texas, Oklahoma, New Mexico, Arizona, Colorado, and California."[7]

While Ramos and friends were unable to motivate the Mexican population to slaughter every Anglo they knew, and many that they didn't, he did manage to motivate the Anglo population to believe that they were the targets of a race war that would happen eventually, if not in 1915. The existence of the Plan inflamed the population along the border and a series of border raids irritated them still further.

The raids resulted from a series of political miscalculations made on both sides of the border. The United States had not recognized Venustiano Carranza as the official president of Mexico. In an effort to show that Carranza had power in Mexico a couple of President Carranza's army officers initiated a series of raids into Texas beginning in 1915 and continuing, on and off, for about a year. The intent behind these raids were to show that Carranza was right when he said that some of his opponents in Mexico were causing problems, and when he was recognized as president by the United States, he would gain enough prestige to end these incursions.[8] The raids were sporadic and stretched from the King Ranch in South Texas to as far west as the Big Bend. The raids gradually diminished with the United States' recognition of Carranza, but that move infuriated Pancho Villa who started his own raid into Columbus, New Mexico, in apparent retaliation for the United States recognizing Carranza. The instability of the border situation frightened and angered

Americans who lived near the border and they demanded that something be done to protect them.

Governor Jim Ferguson was always quick to respond to the voting public, and he decided to take the action suggested by many citizens to increase the number of Texas Rangers and move them to the border. He announced on May 8, 1916, that the Ranger force would be expanded to fifty men.[9] He faced an immediate problem: as usual the appropriations for the Rangers would not support the expansion for more than a few months. Ferguson privately planned to pay for the men with a deficit appropriation out of his budget, and planned to ask the Legislature for more money when the new fiscal year began in September. As it stood, he did not have enough money to totally fund the project. While the announcements of expansion were made, new appropriations were not forthcoming and the force that seemed to be expanding to deal with real problems slowly began to revert to the smaller unit it had been. Some of the short fall had been dealt with by attrition, as some of the Rangers had left the force and were not replaced. The new Rangers were faced with a financial problem of too many men and not enough money.

While the funding issue was probably not known by the new recruits, it proved to be an issue that would haunt the Rangers. As a result of the short fall in funding, of the thirty-eight men enlisted between May 10 and May 30, 1916, the time period of the Ferguson expansion, some served for as little as a month and only eight served past December, 1916.[10] The situation was made clear to the Ranger Captains: they could enlist men, but due to the funding short fall they faced limited service. As for the public, they would see the headlines announcing the expansion but in the best traditions of politics, they would not see the reductions.

The Texas Rangers that Graham joined in 1916 was far from the respected law enforcement body that exists today. The well-known Frontier Battalion that had fought Indians and bandits throughout the state had been put out of business. The frontier had closed and court cases concerning authority to make arrests had caused the Rangers to begin a period of restructuring that would move it toward a more investigative body. The emerging force was controlled tightly by the governor, and was deployed to address a variety of new issues that faced the state. They broke up union strikes, shut down feuds, and dealt with problems on the international border with Mexico.

The Ranger companies were dispersed to semi-permanent camps around the state and from those sites they were detailed to various hotspots around the state. Entire companies or as few as one or two men would be directed to problem areas. The Rangers seemed to be brought into a situation only when it became serious enough that local or state commerce began to be affected. If feuds affected an entire town, ranching interests were threatened by rustlers, or lynchings promised to destroy a town, the Rangers put in an appearance. Unlike the local sheriff, the Rangers had no allegiance to the local voters and they tended to enforce the law as they saw it or as they had been directed to do so from Austin. Their appearances were not without controversy.

By 1916 the Ranger force was shaken by reports of its dealings with citizens, both Anglo and Mexican. Rangers had gotten drunk and beaten up waiters in cafés and saloon keepers in bars. They were accused of shooting prisoners in South Texas and fighting with each other in many of the camps around the state. The image that this behavior created was that the man with the badge was corrupt and ignorant of the law. The actions of some of the Rangers showed that the fair treatment of Mexicans, poor people, and minorities in general were a low priority. The view that seemed to be held by many in the state was that the Rangers might be more of a problem than a solution and that the Ranger problem was based in politics. Serving in the Rangers had become a political plum promised to friends of some officials or the sons of prominent backers. If the force was going to be turned around, it would take a lot of political weight to do so.

As early as 1911, an attempt was made by the Adjutant General Henry Hutchings to regain some kind of control over the force. Recognizing that the Rangers now consisted of mostly young, uneducated men who had received appointments to the force as a favor to a prominent political benefactor or placed by a friendly captain, new rules were initiated. The rules required them to be of good moral character, to be sober, to show sound judgment, and to provide references to support that. The rules seemed to have little effect on the men who wished to join and little impact on those already in the force. While some of the discipline issues involved drinking and a general disregard for rules as they applied to them, many of the problems dealt with prejudices held by the men that were typical of the average Texas of the time. Those attitudes dealt with Mexicans and those people some called Tejanos, or Mexicans born in Texas.

Mexicans were viewed by many as people who were inferior in education and ability. They were acknowledged to be good cowboys, farmers, and workers but were not going to be the equal of their Anglo neighbors because of their color, religion, and financial circumstances. They became a commodity. In South Texas they were frequently formed into voting blocs by local Anglo power brokers who then sold the votes to the highest bidder for political gain. They were used to work in the emerging citrus and vegetable farms of South Texas. Pay was usually better than in Mexico but conditions were such that they found they had escaped a Mexican peonage for an American peonage. For all of this, they were virtually ignored as far as their rights were concerned until a crime or a revolution came along which made them noticed. They were the people in the background of Texas, shadowy figures who played a part in the everyday business of the state but were denied full access to it because of who they were. All Anglo Texans did not subscribe to these attitudes, but enough did, which resulted in numerous incidents of lynchings and shootings of prisoners. Those attitudes directed toward Mexicans and other minorities, combined with the reckless arrogance of some of the men in the Ranger companies lead to complaints, and the complaints went straight to the governor.

The new reform rules included the following: "...it shall be the duty of any citizen who knows of any such misconduct or violation of the law on the part of any member of the ranger force to at once notify the Adjutant General in writing of misconduct, and it shall be the duty of the Adjutant General to at once conduct such examination and to take such action thereon as the facts make necessary..."[11] While the rules might have been ignored by some of the Ranger captains in selecting men, the public seemed to catch on immediately to the business about reporting Ranger excesses. Letters floated into officials in Austin describing Ranger activities that were not reported in the Captain's Monthly Report.

An example of the kind of difficulties the Rangers were getting into was illustrated by complaints filed against the company Graham would join: Company B, which was stationed in West Texas with camps in Ysleta, El Paso, and Marfa. Company B's Captain was J. Monroe Fox. Fox was a veteran Ranger captain who had been appointed to that rank as a result of a series of reforms initiated in 1911. He came to the Rangers from a career as a deputy sheriff and jailer in Travis County. He had become the captain of Company A in Austin, but was moved to South Texas and finally to the station at El Paso. Fox was a controversial officer who seemed to be unwilling or unable to maintain a level of discipline that was acceptable to the citizens being served.

Several of Fox's men got into a political dispute with a Hispanic politician named Jose Alderete in Ysleta. While the actions of both the Rangers and the Hispanics involved were probably exaggerated, the results of the harassment and the reactions got more attention than they deserved. The Rangers thought the Mexicans were involved in Revolutionary activities; the Mexicans thought the Rangers were trying to intimidate them. Alderete's wife complained about the Rangers' actions in a letter to the governor with the result that Fox had to do an investigation. While he cleared his men of any illegal activity, he still paid a price. The detachment stationed in Yselta was almost forced to move completely out of town. The men who were stationed there were replaced, and if the Rangers had any respect from the population, it was damaged considerably by the controversy.[12] For most of the men, Mexicans were seen, not only as second class citizens, but in many cases they were seen as non-citizens and as a result were treated in a very brusque manner.[13] The Rangers had the view that Mexicans were decidedly not equals. This attitude, plus the hysteria whipped up by reactions to the border raids and the threat of race war, likely colored the way Company B brought law and order to a society that had a large Mexican population. The entire Ysleta affair was typical of the situation the force found itself in during one of the most trying periods of time in their history. They needed strong leadership in Austin and strong leadership in the field.

The Ranger captains must have been aware of the problems. If they read the newspapers, they should have known that many people in the state were viewing them as being as big a problem as the raiders on the border. The Rangers were caught between enforcing the law as they had for many years, and a changing society that seemed not to want the old style law enforcement anymore. Change was going to be hard to deal with, and the way they carried out that change was going to make the difference between the survival of the Rangers or the complete disbanding of the organization. While the captains may have understood the situation, it is questionable whether many of the Rangers serving under them fully realized the seriousness of the position they found themselves in. With this unsettled situation in place, the Rangers began a limited expansion.

The Rangers opened up enlistments and Graham Barnett raised his hand and became a member of Company B, Texas Rangers, on May 16, 1916. He swore to "faithfully and impartially discharge and perform all the duties incumbent on me as an officer in the Ranger force."[14] The enlistment papers described the new Ranger as being 25 years and 8 months of age, born in Hill County, and employed as a "Ranchman." The physical description was spare, "five foot nine, light complexion, gray eyes and brown hair."[15] With that enlistment, Joseph Graham Barnett officially entered into the world of legal law enforcement in El Paso. He was one of fourteen men who joined Company B between May 8 and May 17. His job was to enforce the laws of Texas as he understood them for $90.00 per month plus per diem of a dollar a day while in the field, not to exceed $30.00 per month. Company B was on the scene and was given the responsibility for policing a huge portion of the border country from El Paso south to near Del Rio.

To accomplish this, the company maintained semi-permanent camps in Ysleta and Marfa, with temporary sites picked when they could be found and paid for. The company was usually divided into groups of two to four men that moved in response to problems or expected threats. The moves were accomplished quickly through the use of railway passes, which allowed speedy movement from El Paso to the site of the temporary assignment.

Some of the men, like Graham, had no formal law enforcement background; others brought limited experience with them. Besides Graham, among the new men in Fox's company were A. G Beard and Nathan Fuller. Both of these men would end up working with Graham on what has become his best known Ranger scout, an extended ramble through the Chisos Mountains. Beard was a burly man, well over six feet, with a heavy build. He had enlisted in Austin and had claimed some law enforcement experience, although that proved to be questionable. Beard would remain with the Rangers until 1919 when he would leave to follow other law enforcement opportunities.[16] Fuller had worked as a "mill man" and became a well-respected member of the Rangers until a political dispute with his captain drove him out in 1919. Fuller later became a railroad detective after he left formal law enforcement.[17]

After their enlistment most of the company, including Graham, Fuller, and Beard, spent time in Yselta. The first few months with the Rangers must have seemed to be anticlimactic. Newspaper stories of the attacks in New Mexico and the Big Bend led to an expectation of bandit fights and raids into Mexico. Reality set in slowly. Before charging off into gunfights, the new men needed to learn to become Texas Rangers since most had been cowboys. There was a small problem: there was no training for the new Rangers. Formal training would not take place until after the Rangers merged with the Highway Patrol in 1935. In 1916, training was left up to the Ranger captains and much of that was hit or miss. Primarily they were involved in an on-the-job training process with the newer, less experienced men working with the older, more seasoned veterans. The system had problems: it was experientially based. If a new man was paired with a veteran who tended to mistreat prisoners, beat them to get information, and abused the local citizens, the new man usually repeated that kind of behavior.

One of the most controversial aspects of border crime fighting was a near universal practice of conducting searches of vehicles and other property without warrants. With a revolution going on literally at the end of the street, people on both sides of the river were breaking laws and making money by smuggling weapons and hiding various members of all of the factions who seemed to use Texas as a time out corner when things got too hot in Mexico. The justification for these warrantless searches was that it is in a sovereign nation's interests to protect its border and enforce the law at that border. While the "border search exception" was not codified until 1953, it was in common usage prior to that. With a war waxing and waning a few miles away, officers enforced smuggling laws with a great deal of intensity.

Service on the Mexican border was considered dangerous for any law officer or military man assigned to the area. The proximity of Mexico meant that a criminal could commit a crime and be out of the country in minutes in some cases. Smuggling and general criminal behavior had increased because of the revolution, and that led to the Ranger force, especially, being seen as having to be uncompromising just to survive. Because of the unrest, the Rangers who served on the border developed a reputation for being hard on crime and criminals. The Rangers had to be tough because the opposition was tough. The question of warrants and other legal considerations appeared to be waived. It seemed that the Rangers were given free rein to conduct themselves as they saw fit as long as they protected the border and reduced crime. When they left the border, they carried the reputation of border Rangers, men who had worked in situations where they were basically alone, with little or no support from the public, and the expectation that they would protect and serve the majority population. The training that Graham received for law enforcement was learned from men who were not overly concerned with the vagaries of constitutional law, but rather with ending the problem that they were faced with.

While their job was to enforce the law, the interpretation of that law was frequently made out in the brush or in a back alley, in the heat of the moment, and often with little thought given to some of the legalities that their prisoners might have expected had they known about them. There was generally no way the Rangers could check with the captain to determine how to deal with a situation. Most communication was face to face and rarely handled via limited telephone lines. A Ranger patrol was on its own, and any errors in judgment it made were owned by the patrol alone and could not be handed off to a superior officer. They had to rely on their experience and a moral code. The problem was what if the moral code was wrong? The moral code reflected much of the prejudice of the time toward not only Mexicans but outlaws as well. Plainly stated, if you were stealing, shooting at people, or extorting money, you ought not to be doing that. That behavior had to stop. The Rangers were there to stop it.

What was taught in a more consistent fashion were skills such as cutting for sign and tracking fugitives. The idea behind "cutting for sign" involved studying the landscape to determine what was there that should not be. The depth of foot and hoofprints told stories about who had passed and how burdened they might be. Animals didn't move without leaving traces of fecal matter and needing water. Both left evidence.

Animals moving in thorny country left hairs on plants, which could be used to determine direction and time.

Cutting for sign also involved general observation. A patrol had to examine cattle brands, note the number of people who might be at a particular ranch to determine who was coming or going, or know what kinds of messages might be sent by the *"avisadores."* The *avisadores* system was used by Mexicans in the Big Bend area to communicate basic information quickly using flashing mirrors or waving of hats or jackets. The *avisos* were critical in quickly passing information about what strangers were in the neighborhood and where they were going.

Many of the new men picked up on the habits of the successful ones. They kept a pocket notebook with scratched down references concerning where they went, what stock and brands they reviewed, how much they spent for meals, and names of the people they encountered. They quickly learned that some of the ranches in their patrol area could be relied on for a place to spend the night and a meal or an exchange of horses. They also learned that some of the ranchmen did not want any Rangers on their place for any reason because of past problems.

For a company that had been strengthened in order to deal with border problems, the period from May 1916, when Graham joined, and January 1917, when he left the Rangers, was a remarkably quiet time for Company B. Ranger records, which may reflect some gaps and some inconsistent reports, show only two Company B men involved in shoot-outs during the period. Despite later allegations of indiscriminate shootings, Graham was not involved in either of the documented incidents.[18] A major reason for the area calming down was not the small company of Rangers, but rather the movement of the Eighth Cavalry under Colonel George Langhorne to Camp Marfa. The movement of federal troops into the area signaled to the malcontents in Mexico that the US government was serious about protecting their people and territory.

Ranger captains were required to keep "Reports of Scouts and Arrests," which were laboriously completed and sent to Austin monthly. The surviving reports provide information about what a company and its men did during a month. Exactly what Graham did from May until July was probably routine, but he was involved in one incident that stood out because of the unusual nature of the crime and the sensational nature of the trial that drug on for years.

In July 1916, a Marfa hotel operator and music teacher named Henry Spannel killed his wife and an army major he had suspected of having an affair. Spannel's wife was from a prominent family who wanted to see punishment carried out as quickly as possible, with or without a trial. Fearing the possibility of having to deal with a lynch mob, the Rangers loaded up Spannel into an automobile and moved him first to Marfa and then to El Paso to protect him. Based on the fact that Graham was subpoenaed as a prosecution witness, it is likely that he was involved in the long drive to El Paso as a guard against the expected mob action. A double murder always attracted a lot of attention, and Marfa, as well as much of West Texas, was divided in their opinions. Was Spannel a man upholding the sanctity of his home by killing everyone involved in what he thought was a breakup, or was he was just a deluded music teacher who misread all the signals he was seeing? The Rangers had no opinion in the matter; they did however plan to see that the man came to trial. Graham made the first trip with Spannel and was destined to see him again months later.

When he was not guarding prisoners, Graham continued with whatever duties were assigned to him. What else he did must have met the approval of Captain Fox because he was not disciplined, and none of his activities turned up in the newspapers. Keeping your name out of the papers was a good thing. He began to show up in the scout reports in October of 1916, when he and fellow Rangers A. G. Beard and Nate Fuller got an assignment to break the monotony of camp life. In autumn, the three new Rangers saddled up and began a series of scouts that took them from Marfa into the Chisos Mountains searching for bandits and any other lawbreakers they could find. The purpose of the scout was not just to search for outlaws but to show the isolated ranchers in the area that their requests for protection had been heard, and that the government in Austin was actually doing something in response to the complaints. They were to provide a law enforcement presence in a part of the state that was invisible to much of the rest of it. Their patrol centered on one of the most beautiful and isolated parts of Texas.

The Chisos Mountains were a range of mountains that extend about twenty miles across what is now the Big Bend National Park. They represent some of the roughest country in West Texas and consist of high desert as well as forested areas and a series of four of the five tallest mountains in Texas. The elevation ranges from about five thousand feet to the tallest mountain, Mount Emory, at 7900 feet. The mountains provided some break from the typical heat of that part of the desert and in October they were experiencing the last part of the rainy season, or what passes for it.

The mountains break down into ragged canyons framed by lechuguilla, a small, foot-tall succulent with dagger shaped foliage, and prickly pear cactus. Yucca stood on grayish trunks and seemed to watch the movement of man and animals. The grass that sprang up after the rains grew thick and nutritious for a while and then seemed to shrink in the heat. Oak trees were found near water, but the more drought resistant mesquite seemed to be found everywhere, twisting its way up through the shale and rock and that clung to the sides of the hills and canyons. In some places, alpine meadows provided grass for grazing sheep, goats, and some cattle.

It represented a beautiful, remote land that was home to antelope, an occasional bear, and all of the outlaws who thought that no one would ever find them in a place that far from civilization. The temperature in the night dropped into the forties, and daytime on the flats would see mid-nineties. The isolated ranch houses were centered on springs and creeks because water remained the most precious commodity in this high desert. The people who ranched there were constantly struggling with weather, absence of rain, and the threat of banditry. It was about as far away from civilization as you could get in twentieth century Texas, and both the Rangers and the outlaws were basically on their own as far as support or control was concerned.

Beard, Fuller, and Graham left Marfa in October 1916, and, accompanied by a pack mule, began a sweeping series of patrols that took them over some of the roughest country in West Texas. Of the three Rangers, Graham was the one most familiar with the Big Bend. Compared to the other two men, he had spent a considerable amount of time in the area, and had at least a passing knowledge of the general locations of some of the most important land features and a knowledge of many of the ranches in the area.

It is doubtful that any of the men were designated as leader of the patrol, but Graham's knowledge made him a natural for that role. He had chased cattle for his uncle there, and presumably had some personal contacts with ranchers and other people seeking to make a life in the high desert. It must have been like going home for him. With recent rains in 1916, the country showed its spectacular potential, and that must have impressed him. This would be the place he hoped to establish a ranch that would rival his uncle's. It was a place he hunted deer and bear. Now he and the patrol were hunting men.

Bandits from both sides of the river used the Big Bend country to move and hide contraband and stolen animals. The bandits couldn't move without leaving some kind of trail, and the type of trail pretty well defined what they might be carrying. A narrow path usually meant mules that tend to follow nose to tail in a line making it easier to manage a large group carrying smuggled items. Horses, cattle, and sheep open up, move as a group, and need a wider area to move in, leaving a broader path. Both smugglers and stolen stock needed grazing and water, which meant that the trails would eventually have to end up at a water hole or windmill. This knowledge gave the hunters a place to start. The patrol would move from water hole, to creek and seep in order to cut for sign and determine if anyone had watered animals at that site recently.

Maps indicated a number of named and unnamed sources of water in the Chisos, and these tiny sanctuaries provided water, shade, and limited grazing for the animals of the bandits and the men who pursued them. Isolated goat camps and line shacks provided information from the cowboys and shepherds who worked in the area. The question would have always been the same: "Have you noticed anyone moving in the area, someone you don't know?"

As they worked the waterholes they probably moved east to west cutting for sign. They looked for anything indicating men and horses moving north to raid, or moving back south with stolen stock or other plunder. They scouted well inland from the Rio Grande. If they stayed too close to the river, they might find a trail only to follow it further north and find the group had split into two or more raiding parties, which would then split the tiny Ranger force beyond the level it needed to be effective. By staying inland, they would pick up the trails after the raiders had committed to a particular direction. They looked for brush that had been broken by the passage of animals. They also watched for the telltale signs of animal droppings or a poorly concealed campfire that would testify to the passage of men and animals.

They took with them a pack mule that carried some of the state approved issue of food or whatever they could pull together. Ranger regulations allowed for twelve ounces of bacon or meat a day along with flour or corn meal, peas or beans, rice, coffee, sugar, and "one gill of vinegar or pickles," along with a few other condiments such as pepper and some baking powder.[19] Whether they had all of their supplies at all times is still a question. Many of the Ranger captains ran short of supply money for both men and horses. Rangers were paid with state vouchers and that meant that cash was not always at hand. The mule may have been packed a little light on food but it did carry their camping gear and whatever provisions they could buy on vouchers from isolated stores. Additional supplies might be provided by ranchers in the area or purchased when the scout was broken up by trips to return prisoners.

If this patrol was like most of the other Ranger patrols, it was not a long seven-week camping trip but was broken up by periodic returns to Marfa or another site.

The ranchers in the area played a critical role. They were, after all, the reason the Rangers were there. Most of them welcomed the Rangers and provided a place to camp or a meal or two while the patrol was working on a particular ranch. It was not unusual for the Rangers to leave a tired horse in a man's pasture, borrow one to replace him, and pick up the first horse when they swung back through the area. They brought news for the outside and a level of security for the ranch while they were there. A rancher might provide additional support by riding with the patrol or sending a hired hand who knew the country to help the Rangers check for suspicious activity or to move them quickly through rough country. When the patrol was photographed on October 16, 1916, a photographer caught such a moment. When they stopped at Jim Teague's store for information and supplies they were joined by Walter Good, a local rancher, who rode with them for a short time. In the photograph, store owner Jim Teague is pictured on Graham's horse with Graham hopping on the pack mule to provide a complete picture.

Since this was first and foremost a law enforcement activity the men were well armed. The state had standardized some of the weapons the Rangers used and had settled on the Winchester model 1895 in the caliber of .30-'06 Government. The 1895 was the only Winchester to dispense with the usual magazine tube under the barrel. Instead, the five reserve cartridges were held in a fixed, external box magazine in front of the trigger guard. The .30-'06 ammunition had a sharp pointed bullet which made it impossible to use in tubular magazine where each point rested against the primer of the shell in front of it, possibly leading to an accidental discharge in the tube magazine. It was a powerful round and was the same used by the Springfield 1903 that was issued to the National Guard and regular army troops in the area. The Winchester '95 was noted to be a fine weapon but its stock design made for memorable recoil.[20]

If an incoming Ranger did not have such a rifle, one was provided for him, and the price of the rifle was deducted from the man's pay. It became his personal property. Graham's rifle was branded with "O2," possibly from a ranch he had worked at before.[21] The rifle has a full-length forearm characteristic of what Winchester called the Standard Musket, many of which were sold on the surplus market in 1909. Fuller carved two stars in the stock of his. Their personal side arms were generally allowed, and both Fuller and Beard favored single action Colts. The only record of what handgun Graham carried is indicated in the photograph that was taken at Teague's Store. Graham is not seen wearing a gun belt but instead is carrying an early model Colt semi-automatic pistol tucked into his cartridge belt. Based on the rounded grips, the pistol was probably either one of the early 38 ACP models, perhaps a 1903 Pocket Hammer, or a 1905 .45. It is not the more familiar 1911 model that Colt had begun to sell commercially in 1913. It is likely that he is carrying one of the first semi-automatic handguns seen in Ranger service. So, armed and ready, the patrol rode into the Big Bend in October of 1916.

Illustration 8. Rangers of the Big Bend

(Courtesy John T. Barnett)
This photo was taken October 16, 1916, in Glen Springs, Texas. (From left to right) Nathan Fuller, State Ranger; Walter Good, rancher, Chisos Mountains; A.G. Beard, State Ranger; Jim Teague, store keeper, Glen Springs; Joe Graham Barnett, State Ranger.

Illustration 9. Zoom of Graham. Note the early Colt automatic pistol on his left side.

(Courtesy John T. Barnett)

They scouted south of Marathon, and the scout was almost immediately successful. On October 28 two smugglers, Francisco Elizondo and Alfonso Benavidez, were arrested near Marathon, and Graham turned them over to the US Marshal in El Paso.[22] On October 30 Fuller returned to Marfa with two prisoners and then went back on patrol. In November, the three picked up several head of "wet stock horses" from Vicente Santiago and held them to be turned over to the River Guards, a precursor of the Border Patrol.[23] "Wet stock" referred to animals that had crossed the river.

The patrol continued through November and into December. Ranger records show that the three were "on scout in the Cheasps [sic] Mountains" during the first part of the month. Fox reported that in the first part of December they "seized 28 head [Cattle Raisers] Association's marrs [sic] and hold same for Association Inspector."[24] With all the seizures, there is no mention of gunfire.

The results of this ten week patrol are hard to estimate. It was typical of many of the Ranger patrols of the time to spend more time on scouting and trailing than shooting at people. This active pursuit of potential outlaws was typical of the period and required the men on the patrol to exercise an enormous amount of discretionary law enforcement. The theft of several horses might take a back seat to the roundup of fifty stolen cattle. Whatever the three Rangers did on the patrol, they conducted themselves so that there was no question asked about who was arrested or returned to the hands of other law enforcement.

The patrol ended in December. Other cases required that the men pick up other duties. Graham and A. G. Beard were detailed to provide security on two separate murder cases, both of which would make the front pages of newspapers across the country. A. G. Beard had planned to take a short vacation and return to Austin, but on December 6, he was sent to Sweetwater along with John D. White to act as bodyguard for Gladys Johnson and her brother, Sid, who were to be tried for the murder of her estranged husband, Ed Sims. Sims was killed in a dispute over temporary custody of the couple's children. The shooting had occurred in downtown

Snyder after a particularly ugly divorce. Despite the rather public nature of the killing, the two enjoyed considerable support from the community. Beard remained there for several months acting as a bodyguard.

Graham began a similar task in guarding Harry Spannel, the music teacher who had murdered his wife back in July. Several of the Company B men transferred Spannel to San Angelo on September 22, where he was jailed until his trial date in January. The Rangers had provided bodyguard services since that date, and in December the task fell to Graham. He was probably familiar with the case.

Harry Spannel was a 20-year-old Baylor University music instructor when he met Crystal Hope Holland, a 19-year-old Baylor student from Alpine. They married in June 1906 and moved to Alpine. Spannel became manager of the Holland Hotel, which was owned by Crystal's father, John Holland, a prominent Brewster County rancher. The young couple took a suite of rooms in the hotel. They had a daughter, also named Crystal, in January 1910. In early July 1916, they met and befriended 52-year-old Major Matthew C. Butler and his wife, Margaret. Butler was a career army officer who was assigned command of the First Squadron of the Sixth United States Cavalry. He and his wife took a suite of rooms in the hotel because of a lack of appropriate officer quarters at nearby Camp Marfa.

At some point early in the friendship of the two couples, Harry began to worry that his wife and Major Butler were becoming more serious than friendly, and he talked about it to anyone who would listen. The people who listened must have been few because Crystal was described by her friends as a woman with a spotless reputation. The community said Harry's suspicions about Crystal and Major Butler were groundless, and revealed more about Harry's character than any misconduct by Crystal. For their part, the Butlers seemed to ignore Spannel's actions. Butler took care never to be alone with Crystal, but that precaution only seemed to make Spannel more suspicious.

Despite his jealousy, Spannel and his wife continued to see the Butlers. He seemed fixed on the idea that the Major and his wife were involved and that all he had to do was to catch them to prove it. What good that would do he didn't know, but he was fixated on finding some indiscretion. The couples took drives in the country, often met for meals in the hotel's dining room, and went to the movies. On at least one occasion they went to a dance in Marfa.

On the night of July 20, 1916, Spannel claimed that his wife and Mrs. Butler had gone to wash their hands after dinner. He alleged that Colonel Butler (Butler had been promoted that day) entered the room, said or did something, and then left. Crystal Spannel told Spannel that "something had happened" and she would tell him more later.[25] Inexplicably, Spannel invited Butler to join them for a ride around town, which he did. Spannel claimed that he had asked Butler about the incident and the colonel denied it, tried to get out of the car, and the two men struggled with Spannel in the front seat and Crystal and the colonel in the back seat. Witnesses said the Hupmobile proceeded a few blocks down the street, suddenly careened into a fence, and stopped. Several shots were heard, followed by a woman's desperate plea, "Oh, Harry, please don't kill me."[26] A man was seen to stumble from the car and return. More shots were fired.

In a matter of minutes, a clearly disoriented Spannel wandered into the jail beside the courthouse. When the local constable, W. J. Yates, rushed in he found Spannel. Yates, who had been outside near the car, asked him if he had killed his wife and the colonel. Spannel replied that he didn't know. Yates knew immediately that something had to be done to protect Spannel. A crowd had begun to gather, and while no one seemed to know what might happen next, the threat of a lynching occurred to Yates. He contacted the Rangers, and they quickly moved Spannel to Marfa, then Valentine, and on to El Paso. When questioned about the shooting, Spannel admitted what he had done. At some point he mumbled through a wild story about Butler shooting Crystal and Spannel then shooting the colonel, but that story soon disappeared. He admitted shooting them, but when he was asked for the reason he replied that he didn't know. Spannel was locked away from the lynch mob, and indicted on two counts of murder. He remained jailed in El Paso for a time.

The Holland family was a prominent one and emotions in the small town ran wild. John Holland had worked to bring the railroad to Alpine; he had built the hotel to be a showplace because he thought the previous hotel wasn't quite good enough for the town. In his grief, he wanted to see justice done, and wanted to see it done quickly. He wasn't the only one. The army was astounded that one of its up and coming officers was assassinated on a city street, and they began their own investigation.

The newspapers recognized a story that would sell and covered it in depth. The *New York Times* claimed Clay Holland, Crystal's brother, was returning from Colorado to avenge his sister's death.[27] A group of local cowboys were supposed to be roaming the county looking for Spannel. The army had dispatched an officer to conduct an investigation separate from that of the county sheriff. Feelings were so strong that the commanding officer at Camp Alpine had already stated that the incident was "a cold-blooded premeditated murder, committed by a man crazed with jealousy."[28]

The "crazed with jealousy" fellow was making out pretty well. All of the people in the county weren't anti-Spannel. Collections were being taken up to see that he received an adequate legal defense. While these collections were being made, Spannel remained in jail, and the Rangers continued their guard duty. The responsibility fell to various members of Company B, and during the trial it was left to Graham.

The trial was set to begin January 15, 1917, in San Angelo. Graham and two former Rangers were already under subpoena to be there, and Graham drew the assignment of having to collect the witnesses in the Marfa area and to make the journey by train to San Angelo. Graham armed himself with subpoenas and rounded up a number of witnesses in Marfa, Alpine, and El Paso and shepherded them to San Angelo by train. As the Tom Green County sheriff, Hawley Allen, checked his list he found several of the witnesses who had received papers didn't see fit to show up. In the late evening, Graham gathered up additional subpoenas and caught the west bound KCM&O back to Alpine. He corralled the witnesses, some of whom were sick and others who swore that they were confused about some detail, and headed back to San Angelo for the start of the trial.

The nature of the trial was well-known, and the expectation was that there would be a full house of spectators. Sheriff Allen expected not only large crowds, but he also that most of them would show up "heeled," that is armed. While he didn't expect any problems, with a crowd that large it was almost a guarantee that someone would have a dispute with someone else. Graham was recruited to provide security in the courtroom.

By this time, Harry Spannel had developed the role of the outraged husband, and now played it out like a master at the Old Vic. He wasn't worried about the outcome of the trial; it was only his young daughter who dominated his thinking, or that is what he wanted his large audience to believe. He ate three meals a day, two supplied by the county, the third supplied by a local restaurant funded by his family. He prayed daily, and taught Sunday school in the jail for those who were determined to turn their lives around, or at least, make the gesture, and prepared himself for the oncoming show.

The decision was made that Spannel would be tried separately for each of the killings. The first trial would be for the murder of his wife. It would be followed immediately by a second for the shooting of Colonel Butler. The hushed crowd heard his defense. He maintained that he had shot Crystal by mistake while in the process of shooting Colonel Butler. Despite his earlier confession and his inquiring if both victims were dead, Spannel continued to maintain that it was an accident when he shot his wife five times.[29]

In a trial that involved some extramarital activity, someone's virtue is going to be destroyed and this was the case with the Spannel trial. Crystal's reputation was above reproach so that left Colonel Butler. The defense painted him as a bon vivant and man about town with a reputation as a womanizer. Spannel's testimony, alternating between sobbing and praying, told a story of Butler forcing his attentions on Crystal. According to Spannel, it was Crystal's idea to confront Butler and to do it in the car. "No, not here," he said his wife replied. "If you want to have it out with him, call him over to the car."[30] The two exchanged words, and Spannel picked up one of two pistols in the car, they struggled, and after losing one pistol to Butler, he pulled a second gun out of his pocket. He described how he found himself outside the car watching the flashes of the gun shots. "Butler seemed right behind Mrs. Spannel...I fired at him, I don't remember how many times."[31] Spannel lapsed into a rambling sob describing how he had gotten out of the car, thought Crystal had fainted, found she hadn't, and was stopped from shooting himself by either his daughter or a bystander. When he was asked what position he was in when he shot his wife he replied, "I never shot my wife. Butler moved out of the way and Crystal fell, Butler also fell."[32]

The lack of witnesses and the apparent confusing testimony given by Spannel on the stand when compared to the original statements he made should have caused problems for the defense. Apparently little consideration was given to Spannel arming himself with two pistols, firing a number of shots into the couple, walking away, and returning to the car to fire again. It was the return trip to the car that should have provided concern for the defense. Spannel had said on one occasion that he had intended to shoot the Colonel and that Crystal got in the way and her killing was an accident. The problem seemed to be Crystal's pleading scream for help, and Spannel's return to the car. In additional testimony he claimed that Butler had killed Crystal, and he had then rushed back to the car to finish off the man who had killed his wife.[33] The testimony was given through tears and long pauses. It was a bravura performance.

Other testimony was heard, but after Spannel testified, the trial was a good as over. He was acquitted for the murder of his wife. The jury decided that her shooting was as accident that had happened as Spannel tried to kill the Colonel. The verdict was not unexpected. Almost immediately he was taken to Coleman for trial for the Colonel's murder where he was found guilty and given a five year sentence. That sentence was overturned on appeal. Tried again in Brownwood he was found not guilty in Butler's death. A day later, the music teacher headed back to Pennsylvania.

One week later, on January 28, 1917, Graham Barnett's career as a regular Texas Ranger ended. The funding problem had caught up with him and the others hired the previous May. One of the questions that needs to be answered is: Was he a good Ranger or a bad one? It is difficult to characterize his career in the Rangers as a successful one or not. It was simply a job he did. He followed the rules, as far as it can be determined, and he left when the job ended. Far from being a killing machine that caused the organization to fire him for too many killings of prisoners, Graham did his job without a great deal of fanfare. For years people commented that Graham was thrown out of the Rangers for shooting prisoners or some other impropriety. There is no indication that any of that ever occurred. No reports from other Rangers or civilians have surfaced to indicate that he did anything other than what he was required to do.

There were a number of Rangers who were involved with criminal activity during this time. Some were disciplined, some were not. It was not unheard of for Rangers to be indicted in shootings; the case of Will Sands who shot an army sergeant in 1916 is one example. W. T. Vann arresting three Rangers for killing a prisoner, Florencio Garcia, in Cameron County is another. Graham's brother Boog was investigated as part of the Canales Investigation for shooting at two Mexican cowboys. Not hitting them, shooting at them. For Graham to have killed prisoners during this period, he would have had to shoot only orphans or people that no one knew because no uproar was raised over a father, brother, or husband turning up missing. If he had killed a number of people during the long patrol in the Big Bend it would have required that Fuller and Beard, both men who lived fairly rough lives and were not too worried about the consequences, would have had to refuse to comment on anything relating to the patrol for the rest of their lives. Without any proof it is impossible to say whether the killings attributed to Graham ever occurred.

There is no record that Graham was indicted or disciplined during his period of time in Ranger service. The Graham Barnett legend seemed to demand that he be one of the primary miscreants in this period. When he entered the Rangers he brought with him a backlog of stories concerning shootings or near shootings that impressed people. It seems likely that these stories combined with stories of Ranger misbehavior led many observers to lump Graham's name in with others. For a number of years there was speculation that he was involved in the massacre at Porvenir when the Rangers and some army troopers raided a small community in Mexico. This occurred in December of 1917, well after he had left the Rangers. There is some evidence that Boog claimed he and Graham were both present, but recent investigations identified the men who were part of the raid and neither brother was included on those lists. What is more likely is that some of the stories from Graham's time working for his uncle led people to move those stories into the present and comment "That sounds like something ole' Graham Barnett would do."

Graham may have contributed to this himself by embellishing the stories that were already in place. There is no way to know, but of the men who served with him, none left any indication that he shot anyone. Captain Fox may not have been too strong a leader, but since he had had problems in Ysleta he must have realized that the Rangers as a whole were being watched. Any unjustified violence could only result in problems for both the force and for him as captain. Neither could afford that kind of bad publicity. Graham may have had a reputation but there is no evidence that his actions during this enlistment were anything other than acceptable. Questions of good or bad Rangering can't be answered at this point without more information. He did his job, and then he went home.

His career in the Rangers ended on a prosaic note. Like many in the emerging twentieth century he became a victim of funding cuts. The Rangers had been expanded without sufficient funding, and now they were being cut down by that action. The activities of politicians in Austin reached as far as West Texas and without funding Governor Ferguson's Ranger initiatives had faltered and stumbled to a halt. Graham's law enforcement career fell victim, not to gunfights and missing prisoners, but to politicians and absent funding. He was 26 years old, he had a family, and he was unemployed.

Chapter 7

"Wild West—Wont do"

1917-1925[1]

Graham went home, not to Sterling City, but back to Uncle Joe Graham. Graham, Annie, and the baby moved to Alpine, although he ended up working in the Big Bend. Everyone expected that Joe would provide a job for Graham, and with war-driven prosperity there was plenty of opportunity to work. Agriculture was booming because of the First World War. Beef, wool, cotton, almost anything that could be grown and sold was in demand, and Joe Graham was not sitting by and watching other people make money.

While Graham had been away in the Rangers, Joe had expanded his operations. He had bought the one hundred section Buttrill Ranch in what would become known as the Big Bend National Park.[2] The ranch was in the Rosillos Mountains, northwest of where Graham had scouted with the Rangers just months earlier. The Dead Horse Mountains where Graham had self-exiled himself after the Babb shooting was east of the new location. The Ranch consisted of several smaller parcels of land primarily controlled by two headquarters ranches known as the Wade Place and the Buttrill Ranch. The Buttrill became home to Graham and

Annie Laura while Joe occupied the Wade Place on the other side of the mountain.[3]

Annie later recalled the time spent on the Buttrill place as one of the best times of her marriage.[4] The Buttrill Ranch house itself was a structure of rock, adobe, and hand-hewn cottonwood timbers about halfway up the rocky northwest slope of the 5,500 foot Rosillos Mountain. The main house was connected to a small, two-room wooden structure near the creek by a breezeway. There was an adobe house and dugout downhill from the main house that was used for the family of one of the ranch hands. Stock pens and a chicken coop were down slope from the house and spring. The Buttrill's had laid pipe from the creek to the kitchen and provided running water to the house. "We were the only people who had a bathtub and running water,"[5] Annie recalled. However, the toilet was an outhouse and if they went out there at night they carried a gun as protection against mountain lions, rattlesnakes, and a host of other nocturnal wanderers. With all of these luxuries, Graham and Annie lived a better life than most married couples in the area.

Part of the area had been terraced for fruit trees. An orchard of fig, peach, pear, and apple trees were watered by the spring. During the time they were there, the family took advantage of the crop. Each fall they canned hundreds of jars of fruit, some of which they exchanged for fresh green beans, cucumbers, and onions grown by Ira Hector in his garden near Marathon. The middleman in this barter was Ed Hancock, who delivered the mail every Monday from Marathon and wore two .45's on a belt strapped around his waist. Ed brought dress goods from Montgomery Ward and Sears to be transformed into everyday clothing by Annie on the little Singer sewing machine.

Annie had grown used to the isolation. "I didn't feel life on the ranch was an unusual hardship. I was happy, because Graham was home every night."[6] Years later she recalled some of the stories of their life that made this period special, one with particular humor. It was customary for ranchers to trade out labor from time to time. It seemed as if Graham always picked washdays to return favors. One washday he saddled up to go help on the Rice ranch to brand calves—ten miles away by horseback, twenty by car. Graham crawled on one of his saddle horses and noted that he would be back later. As he slowly rode out of the pen, Annie said, "I hope that old horse bucks you off." Graham must have smiled, but the next thing he knew the horse had shied and began to pitch, dumping him in middle of the yard. Annie claimed later that he went on to the branding but with a little less flair than he had before.[7]

It was not all ideal; the area was still plagued by problems with rustlers. Tensions between some of the Mexican and Anglo ranchers continued to grow, partly as a result of rustling problems, which had continued on both sides of the river. Cuco Torres, a notoriously bad man who never let his victim's race or income stop him from robbing them, received part of the blame for the theft of cattle on both sides of the river.[8] He was not the only source of banditry in the area. The tendency was to blame the theft on "Mexico Mexicans" but Francisco Villalba, a pioneer Mexican rancher in the area, knew that wasn't always the case. He tried to put an end to that story when he collected information that some of the cattle being sold in Mexico to ranchers were sold by the Anglo foreman of one of the large Big Bend ranches.[9] He didn't make many friends, and probably set back the cause of Anglo-Mexican relations several years by pointing out that the theft went both ways. He was ignored and the rustling continued but it was getting ready to take a back seat to a somewhat bigger contest. The war in Europe was coming to call.

The revolution in Mexico had slowed and a central government began to emerge. In a desperate attempt to tie up expected American support for the allies, Germany made a play for Mexican support. Germany suggested that the two countries support one another and Mexico could take back Texas, New Mexico, and Arizona along with the possible collection of most of the American west at a later date. Even the Mexican government saw this as a bad move. Mexico turned the offer down, and after a promise of neutrality, the Carranza regime was recognized by

Washington. Coming on the recent upheaval over the Plan of San Diego, the threat created by the mere contacts between Mexico and Germany contributed to the anger and fear felt by people along the border. The uneasy feeling expanded across the nation.

Patriotism was on the rise and the call for men to take part in the draft received quick response. Graham signed up for the draft in July 1917. His draft card served as a brief resume of the gunfighter's life to that date. He was married, had a child, and a case of "chronic appendicitis." That malady in the early 1900s was a blanket term for generalized stomach problems. Because of his marital and family status, he was probably ruled Class II: "Temporarily deferred, but available for military service." This classification was for men who were married and had children but whose family had sufficient income to survive if the husband went into the army. The next classification was for men whose family did not have sufficient income. With either classification he probably would never have been drafted.[10] While some maintain he was a World War I veteran, there is no indication that he served in the army. There was a family story that he broke horses for the army and made a bundle riding a horse no one else could ride at Fort Bliss. He may have worked as a civilian contractor breaking and delivering horses to the army during this period but by November 1918, he was back on the border. There were rumors that the Rangers were expanding and Graham wanted to get back behind the badge. That proved to be more difficult than he could have imagined.

As long as the war was going on, patriotism had been running loose in the streets in Austin, and legislation was introduced to expand the Rangers. The winding down of the war in Europe appeared to make this move unnecessary, and that fact, along with the actions of some of the Rangers themselves, made expansion difficult. In order for the Rangers to be expanded, some changes had to be made and those changes were going to be directed toward personnel and conduct.

Ranger abuses directed towards the Mexican population resulted in an investigation conducted by Representative Jose T. Canales. Canales looked into a number of incidents involving regular and special Rangers chiefly in their dealings with Mexicans. The hotly disputed investigation actually served to exonerate the Rangers as a whole but still identified the considerable criminal activity that some of the Rangers were involved in during the unrest in South Texas. Canales introduced legislation to restructure the force and it was met with tepid support.

Governor William Hobby realized that changes would have to be made not only in the regular Rangers but also the Special Rangers, and he instituted a series of reforms in the Ranger service before the reforms were forced on him. Leadership was the key and that started at the top. To achieve this James A. Harley was appointed as adjutant general with total control of the Rangers. Harley was an old-line county attorney who had just completed two years in the Texas senate. He was not especially supportive of change for the Rangers but his political sense told him that the continued excesses could not go on. He and Hobby set out to "select for the Texas Ranger's Service men of the best type and best character."[11] One of the most ambitious of these high character criteria was a no drinking policy, on or off duty, which impacted a number of the Rangers. Other changes included a dress code demanding that the Rangers not wear their border or scout belts, generally a three-inch gun belt holding both pistol and rifle ammunition, unless they were on a scout. In town a little bit more restrained behavior was expected and the image of the border gunfighter had to fade from the public's view. Too many visible guns tended to alarm the civilians.

The reforms requiring men to show a little more character didn't impact the Rangers immediately; decisions made by the legislature did, however. Convinced that the threats from Mexico were over and the war in Europe would not last much longer, the legislature began a series of budget cuts. On September 1, 1918, budgets began to be slashed and the Ranger force, swollen to 150 Regular Rangers, began to be cut.

Even with the reforms and despite the budget cuts, some companies continued to recruit men who knew the border. On November 8, 1918,

Graham signed enlistment papers with Captain Will Davis' Company L, tentatively stationed in Del Rio. The Ranger warrant shows something about how quickly changes were taking place with the Rangers: the "L" is marked through and "C" is written above it.[12] The date and the location cast some doubt on his army service since the war ended on November 11. While he was accepted in Del Rio, he was not in Austin; he had come up against the new reforms. At the bottom of his warrant, or official authorization papers, is scrawled "wont [sic] do Wild West." While the exact meaning of this phrase has eluded people for some time, it is highly likely that Graham's reputation as a drinker and a man who had pulled a trigger a time or two caused him to be denied the job he wanted. Scrawled across the inside of the warrant is the handwritten statement "Not issued."[13] He wouldn't do for the new Rangers. His "wild west" mentality had no place in a Texas that was trying to find a different direction, at least politically. It didn't pay to be too much of a legend. At the age of twenty-eight, he was considered a liability because of the experience he had gained and the reputation that had grown around it. The world was changing; a new era of optimism was taking over. The war was ending and people wanted a quieter place, one without shooting or memories of those years past that had been dominated by threats and raiders from across the border. While Graham's reputation undoubtedly opened a few doors for him, doors in the capitol building remained closed. If Graham was going to have a future in law enforcement it wouldn't be with the Rangers. He turned back to ranching.

Perhaps with Joe's support, or maybe buoyed by the promising market in cattle, Graham and Annie went into debt to buy seven sections of land in the Big Bend owned by W. R. Wyatt. It was just about the worst time to try to expand a ranch. Two natural disasters and an economic one were stalking the Big Bend.

In the fall of 1918, people began to get sick with a respiratory infection that, oddly enough, struck young and vigorous men and women more severely than children and middle-aged people. The infection, soon referred to as the Spanish Flu, swept the border country. The people in the isolated ranches seemed less likely to get the flu, but it still impacted the Big Bend. The illness spread throughout the United States and the economy, which had begun to slow with the winding down of the war, was hit hard again. While the Barnett family, protected by their isolation, escaped the Spanish Influenza, they could not escape an economy that continued to fail.

When World War I ended, demand for cattle slackened and the market collapsed. By spring 1919, prices began to drop and they didn't stop. A cow that brought $50 in 1918 was worth $30 in 1922, and prices were spiraling lower in isolated sections of the country far from markets, such as the Big Bend. Panicky bankers started calling in loans. Joe Graham took desperate steps and sold off thousands of head of cattle in Kansas and Oklahoma to pay down his debt. If the depressed market wasn't enough, it seemed as if it just quit raining.

The drought of 1918 remains one on the three most severe in Texas history. Pastures baked under cloudless skies, grasses died, and nonstop winds blew West Texas topsoil to the ends of the earth. Springs dried up and water holes became dust bowls. To keep cattle alive, ranchers such as Joe Graham had to spend cash reserves for hay brought in by rail from other regions of the country. When the money ran out, they borrowed from the banks to buy more hay. Joe Graham owed a San Antonio bank $170,000 on his 134,000 acres. His son Frank took over management of the Buttrill in 1918 and the family suffered through the worst of the drought but in the end, it proved too much. Joe began one of his many series of transactions intended to save the majority of his land and cattle holdings: moving stock, selling what he could, and juggling payments to the banks.

Joe lost a thousand of his best black cows to tick fever, despite all-out efforts of a San Antonio veterinarian he hired to save them. Since Graham was managing that part of the ranch, some members of Joe's family began to question exactly how much he knew about the cattle business. Joe stood by Graham and despite the awful losses, he stayed with the ranch.

The Rosillos became a giant infirmary for sick and dying livestock. Of Joe's 6,300 sheep, only 700 survived. "I lived on pulled wool for a year," Joe said.[14] As a dead sheep decomposes, its wool loosens and can be removed easily by "pulling." Pulled wool is salable, but brings less than wool from live sheep. Joe might have mentioned that the odor of a putrefying sheep is overwhelming, but willingly endured by a broke rancher.

The economy continued to spiral downward. The depression of 1920-21 has been viewed as more terrible than the one beginning in 1929, just not lasting as long. Graham and his family were searching for some way to survive. On August 10, Graham and Annie sold their interest in seven sections of land to J. W. Potter for the sum of one dollar just to get out from under the loan payments.[15] By January 1920 they had moved in with Boog and Chicora. In a few months they moved again.

The family moved to the Wade Place, a house originally owned by Lloyd Wade, and stayed there for nearly four years. The house was small and a little more basic than the Buttrill house. This one had no windows in it, and they had to ask friends who came to visit to bring ice for the icebox. Most of them did so, with the cargo wrapped in newspapers and blankets to survive the journey. There was a stream nearby where they kept canned milk and other items cool between visits. In later years as the family grew older Graham stayed at the Wade Place most of the time, and Annie moved with the kids to Alpine so they could attend school.[16] They returned to the Wade Place in the summers.

Graham was gone much of the time, working for various ranchers and local law enforcement. He accompanied Jack Allen, sheriff of Terrell County, into Mexico to recover some stolen horses. He worked with Dudley Barker, sheriff of Pecos County, as a jailer and investigated cattle theft cases.[17] While he was gone, Annie was in charge and she took care of things as he would have. Graham had left her a small Colt .380 automatic pistol, which she kept with her most of the time. Joe Graham recalled that one day, Graham was late coming home and two Mexican cowboys rode up to the place and asked for something to eat. Annie never faltered. She fed them, and while she did she made sure they could see the Colt she kept with her. The *vaqueros*, friends of Joe's, met him on the road and told him of their adventure. Joe recalled they all laughed about it, but the incident provided testimony that the country was still dangerous and as long as they lived there, Graham and Annie would have to deal with the possibility of danger.[18]

The family settled into a pattern of Graham working anywhere he could find a job. Work with Joe Graham remained somewhat stable, and he could do day work for neighbors, but all that slowed with the drought and depression. What seemed to be more promising were the contacts that he was making in law enforcement. His work with the Rangers had given him a feel for state-level law enforcement. Now he was working a lot closer to the people he was policing, and he found that working for the sheriff required a different kind of enforcement.

As a stock detective he had no restrictions on what he did. It was an unofficial job, and it amounted to a hunting license for rustlers. With the Rangers he had enjoyed a sort of legal immunity, because the Rangers were considered the governor's men. They were state officers and didn't answer to the local population through elections and local controls; while they could be ordered out of the county, they could not be voted out. Graham had to learn that when working with the sheriff's office the people he was working with demanded a gentler hand. They did, after all, elect the sheriff, and they could vote him out if they wanted. Graham was not used to this. His experience had been that he had the badge, and he was the man in charge. He required people to do as he demanded, and do it immediately. As a deputy, he found that people didn't like that approach. It was a difficult lesson for him to learn.

In the late spring of 1920, Graham Barnett formed an acquaintance, and later a friendship, with two men who would remain influences on him for the rest of his life. The two men were lawyers John Sutton and Brian Montague who had had a law partnership in Alpine. Over the next twelve years the paths of the three would cross again and again, driven by mutual respect, professional needs, and violence.

When the three were seen around Alpine they would have attracted a second look because of their differences. Graham stood 5'9" and weighed about 165 pounds. He continued to merit the nickname "Bush" because of his rough, unshaven appearance. He wore work clothes, usually with the bottom button of his shirt undone to allow access to the pistol tucked inside his shirt in his belt. Graham was a man who loved to drink, gamble, and tell stories, all of which provided a black and white contrast with his lawyer friends.

Montague was smaller, no more than 5'6", thin, with a shock of black hair above heavy horn rimmed glasses. He spoke in a low voice with a courtly manner that contrasted with most of the people he defended. Montague was a veteran of the First World War who had seen combat and had been commended for his bravery in defending an ammunition dump under fire. He had passed the bar in 1920 and moved to Alpine shortly after. He had a long and distinguished career, becoming district attorney for Pecos County in 1922 and moving in and out of private practice for the remainder of his career.[19] When Montague moved into the area he met Joe Graham and immediately struck up a friendship with him, calling him "one of the best men I ever knew."[20] Originally, it was probably the relationship that Montague had with Joe Graham that brought him into contact with Graham Barnett. He found that he and the ex-Ranger had a number of common interests. Both were of fond of guns and collected them. Both also collected stories about the borderliners they knew. Graham kept them in his memory; Brian Montague kept meticulous notes about the people and events that he encountered. In a loss that could only be considered tragic, most of the files that he kept over the years were destroyed after his death. The friendship went beyond the two of them. Brian was friends with Graham's family and his brother Joe would be brought into the friendship when he moved into the area in the mid 1920s. Montague's partnership with John Sutton was critical for all the three men.

John Sutton was a tall, thin man who was married with one child, a son. Sutton had moved to Alpine before the end of the war and had set up a well thought of law firm. Montague joined him after being released from service with the army in World War I. By 1920, Graham was already involved with Sutton's office and had had occasion to make use of John Sutton's political acumen. He had written the adjutant general in Austin on Sutton's letterhead requesting an application to rejoin the Rangers.[21] The letter was very short and to the point and it isn't known if the adjutant general even responded, but it is interesting that by requesting enlistment papers on the lawyer's letterhead that Graham was implying some sort of working relationship with the Sutton law firm. The implied relationship apparently made no impression on the adjutant general, and Graham was not rehired as a Ranger.

When Brian Montague joined John Sutton they both had occasion to work with Graham, but Brian formed a closer relationship than Sutton did. Brian later wrote a fourteen-page memoir of his friendship with the gunfighter that provides some of the best insights into both their characters. Over the years, Montague collected a number of the stories, some he questioned, others he did not. Together they make up a large part of the Barnett legacy. By the time Montague came into the Sutton law firm, Graham Barnett had a well-established, colorful reputation that fascinated the young lawyer. The stories that fueled the reputation both intrigued and disturbed the attorney. He described Graham as having "the reputation of being a very dangerous man and extremely accurate in firing either a rifle or a pistol."[22] While he was impressed with some of the stories that Graham told, he was horrified by others. One that stuck in his mind was that Graham occasionally sat on the bluff above the Rio Grande and took a shot occasionally at people on the other side. The issue of sniping across the river was an activity engaged in from both sides at that time and into the modern era.[23] While that doesn't excuse it, it does explain something about the lack of respect for both sides during this period. There were other tales that impressed the lawyer enough that he noted them down. All of them contributed to the mythology of Graham Barnett. The story about how Graham became a Brewster County deputy sheriff was one.

Graham explained to the lawyer that he was known through the area as a man who carried a gun on just about all occasions, and usually carried it concealed under his shirt or his coat. The habit had caused some concern from enough citizens that a sheriff and his deputy, who were not named by Montague, decided to visit Graham and discuss the issue with him.

While Montague does not name the sheriff, it was probably E. E. Townsend, who was a friend of Graham's since the Babb trial. In his memoir, Montague stated that the sheriff and a deputy went out to the ranch to talk to Graham, apparently about his tendency to carry a concealed weapon in town. When they got there they couldn't find anyone home, so they sat down on the porch to wait for his return. After a short time Graham rode up, and the lawmen told him why they were there.

Graham invited them into the house for a cup of coffee. The talk turned to concealed weapons and for some reason, Graham decided at that point to demonstrate his quick draw. Because he was working in the country Graham may have been carrying his pistol in one of the pockets of his chaps.[24] That method of carry is not unusual, but it is awkward. The unnamed sheriff was sufficiently impressed with the move and the reputation that Graham had that the two came to a settlement. Graham would serve as deputy when he was needed. Many counties had a policy of enlisting unfunded deputies to assist the sheriff when, usually because of the distances involved, the sheriff was unable to reach an isolated part of the county. As a part-time deputy, the legality of his concealed weapon was somewhat addressed. However, it wasn't the legality of carrying a pistol that brought Graham into the lawyer's office shortly afterward. It was a potential feud with the Texas Rangers.

In late 1920, Graham came by the law offices with a potentially explosive question. He told Brian Montague that he and Annie had gone to a dance in Marathon. At some point, Graham got a little too exuberant in whatever he was celebrating, and drew the attention of two of the most well-known Texas Rangers in the area, Arch Miller and John Hollis. Miller and Hollis decided they would try to arrest him for either disturbing the peace, or being drunk and disorderly. The arrest didn't happen. It is likely that when the Rangers began to show interest in him, Graham or Annie decided the evening was over with anyway and left the dance. But words were exchanged and the Rangers marked Graham as a man who they would be watching. He couldn't have chosen two more difficult men with which to have a feud.

Arch Miller was a veteran Ranger who was well-known for two reasons: his ability as an officer and the fact that he had only one arm. The loss of his arm was the subject of a number of stories ranging from a knife fight in Mexico to a gun fight with bandits in Texas. The storytellers should have stuck with the truth. Miller and fellow Ranger Lee Trimble had a Ford Model T that they used for transportation in the Big Bend and at times for personal amusement. Part of that amusement involved chasing cattle and roping them out of the car. On one occasion they were roping out of the flivver and wrecked it. A car wreck tends to be a little more serious than a horse wreck, and Miller's arm was mangled terribly. The pair started an epic journey to find a doctor to fix the busted up arm. By the time they found one to do the work, gangrene had set in and the arm had to be amputated. Shortly afterwards, an additional surgery had to be done to clean up the job and the pair went by train on to San Antonio where that surgery was performed. Miller later claimed he was the only man to have his arm amputated twice.[25] Miller wanted to stay with the Rangers and his captain, Charles Stevens, told him he could stay if he could get his gun belt on. Miller developed a technique, demonstrated it, and remained in the Rangers until 1933, retiring as a sergeant.[26]

Miller was partnered with John Hollis who was known universally as "Ricochet John" because of an incident that occurred when he shot at a Mexican horse thief. Hollis was trailing a group of bandits and decided to take a shot at them. In the changing political climate, Hollis always said he decided to take a shot at the outlaws just to scare them. He said that both he and the bandit had some bad luck. According to Hollis he fired and the bullet hit a rock, ricocheted off, and killed the fleeing outlaw. The story of what was supposed to be an accidental shooting spread across the border and John Hollis quickly became known as "Ricochet John."[27] Hollis remained with the Ranger force until 1927. The two men became a well-known pair and it was inevitable they would cross Graham Barnett and have what he referred to as a run in.

Shortly after the dance at Marathon, the Rangers were on a scout on the Joe Graham ranch and met Graham again. The three men exchanged some conversation in the pasture, and the subject of the problem in Marathon came up. According to Graham something was said that made him believe that that two were going to try to kill him.

The next day, he told Brian Montague, that while he was driving into town he saw what he called "a grass sack" somewhat concealed in a rut on the road. He stopped the car and found that the burlap bag held several sticks of dynamite, creating a kind of 1920s improvised explosive device. Graham told Montague that he believed the Rangers had planted the bomb and intended for him to set it off as he drove over it. Montague was skeptical. "Neither he nor I knew whether contact made by the wheel of the car and sack would cause the dynamite to explode but he was absolutely convinced that the Rangers had placed it there. At the time Graham related this story to me, I wondered if it were true or if it was a figment of his imagination, and, too, the thought occurred to me that Graham was probably laying the foundation for a defense if later he became involved in a shooting scrape with either or both of the Rangers."[28]

The expected shooting scrape never did take place. Whatever differences the three had remained unresolved and the question of the dynamite bomb was never settled, either in court or in a gunfight. It did establish that perhaps Graham was not as impulsive as some of his actions might indicate. He anticipated having to have an alibi for what he had decided was an inevitable gunfight. Should he have another run in with the Rangers, the story could have been seen as justification for a plea of self-defense. Montague, or another lawyer, might have been able to establish that vague shadow of a doubt in the minds of jurors that might have made the difference between an extended time in Huntsville or continued freedom on the ranch. No one ever mentioned what happened to the sack of dynamite.

Life was still unsettled in the Big Bend area; it didn't do to just ride up on someone's house without a little warning. A neighbor, Tom Henderson, remembered how tough and careful the man he called "Bush" was. "Whenever you saw Bush in Marathon he didn't wear a six-shooter in sight but if you looked close a shirt button was always unbuttoned just above his belt."[29] That unbuttoned shirt gave testimony that Graham was using the belt carry in town. Outside of town it was different.

Henderson was sent on an errand to the Barnett outfit and it proved to be memorable. "In 1922, mama sent me to Bush's place to pick up a horse and mule we owned that kept running off. Bush lived about twenty-two miles from us. I saddled a good horse and got there about noon, my stomach told me. I rode up to the front of their house and hollered hello. About two minutes later, Bush's wife came out on the porch and, recognizing me, told me to unsaddle and come in and eat. About that time, Bush stepped from around the corner of the house with a cocked .45, let the hammer down and dropped it in his holster."[30] Later when they ate, Tom noticed that Graham sat facing the door with his pistol on the table to the right of his plate. It didn't pay to take chances, even in your own home.

Graham expanded his law enforcement experience by working for E. E. Townsend, Brewster County sheriff, as a part-time jailer and occasional deputy.[31] It was a beneficial arrangement for both men. Graham needed the money and Townsend needed a ready-to-work man who carried enough of a reputation that generally no one would cross him. Being a deputy was part of an intricate political labyrinth in which every arrest or miss-step by either the sheriff or the men working for him would have an impact on elections. The sheriff had to be cautious how he dealt with crime in his county. He needed tough men with good judgment. What Townsend got was Graham Barnett, and he knew that Graham was not the only tough man in the Big Bend. The scene was set for a memorable tale.

Again, Brian Montague was a willing listener and Graham, or one of his friends, were willing story tellers. As Montague later recalled, this story involved murder, an attempt at rough justice, and a local man named Ed Caulder. While Montague was not there to record all the details, he was there to record those details people choose to tell him about the time Graham went up against another man with a reputation.

In November of 1922, Townsend was called to investigate what appeared to be a murder in his jurisdiction.[32] Murder seemed to be the proper call since the victim, Bill Harris, had been found sunk in the Rio Grande with two large rocks tied to his body. Harris's longtime partner in ranching and crime was a man by the name of Ed Caulder. The two had met when Caulder had moved to Edwards County with a herd of sheep, goats, and a shady reputation. Harris and Caulder had drifted into Crockett County where Caulder had been accused and acquitted in the drowning of his baby daughter. The pair, along with Caulder's wife, slipped into Brewster County and set up operations in the southern part of the county in the Chisos Mountains. They ran their combined herds on the free range in the area, but they just could not avoid the attention of the law. Caulder was in and out of jail.

Caulder's wife disappeared in 1918 or '19. The exact date was hard to pin down since, after a while, Mrs. Calder just failed to show up in public anymore. She was not there in January of 1920 when census records show that Ed, his daughter, son, and nephew were all living together in Brewster County. [33] At that time, however, Ed was not at home. He was in Alpine, in jail during the census.[34] John Sutton, who, along with Brian Montague represented Caulder in a civil action in 1919, remained convinced that the late Mrs. Caulder was now occupying a hole in the ground in one of the many caves in the Chisos Mountains.[35] No charges were ever filed in the case, so apparently no one missed Mrs. Caulder any more than Mr. Caulder did. Her disappearance only seemed to enhance his reputation as a man who should not be crossed. Caulder apparently was aware that neither of his lawyers, Sutton nor Montague, really cared for him as anything other than a paying client. He always ended his letters to Sutton with the enigmatic phrase, "Give my love to Mr. Montague."[36] Caulder was tough, he made his own rules, but when he became a suspect in Bill Harris's death he was introduced to Graham Barnett.

After hauling the heavily weighted body of Bill Harris out of the river, Sheriff Townsend considered his options. He had a body, and with Ed Caulder he had a man with a reputation that indicated that he was no stranger to violence. It seemed reasonable that while Caulder might not be the only person with a motive to kill Harris, he was closest to the situation and would benefit the most from Harris's death. In the best traditions of the frontier west, the sheriff formed a posse that included Graham and rode out to find the suspected killer to see if some kind of justice could be administered. Caulder wasn't too hard to find; he did, however, refuse to admit anything with regard to his suspected role in the murder. After some extended discussion, Townsend announced that he needed to go to use the telephone. It isn't clear why at this particular juncture in the interrogation the county sheriff suddenly remembered that he had to make a call, but he rode off to the nearest ranch to find a phone and left Graham in charge of the proceedings. If Ed Caulder didn't know Graham Barnett before, he was getting ready to meet him.

Since everyone had already decided that Caulder was guilty, the only thing missing was the confession. Graham tossed a rope over the limb of a handy tree, and slipped the noose over his prisoner's head and pulled him up. Whatever encouragement the hanging might have provided to Caulder did not result in the voluntary confession that Graham had wanted. When Caulder's tongue was sticking out of his mouth, Graham dropped him back on the ground and waited for the anticipated confession. Ed Caulder was not a man who would let something like a lynching impede him too much. "He gave me the worst cussing out I ever had," said Graham.[37] Just as Caulder wasn't intimidated by the hanging, Graham wasn't intimidated by the cussing.

He hauled him back up into the air and left him a little longer with a similar result. "If it was possible, I got a worse cussing out than I did the first time."[38] Just to make sure that Caulder was thinking straight, Graham pulled him up a third time with the same result as the other two. The posse was puzzled. They had who they thought was the right man, they had a body, they had everything but a confession, and the confession did not appear to be forthcoming. The posse seemed to have run out of ideas about what to do with the unrepentant and still untried Ed Caulder. A decision had to be made about what to do and Graham made it: "We just gave up and let him go."[39]

In a footnote to the incident, the grand jury met in January 1923 and could not find a single bit of evidence linking Caulder, or anyone else, to the murder. Caulder was not charged in the matter, and, interestingly enough, Graham was not charged with anything either, although it is doubtful that the two of them ever exchanged the kinds of greetings that Caulder sent Montague.[40]

It wasn't only the lawyer-client relationship that drew Graham and Brian Montague together; the pair enjoyed some other common interests, among them firearms. While Brian was concerned about stories he had heard about Graham sniping at people along the Rio Grande, he was not concerned about the trunk of guns that he had heard Graham kept.

The two men kept each other aware of their gun trading. Montague had a long barreled .38 special that he had won playing poker in France during the war. He didn't like the gun because the barrel was too long for him. He was approached by Joe Velasco, whom Montague described as a "notorious killer"[41] and a man he later prosecuted for murder, who offered him a single action .45 Colt in trade. Brian jumped at the chance. It was a .45, it had a shorter barrel, and it was something he wanted. They cinched the deal. Brian was showing off his new trade to Graham who offered to "train" the new gun for him. He took it, worked the action over, and returned it, telling the lawyer that it was a very good gun but he had not made the gun as light on the trigger as he could have. "You don't need one as quick as mine," he grinned.[42] Brian was pleased with newly slicked up pistol and fascinated by his gunsmith.

Brian Montague continued to learn more about his new friend and learned pretty quickly that with Graham it wasn't all about being a gunfighter. He must have suspected that there was a difference between the man and the stories he continued to hear. At times it seemed that he knew two different people: the man he told stories and traded guns with and the man with the reputation as a manhunter. But which was real? For most of the people who knew him, including Brian, Graham showed two sides of his personality that contributed to his reputation as a mysterious cowboy. One side was the cowboy who came to town from time to time, and then a darker side that not everyone saw, but it seemed everyone heard about. The dichotomy was what made Graham interesting to many people.

Graham was known for his skills as a cowboy. He was good with stock; he broke horses, although he was known for being hard on them. He had a good record with Joe Graham's sheep herds and he had learned the cattle business from that master. There was no doubt that he loved his wife and family. The extended family meant almost as much to him as his immediate family. The problem he faced was that a cowboy with a family was a man who was never going to make a lot of money. The dream that many cowboys had was buying a small place and expanding the operation the way the old style cowmen had done in the past. With the economy dropping as quickly as it was the odds of that happening were somewhat less than getting struck by lightning during a drought. He faced some other problems as well.

One of the other problems was the reputation he was beginning to get as a man who drank too much. Montague was just one of the people who had heard the stories of typical Graham Barnett drinking bouts and what went along with them. "Graham was a congenial, nice fellow until he started drinking, then he got mean and started looking for somebody he didn't like," said Sam Haynes, one of the few lawmen Barnett would let lock him up when he was drunk.[43] James Weatherby, a family friend at Big Lake knew the behavior and said, "Graham was a mean son of a bitch when he got to drinking."[44] Charles N. Hickcox, a steel tank builder, remembered, "He liked to play poker and drink whiskey. He usually didn't get falling down drunk but he was mean when he was drinking."[45] When he got drunk he wanted to fight somebody and as often as not he would begin to list the people he was going to kill. It was a pattern that would be seen for the rest of his life: drinking, some thinking, some fighting, and some threats. It didn't make much difference if you were a friend or not. When Graham drank, he changed.

As an officer of the court, Montague heard stories about his friend, and usually he noted some details. Among those details were that there were very few people who could handle Graham when he was drinking. One of the only people who had any ability at all to deal with him during one of these episodes was Vern Davis, the sheriff of Sterling County who had grown up with him. Vern had had a lot of practice dealing with Graham.

Since Graham and Annie had relatives in Sterling City and he still had some ranching interests there, the Barnett's visited Sterling County often. Graham developed the habit of coming by the courthouse to tell Sheriff Davis he was in town and to visit with him about the activities of the day. Whether it was intended or not, the visit also alerted Vern to the possibility of trouble, and the trouble was usually predicated by a bout of drinking. When he drank Graham changed, and he became the man who was going to get even with everyone and everything that had shorted him in life.

After watching Graham for a number of years Vern was able to predict the cycle of drinking, anger, and Graham's failure to consider the consequences of what he was doing. "He just got ornery and mean... he would go haywire [and] after he went haywire he had no physical fear"[46] This lack of fear went a long way to explain some of Graham's more erratic behaviors such as taking on, or trying to take on, anyone who showed any opposition to him. As sheriff, Vern Davis was more than aware of the pattern. He arrested Graham at least four times but he never approached him without being cautious. "He never gave me a minute of trouble; I arrested him for drunkenness, for carrying a six shooter, for fighting with fists and for gambling."[47] It was the arrest for drinking that might have given him a little concern. "I got word that he was drunk and had announced publicly that he was going to kill me. But when I arrested him he had no gun and made no resistance."[48] Graham didn't give Davis any trouble because, as Davis recalled, "I figured it this way, he was a good friend and, even though he could best me in a gun fight, he knew I wouldn't fool with him."[49] The implication was clear; Davis was not going to allow Graham an even break on an arrest. If it meant a leather slapper across the head or a double barreled shotgun, Vern and Graham both knew that there were some people who could play as rough as Graham did. It worried Annie: "I was always afraid that he wouldn't come home some night"[50]

When Vern Davis arrested him after the threats, the sheriff noted that he didn't have a gun on him. Not having a gun was not a normal situation for Graham Barnett. It was expected that Graham carried at all times. He had a gun in the car, and when he went to bed a pistol was within easy reach on a chair. For a man living a life of isolation, and who might have to face a rustler, a rabid dog, or a crazy steer before the day was out, carrying a weapon was more than just an affectation; it was a matter of life or death. Having a gun on you and not needing it was a lot better than the opposite. The more he practiced, the more people noticed and as they did, they talked. The talk became gossip and the gossip became legend. Vern Davis, who watched him, described his speed as "pretty salty." If his speed was salty, his accuracy was more so. The sheriff saw the gunfighter shoot one time. "He and I were driving around and I had an old thumb buster .45, a single action. We were driving down the road at about 45 miles an hour. He shot at fence posts and never missed a one. That convinced me."[51]

Over time, Montague and others developed a view of Graham Barnett that approached nearly mythic qualities. Partly because of the reputation he carried after the fight with Will Babb, and partly because of stories that still circulated of Graham's activities as what Brian Montague called "a dangerous man." Graham was seen as a shadowy figure that had fought with guns and fists and if he lost one of the fights, you could rest assured that he would even the score later. Stories circulated about men he was supposed to have killed and how he done it, and it made no difference if it had actually happened or not; the stories were too good not to repeat. It was all part of the Graham Barnett legend that seemed to grow out of people's need to see a hero from the past deal with the problems of the present. In reality he was a man long on reputation and short on cash. He had a growing family in the middle of a drought and he was dealing with a loss of a lot of cattle. He was a legend in need of a job. So he found one. He became a bootlegger.

Bootlegging was not considered a particularly honorable business, but it was one that a number of people got involved in because of the unpopularity of the progressive movement outlawing liquor. Bootleggers were found in all places and among all social groups. In one well-known case that smacked of the pulp magazine "Flying Aces," several professors at Sul Ross University ran an airborne bootlegging business using a small airplane one of them had. They finally nosed over into a ploughed field and were put out of business by Prohibition agents.[52] Graham didn't get that fancy. For him it was a normal activity; he was supplying a service to people who needed a product and he didn't see it as a particularly risky endeavor.

Even with the bootlegging, money was still a problem. He told Brian Montague that the family was starving and he borrowed money to pay for food and, probably, ammunition and gambling debts. At that point, fate, as it sometimes does, took a hand.

In May of 1923, Graham heard that there was a huge oil boom going on at the Santa Rita oil field near the small town of Big Lake. The boom had created two more towns, Best and Texon. The county was filling up with drillers, speculators, oil scouts, and the attendant groups of workers and camp followers that created a somewhat lawless atmosphere in the oil patch. The oil companies hired men to provide security on the oil leases and those men were frequently co-opted by the local sheriff's department as deputies. He also heard that the sheriff of Reagan County was looking for a deputy to police the new towns and work jointly for Big Lake Oil. Graham decided it was a job made for him. There were problems of course.

He went to Brian Montague and asked him for a recommendation to Sheriff L. M. Rankin. "I told Graham that I just simply could not in good conscience do so because of his doing so much gambling, drinking, and bootlegging, at least I suspected him of bootlegging as about the only means of making a living."[53] Graham was desperate. He waited a couple of months and came back to the attorney to ask him again for a recommendation. The job was still open, the situation at home was worse, and the family was starving, he claimed. Montague weighed the choices he had: helping a friend who had potential to be an outstanding lawman against putting a man behind a badge when that man might prove to be as dangerous as some that he opposed. As he struggled with the decision, Montague played off his reluctance against Graham's high potential. "I knew he would make a good officer if he would conduct himself in accordance with the law."[54] But it was the gambling and the drinking that still concerned Montague. Graham made a last plea. "He got up out of his chair and held his right hand in the air and said, 'If you will just recommend me to Mr. Rankin, I swear I will never touch another drop of liquor or flip another card as long as I live.'" Montague rationalized that Graham had always kept his word, and was as desperate as he had ever seen him. He agreed. "Graham said 'Pick up the phone and call Mr. Rankin right now.' Which I did and Mr. Rankin told me to have Graham come right over to Reagan County and he would make the appointment."[55] Graham would become a special officer for Big Lake Oil as well as a deputy sheriff for Rankin County. He was back in law enforcement, but it would only be for a short time and that time would be controversial.

CHAPTER 8

"COME ON IN, YOU'RE AS
WELCOME AS A CORPSE"

1924-1925[1]

The world of law enforcement that Graham was going to reenter was different from law enforcement as it is known today. A major difference dealt with the expectations the public had for law enforcement then and how those expectations differed from place to place. The law in Texas, from 1900 until deep into the 1960s, was primarily centered on small towns and small town attitudes. It was heavily influenced by political considerations and use of a roughly defined concept known as discretion. Discretion was an unofficial concept that maintained that law enforcement had a certain leeway in enforcing the law. When law officers faced a situation they could make decisions based on a number of considerations, including what was best for the individual, the community, or themselves. The result of the application of discretion led to both positive and negative results.

In early twentieth century Texas, the sheriff held most of the discretionary power and used it in a variety of ways, which led to a certain milieu. Thad Sitton described it as follows: "Rural and small-town Texas...

was a strange, often violent, complicated place, where nineteenth century lifestyles persisted, blood ties held, racial apartheid remained rigidly enforced, and sheriffs played the key role in keeping a lid on things."[2] Keeping a lid on things was a full time job. The sheriff was selected by the local political machine, and served based on the desires of the voters. It was expected that the sheriff would enforce the law based on the needs of those same voters. He would do this through the exercise of a certain amount of discretionary law enforcement. One man driving drunk might be taken to jail, another might be given a ride a home and a stern warning. People understood that the sheriff was going to do what he thought was the right thing for the community. In most cases, the sheriff was not a professional lawman, but a local man who was selected and voted on by his neighbors. If he wanted to remain sheriff he needed to remember that in small towns, he was never far from his neighbors.

Most sheriffs in West Texas didn't think too much about dealing with organized crime. They were too busy dealing with the kind of disorganized mischief that had them facing belligerent drunks who just wanted to fight somebody on Saturday night. As often as not, the fighting was a carryover from the election; there were very few good losers in Texas. Once he was elected, the fights were just starting for the sheriff. He dealt with crime as well as domestic disputes, policing high school football games, the removal of skunks, possums, and other undesirables from under people's houses, and the constant monitoring of dance halls and beer joints. He used what he had at hand to deal with the public. Fists, leather slappers, and lead-loaded saps helped to pacify the more enthusiastic members of the population. The sheriff might use a gun if necessary, although shooting a member of the voting public was always awkward.

The sheriff would also define the conduct of his deputies. Sheriff Walter Ellison of Caldwell County was one of the few who had a deputy and explained to him what was going to happen: "Now they're going to try to run over you. If you give one inch, you might as well quit. Whatever you do, I'm behind you."[3] The idea that people would "run over" the deputy, intimidate him at best, beat him to a pulp at worst, drove a lot of decisions that were made in small town Texas. The idea that the deputy couldn't give an inch sealed a lot of those decisions. The sheriff could not afford to have someone run over the local law. Fighting with the belligerent civilians kept many deputies occupied before the actual business of dealing with recognized crime began. Small towns always seem to have people who believe the rules don't apply to them and that there is no better fighter, drinker, lover, or brawler than they are. If a man was going to be in the sheriffing business, he had better be prepared to deal with the toughest people in the county because he would see a lot more of them than he would the good people.

As crime became more of a business with the coming of Prohibition and the expanding oil economy, the country sheriff found that he might have some resources that were not available ten years before. In a number of situations businesses brought in their own private officers. Railroads, the new oil companies, and some large ranching interests generally employed their own security people. In many cases these private officers were deputized by the sheriff or held special Ranger commissions. They did not, however, have the same political base as the sheriff. As federal prohibition agents, the Bureau of Investigation, and other state and local entities came on the scene, the local sheriffs often found themselves at odds with their new allies. Typically, the state and federal officers ignored the concept of discretion. They were committed to a different kind of law enforcement than the local officers and this difference led to some divisions between the two groups.

It became harder to keep a lid on things as Texas began to move into the twentieth century. Times were changing. Fueled by the oil boom, the economy was exploding. People had money, and were willing to spend it on things they wanted, and they wanted liquor. Prohibition had been in place for four years and had opened a new world of bootlegging and smuggling. Everyone who wanted liquor seemed to be able to get it. The unpopularity of the liquor laws led many in the population to become disillusioned with the law and those who enforced it. Texas in 1924 was a dramatically different place than it had been ten years earlier, but the county sheriff was still the key player in the enforcement of the law in contrast with the new state, federal, and private lawmen who were spreading across the state.

Most of the sheriffs realized that the nature of crime was changing. It was expanding, and it touched more people than it had before. Crime during this period could be classified into two categories: crime that denied something to someone, which would include theft, rape, and murder, and crime that provided something to someone, which would include gambling, prostitution, liquor, and drugs.

The first category of crime was opposed and generally not tolerated by most of the population. The second category, the criminal provision of services, seemed to be supported and even encouraged by parts of that same population. Vice, composed of alcohol, prostitution, drugs, and gambling, was wildly popular in Texas. A large number of Texans did not want a government that told them when and where to drink, how to lose their money, and with whom they could become involved in short term commercial affection. The Progressive Movement attempted to force a more moral atmosphere in the state, but for most people this movement was an unwieldy intrusion into their lives. This attitude affected the way people viewed the lawman who attempted to enforce the laws.

At the beginning of the century, vice was viewed as major problem and attempts were made to make it less available and simpler to police. To make it easier for everyone, saloons, parlor houses, and gambling dens were set aside in special zones in many large cities. The zones had their own advertising booklets, and people generally believed that this placement allowed more control by providing a centralized area that could be patrolled better. The advent of World War I put an end to many of these vice zones although San Antonio and Galveston maintained theirs until later in the century.[4] By the 1920s vice had gone back underground and it became much harder to combat. Both police and criminals found that possessing information about the activities of the other side was the key to everyone being successful.

A symbiotic relationship sprung up between lawmen and outlaws. In an effort to gather information about what was going on in the world of crime, lawmen expanded their informant system. In response, the crime bosses did the same thing. The two groups passed information to each other via informants and casual spectators supplied data to both sides. Part of this flow of information and money was directed by greed and part of it was concerned with keeping a handle on what was happening with the opposition. Cops provided advance warning on raids. Criminals responded with the locations of certain stills or the time of an arrival of bootleg liquor. The brothels, bars, and gambling houses paid for protection from the police and in turn, the police kept the fighting and nonsporting behavior to a manageable level. In the middle of this ongoing struggle, information was exchanged that benefitted both parties.

An example of this relationship was the arrangement between Sheriff Will Loessin, sheriff of Fayette County, and Miss Jesse Williams of what was known at various times as Edna's Fashionable Ranch Boarding House or, during the depression, as the Chicken Ranch in LaGrange.[5] The brothel had operated since 1844, in one location or another, in La Grange. It had become a functioning part of the community and, while not completely respected by all, it was tolerated and accepted by many. Loessin was sheriff from 1925 until 1946 and recognized the usefulness of the business as well as the information that came to him out of the ranch. Loessin received daily reports from the local madam, Jesse Williams. Miss Jesse knew that criminals and everyday sporting gents loved to talk about themselves to the girls. The girls reported the customer's comments, first to Miss Jesse who then relayed pertinent ones on to the sheriff. Will made a daily trip to the Chicken Ranch to collect the latest criminal information. The model was continued by Loessin's successor, T. J. Flournoy, who kept the contacts but established a telephone line when he became sheriff.

This type of communication made for close contact between law officers and lawbreakers. The relationship benefitted both, but also gave the impression that lawmen sometimes crossed the line between the two sides. Having an informant and being an informant were two sides of the same coin, just as enforcing some laws and breaking others became an extension the concept of discretion, which had driven local policing for years.

The information that moved between law enforcement and law breaking dealt with a number of activities, most notably those related to the Volstead Act. With the Volstead Act prohibiting the legal sale of most liquor in the United States, the country reached an epiphany of enforced morality. It also led to the greatest disregard for the law that ever occurred in the country. The Volstead Act was passed in 1919 and became the Eighteenth Amendment to the Constitution in January of 1920. Its intent was to control the liquor industry, to make sure that there was sufficient alcohol for legitimate purposes, as designated in the bill, and to regulate the manufacture, sale, and transportation of liquor. In addition, it stated that "no person shall manufacture, sell, barter, transport, import, export, deliver, or furnish any intoxicating liquor except as authorized by this act."[6]

In response, distilleries and breweries moved lock, stock, and aging barrels to Mexico in order to continue to produce the booze that the people wanted. What was shown in the voting booth and supported in town meetings was frequently not the way life was lived. In reality, it was a case of many people voting "dry" and living "wet." In many towns, pharmacies began to sell alcohol that had been prescribed by local doctors in a system that allowed a gentleman to enter the front door, pick up his prescription, walk to the back, have his drink, and drop the prescription off to be used again the following day. Presumably, ladies had to drink on their own.

What the Volstead Act accomplished was to create a number of criminal centers in larger cities that interacted with each other and with the civilian population. In the eyes of many people, the bootlegger wasn't the enemy. He was the kid down the street who provided beer for the Knights of Columbus. He was the banker who stored booze in the bank vaults. He was the deputy sheriff who let the loads run, and in doing so didn't enforce a law that most people found odious. In Texas, the flow of liquor centered on the Mexican border, both a source and a destination for criminal activity for a century.

Smuggling had been a way of life for years on the border. For men who had smuggled guns in the revolution, moving liquor by mule train was no problem. The bottles were wrapped in tule grass and strapped into *aparejos*, the commonly used Mexican horseback pack. The 1200 miles of border was riddled with fords, crossings so narrow you could walk across, and places that a supplier on one side could float liquor on a raft to a cohort on the other side. The mule and horse trains slipped across the river and headed to distribution points in South and West Texas. There they were met by distribution gangs and the liquor transferred to cars and trucks where it was quickly transported to the larger centers such as Austin, San Antonio, and Dallas. The smuggler's trip home was made with the same *aparejos* full of items that were hard to find or heavily regulated in Mexico. Competition between the smuggling gangs made the need for protection intense, and while some organizations provided it themselves, others involved local law enforcement. Who better to provide protection than those people already set up to do so? Many law enforcement agencies were faced with an unpopular law and pressure from the public to ignore it. That pressure, combined with the flow of money controlled by the bootleggers, convinced many local officers to selectively enforce the law through their discretionary policies. The local officers would protect some of the bootleggers, arrest others, and in doing so, appeared to be conducting a serious campaign against lawbreakers. Almost no one was fooled by it. What prohibition managed to do was to create an eminently successful and corrupting business of extortion and bribery. It was not that many people in law enforcement were corrupt, it was that they were accommodating to the attitudes of the communities they lived in. The policing of other activities was viewed much the same way.

Gambling was part of the triumvirate of vice that included drinking and chasing around with the opposite sex, and was part of the Texas lifestyle for people who made the headlines and others who wanted to make them. Conventional wisdom held that the way a person lost their money was their own business and not that of the state. It was something people did and as more and more people began to gamble in earnest, the community of gamblers began to get organized in order to provide an outlet for gaming and a place to do it. In Dallas, the high rollers made their bets with an ex-horse trader and emerging numbers man named Benny Binion.[7] The Sicilian brothers Sam and Rosario Macio controlled most of the vice activity in the Free State of Galveston and policed their own territory.[8] In Houston, Jakie Freedman controlled the punchboards, cards, and roulette.[9] The bosses weren't just limited to life in the big cities, the gambling families or branches of them reached out into West Texas, into the small towns and oil fields.

The discovery of the large oil fields in West Texas shed new light on the problems. The discovery of oil began in 1920, but it was not until 1923 that the big field on the 421,000 acre University of Texas land came in. When Santa Rita Number One blew on May 28, 1923, life changed, not only in Reagan County, but all over West Texas. The rig itself became a monument to the industry and was dismantled and hauled to Austin to be put on permanent display on the grounds of the University of Texas, honoring the original source of that universities wealth.

Oil also brought wealth to the ranchers and farmers who leased their twenty acres or twenty sections to the oil companies and stood back and waited for changes to their bank accounts and to their land. The oil patch, as people referred to it, changed West Texas forever.

When the oil boom hit, towns developed around the drilling sites, railroad sidings, or the archetypical wide spot in the road, any place where people could set up offices and places to sleep and eat. Literally one day there would be no town, and within a week, a settlement would appear. In Reagan County, the story was repeated twice in the fields leased by Big Lake Oil. The towns were Texon and Best. Both sprang up from the oil and dollar soaked West Texas prairie but with decidedly different visions. Part of the ongoing conversation concerned which of the two towns would last. As it turned out, neither did.

When the drilling first began in that area in 1923, most of the drillers lived in Best. As the area west of Best was being developed, the Big Lake Oil Company decided to try something new: a planned company town. The general manager of Big Lake Oil was Levi Smith, a man with extensive experience in the oil fields and some definite ideas about what would work and what would not. He believed that a company benefitted from a stable labor force that could have their families close at hand. The only way that was going to happen was if a new town was developed in the area owned or leased by Big Lake Oil. Smith was determined to provide his people with amenities that would have been found in larger towns such as a drug store with a soda fountain, a barber shop, separate dormitories for single workers, and small houses so that families would be able to spend their off hours together.

When Smith built Texon he laid the groundwork for a town that would eventually have a public school, church, hospital, theatre, ice house, and a boarding house. The houses were built on streets that had names rather than being just a bungalow with a number. Meals were available at Mrs. Walter Mann's boarding house for .50 cents and a night watchman patrolled the town's streets to provide security for the sleeping families. Before the town disappeared in the early 1960s, it had polo grounds, tennis courts, a golf course, and a baseball field. Smith loved baseball and sponsored a semi-pro baseball team that played where it could get games. At its peak Texon had a population of about 1800.[10]

Texon's neighbor, Best, fit the more traditional view of an oil field town. Best was located west of Big Lake also, about four miles from Texon at the Orient Railroad siding. It started out as part of the supply system for the oil fields, but boomed quickly, growing to a population of about 3500 by 1925. It became "Vice Central" for that part of West Texas, providing just about any kind of pay-as-you-go sin that might be sought after by young men who worked hard and had more money than they had ever dreamed of having. Bootleggers, gamblers, and hookers followed the money to Best. There was generally a Texas Ranger stationed there or in the area until the big raids of 1925 made that presence a little less necessary. It was known as the town with the best name and worst reputation in Texas.[11] Oddly enough Best had the only school for the first year of Texon's existence and all the children went to school in Best. The contrast between the two towns was dramatic: one a site for families and quiet evenings watching the kids play baseball, the other a booming, violent place that seemed to be a twenty-four hour a day carnival that showed no signs of slowing down.

Law enforcement in the oil fields became a shared responsibility between the company, local law enforcement, and the state. Texas Rangers could be found sporadically in many oil towns but only on a limited basis because of the small size of the Ranger force. Local sheriffs were usually too stretched for resources to provide expanded services to the community and the expanded company-based sites that seemed to emerge daily. The answer to the problem seemed to be the special officers hired and supported by the companies.

The term "special officer" was applied to any number of employees of businesses, governmental agencies, or local agencies who handled security and law enforcement within a specific area of responsibility. Railroads had railway detectives, some large cities, such as Houston, employed special officers for specific problem areas, and in some cases investigators for district attorneys were designated special officers. Graham was hired as a special officer and was paid and supported by Big Lake Oil. Since he would be making arrests he was also deputized by Reagan County, which would authorize him to carry a weapon and arrest people off the oil lease areas. The oil field brought organized crime into rural Texas and that was not something many local officers were prepared for. Since so much money was involved in criminal activities, officers were routinely subject to being bribed, beaten up, or killed to protect the business. The response to this new level of crime was to bring in men who were as rough as the criminals to deal with the problem.

During a hiatus from the Rangers, Manual "Lone Wolf" Gonzaullas ran a security firm for several oil companies in East Texas. He hired as many former Rangers as he could, and let it be known that they were from the border. One man he hired was a former Ranger named Leo Bishop. Bishop came to the job with some well-respected credentials earned on the border. Bishop recalled that when Gonzaullas introduced him to the rest of the staff and the drillers, he had him come into the meeting armed with a sawed off shotgun and announced that Bishop had just arrived from the border. Gonzaullas knew that reputation was everything. "They thought that because I was from the Mexican border that I'm bound to be a tough son of a gun 'cause they thought the Mexican border was the toughest place in the world."[12] The world of the oil field mixed organized crime with men who wanted to work, make their money, and get out. The workers might engage in some vice from pay day to pay day, but they were more victims than criminals. Dealing with the mix of criminals and workers found in the oil fields required a different kind of policing than was done on the border. Veteran Rangers understood one of the cardinal rules: policing methods were different in different parts for the state. Leo Bishop knew this and remembered it years later. "I've heard a lot of old time peace officers that had worked in different parts of the State of Texas that expressed my view exactly about the difference in the way you had to operate as a peace officer along the Mexican border, compared to North Texas or East Texas or something, just different kinds of people that you worked with and you had to have different tactics to get the job done in different parts of the state."[13]

Exactly what these tactics included was only hinted at by Bishop. Some of it had to do with the fact that many people away from the border were not going to be as easily intimidated as many of the poorer Mexicans who had been kept in a second class or no class position for years. A gambler in an oil field town might have a backup of enforcers to keep him in business in West Texas. Often a criminal enterprise didn't exist in a vacuum, but had connections with officials across the state who were benefitting from the business. Responding to the different situations defined how successful the officer would be. The issue of adjusting from one set of tactics to another to deal with different problems in the rapidly changing world was never made clear to Graham, or if it was, he ignored the advice.

Policing on the oil lease initially was concerned with keeping the holdings of the company secure. The growth of company towns expanded the role of special officer to include not only the company sites, but the new towns as well. Big Lake Oil was concerned primarily with crime on the oil leases. If Texon was going to be an ideal city, it and Best needed policing from the growing crime problem driven by new money. While the Rangers had a man stationed at Best, the volume of crime was more than one man could handle. The geographic size of the oil leases and the continuing high volume of crime meant that the private officers often were on their own to make decisions and handle matters. The understanding that some kind of officer discretion was expected, and a change of tactics was needed from those used on the border, would prove to be a problem for Graham.

For the first time he was accountable to a company and to the electorate for his behavior. Levi Smith provided a Cadillac for the new deputy, and Graham became a familiar figure in creased khakis, a white or blue shirt, and one or sometimes two .45 automatics tucked in his belt. His patrol area took him down the streets of the town, past the planned school, golf course, and tennis courts. The neighborhood was being established and trees were being planted. It was a long way from the Big Bend. Despite the badge and the link to security in the oil fields, not everyone was impressed with Graham. Alex Olivey, who worked for Big Lake Oil, called him "Geronimo" and said the he was the "erstwhile upholder of the law west of the Concho."[14] If Graham heard that, it would have been the "erstwhile" part that would have gnawed at him. While his reputation may have gotten him the job, it appeared that to keep it he would have to develop another reputation. That didn't happen. He fell back on his original on-the-job training from the Rangers.

There is evidence that he was using the same strong arm tactics that he had learned in the Rangers, exacerbated by his lack of experience working both as a security man and as a member of an elected sheriff's department. He apparently ignored complaints concerning the lack of police procedures and also did not pay attention to the people he was policing. He could not adjust from the para-military attitudes of the border Rangers to the different setting of the oil field. That unwillingness to see a need to change and make that change doomed his career. Stories about Graham's conduct as a deputy began to circulate and eventually reached Brian Montague. Like most people he liked Graham, wished him well, but could not understand his friend's behavior. As district attorney for the 83rd Judicial District, Montague naturally received information about the goings on in all of counties he served. "I began to get reports that Graham was conducting himself in a very high-handed manner, arresting people without cause, searching cars, threatening local citizens and strangers alike, and I realized I had made a serious mistake in having recommended him to Mr. Rankin for appointment as a deputy."[15]

What Montague did after he realized his mistake isn't recorded; the indications are that he did nothing. However, he did watch as Graham continued to ignore the changing attitudes toward him and the job he was doing from the people in the towns and oil fields. His behavior was quickly creating himself a new reputation, that of a badge-heavy individual who believed that he could bully his way through a situation. Graham was making adjustments; they just were not the ones that he needed to make.

Another adjustment that had to be made was to the new family life in a company town. For the Barnetts, the oil boom had the potential to change their lives. If this opportunity could work out, everything was going to be different, not just for Graham, but for the entire family. The move in October of 1924 was fueled by optimism and hope. Annie must have felt a sense of relief; they had a job, a level of respectability, and Graham would be at home in the evenings. To her, it must have seemed that their life was turning around from the family of the itinerant cowboy and ranch manager to something more stable.

There were four children now, Maud, who was 6, Bud, 4, Conger, 2, and Jerry, who had been born in August. They set up housekeeping in a new place with a decidedly different environment than they had lived in before. They were in a company town. They weren't tied to the land anymore and they didn't have to worry about the drought or beef prices. They were going to have a steady salary even though it was acquired by trading long hours in dangerous places for the consistency. They could concentrate on doing what a family did: raise children and establish their own place in the world.

Families moved in and by Christmas the Barnett children were joined by several others. Levi Smith loved children and that first Christmas sent around a present to each child in his town. He chose one of the oil field workers as Santa Claus because he had a beard.[16] For Maud Barnett, it must have been a box of stationery because she wrote her thank-you note "on the same paper you gave me."[17] Smith replied with a typewritten letter that said in part "it was a pleasure for me to give you and your little playmates the Christmas remembrance to which you refer."[18]

The kids were well behaved. Annie saw to that. She was the one who tended to wield the rod. It was Graham who spoiled his children. The combination of love and high expectations from their father and their mother produced extraordinarily resilient and reliant children. The children remembered him as constantly showing them affection, carrying the younger ones around the house, and spending time with them outdoors teaching them to ride, work animals, and shoot.[19]

The Barnett family was a little different than most of the others. Guns were a part of everyday life. "Guns to us were like having a coffee pot around the house."[20] The kids all knew that Graham was never far from a pistol. At night he slept with one on a chair by the bed and when he got into the car he slipped the .45 into the pocket in the car door.[21] He carried weapons, maintained them for himself and friends, and kept his famous trunk full of pistols where he could get to it when he needed to. Everyone in the family knew how to shoot; it was just something that was expected.

Graham was involved in a shooting shortly after taking the job and naturally it attracted a good bit of attention.[22] Late one evening he noticed a bootlegger in Texon and the smuggler decided that he could outrun the new cop. Graham and the Cadillac were not going to be out run. It isn't clear who started shooting first, but the lead was quickly flying both ways. If the bootlegger was driving, there probably was someone with him doing the shooting, unless he was a contortionist, or he shot out his back window. Shooting out the side window of a car at a pursuer is a difficult task made more difficult when the individual behind you is shooting at you. The bootlegger raced out of Texon, headed for Best with the night lit up only by the car's headlights and the muzzle flashes of the guns. If nothing else, Graham was persistent and a good shot. The newspaper accounts describe the pursued car as being shot to pieces.[23] The story was that one of Graham's .45 slugs hit the driver between the eyes. The San Angelo newspaper noted, "Barnett had shot accurately, but the distance between them was so great that the bullet had merely lodged in the skin between his eyes."[24] What is more likely is that a fragment of the bullet or a piece of the interior struck the man as he was driving. The wound brought the pursuit to a halt and Graham walked up to the car and pulled the fragment of the bullet out of the man's face. In the best traditions of the western movie he told him not come back to Texon. No arrest was reported.

Whatever he had done in the past seemed to be matched by the stories that were told about his adventures in dealing with crime in the oil leases.[25] In a story that was told for generations he hitched a team of mules to a wagon, and taking a sack full of handcuffs, he drove up to the front door of the number one madam in Best. A short time later, scratched and bleeding, he ushered the shackled proprietor and her girls into the wagon, and hauled them in for the expected fines. The brief breakdown in companionship was mourned by many.

If a man gambled or drank in Best he knew Bill Burke, also known as "Boiler Maker Bill." Burke was known for serving and consuming the drink known as the boilermaker: a glass of beer with a shot of whisky depth charged into it. Both the drinking and the gambling were popular with his clientele and that had attracted Graham's attention. Burke had established himself in a two-story clapboard house and converted it into a one stop convenience store for vice-related activities. The thin walled rooms on the first floor served the drinking crowd while the upstairs hosted the poker, dice, and any other gaming activities that could produce a profit for the house. The drinking or the gambling had attracted Graham's attention. The deputy showed up prepared to arrest everyone he could and that appearance led to one of the most well-known fights of either man's career.

Graham steered the Cadillac to the front of the establishment, strolled inside, and made an announcement that must have stunned the occupants. The place was officially closed pending Bill's arrest. Bill Burke was prepared to contest the issue. After Graham made his speech, Bill sidled up to the deputy and slugged him, picked him up, and threw him out of a window. The fight was on. Bill was prepared to return to business when Graham came through the door with a 2x4 in hand. The lumber didn't have the desired calming effect on the saloon keeper and they began a fight that eventually wrecked most of the downstairs. The fight ended when Bill picked up a chair to batter the deputy and Graham finally pulled his .45, which had the effect of restoring calm to the situation.

Burke was arrested and taken to jail. The next day when he had made bail and gotten out, he encountered Graham on the street and expected the fight to continue. He was more than a little apprehensive about the meeting but Graham, patched up and limping, nodded to him and continued on to his destination, leaving the bruised barkeeper to return to his bar and decide what to do next.[26]

Just as he had done ranch work for whoever needed help when he was cowboying, now that he was carrying a badge he was quick to back up a fellow officer who needed assistance. One of the men he made friends with was a deputy in an adjoining county named Bill Fowler. Graham and Fowler formed a curious alliance. They worked together occasionally raiding bootleggers and busting stills in towns around the oil field.[27] Fowler was a quieter man than Graham, but one that still enjoyed a drink and they both shared an appreciation of firearms. Other officers were not as supportive of Graham. This reluctance on the part of others to get involved could have been based on the disturbing stories of Graham's explosive temper. Officers all over West Texas recognized his abilities and welcomed his assistance but understood that his explosive temper might create a problem for both criminals and the men he was trying to support.

There seemed to be another problem. Graham appeared to stretch the concept of lawman discretion well beyond what was usually seen in small towns. Vern Davis and Sam Haynes, who were both sheriffs during the time that Graham was working, commented that Graham had no use for officers who were on the take from the bootleggers or who assisted them. At the same time, Graham appeared to be able to switch back and forth between bootlegging and law enforcement easily. While there were a number of crooked cops and officials in oil towns, most of them were crooked all the time. Graham seemed to switch back and forth with little regard for what people thought of it.

For the people that knew him, it appeared that Graham had two very public sides to his personality. One was the hard driving lawman who put up very little nonsense from criminals, and the other was a man

who slipped easily into the world of the law breaker when he needed
the money or saw an opportunity. The two sides of Graham Barnett
became more and more apparent as he got older. He claimed to hate cops
who helped bootleggers but he allowed some bootlegging to go on. He
threatened officers who tried to bully his friends but he resorted to the
same techniques himself. Davis commented that Graham would go out
of his way to assist an officer, but many remained fearful that when the
assistance was over and the drinking began, they would have to deal with
the man who had come to their aid.[28] Some of the officers thought highly
of him, as long as he stayed sober and didn't overstay his welcome. He
seemed to make enemies and friends at the same time.

Graham developed some enemies, including both criminals and other
officers. There were ongoing stories that he was involved in selling
protection to bootleggers, and perhaps running a little booze himself. The
stories about crooked officers either actually involved with smuggling or
taking kickbacks from bootleggers were told everywhere. Graham knew
of several men who were dogged by rumors that they were involved,
or rumored to be involved, in the liquor business. Three of the men in
Reagan County whose names came up over and over would be linked to
him a number of times in the next two years.

Carroll Bates, deputy sheriff in Reagan County, along with Harry
Odneal, deputy in Fort Stockton, were both suspected of assisting with
the running of illegal liquor in their respective counties by handling
protection for the liquor coming into the oil fields.[29] Bates had been
investigated for smuggling when he was a Ranger captain on the border
in 1918.[30] He continued to be a suspect and Brian Montague stated that
Bates was not arrested during some of the raids "to the disappointment of
these officers, especially Lee Barler, Carroll Bates was not apprehended, as
he would kill him, which he could have done."[31] Nothing was proven but
both he and Odneal seemed to pop up when Brian Montague investigated
bootlegging. One man was more directly linked to the business.

Since trucks were used so much to transfer anything that came in and out of the fields, there had to be a connection with teamsters. For Brian Montague one of those connections was a truck driver named Kirtley Watson, known to just about everyone as "Noisy." Watson was a thirty-eight-year-old trucker who hauled cargo between oil towns and was in and out of the oil fields constantly. He was a well-known character on the San Angelo scene and a favorite among many people because, in addition to moving cargo, he was known to be able to find liquor at about any time. Brian Montague, who was district attorney at the time, suspected that all three were connected somehow and were involved in bootlegging in the oil fields. There were some informal connections between lawmen and outlaws and they seemed to center on one of the best known speakeasies in the area, a social club in Big Lake run by a man known as Colonel J. O. Brooks. Graham had shown up there a few times and, to make matters worse for the DA, Montague suspected that Graham was getting into the bootlegger protection business. If he was, it would be bad time for everyone. The conflict got personal when Graham and Noisy Watson got into a dispute that turned ugly in the fall of 1924. The fist fight they had was memorable enough that people recalled it for years after. When the fighting was over, Graham had come off second best. "Noisy Watson whipped him one time so they said," recalled Billy Rankin. "Graham got whipped occasionally."[32] The cause of the fight isn't known but the result of it was that Noisy Watson's name was added to the long list of people that Graham Barnett had plans to settle up with later.

Noisy was picked up for bootlegging in Best during a wide scale series of raids conducted during the spring of 1925.[33] Whether his arrest had any connection with the fight isn't known, but he did begin to comment about how he would get even with Graham, and he was known as the kind of man who carried out his threats. He wasn't the only person with a grudge against Graham. A side trip to San Angelo created five more.

Graham was in San Angelo on October 9, 1924, for a trip destined to begin as a comedy of errors and escalate into a serious problem. The Tom

Green County Fair was under way and had attracted school children, parents, and other folk looking for a good time. The attraction also drew a variety of pickpockets, hookers, scam artists, and other small time crooks as well as a number of local citizens who used the occasion to engage in some mischief. Graham was among a large group of officers who were providing security for the fair. The fair had a number of lawmen in attendance, among them Texas Ranger Bob Sumrall, assigned to Company A in Presidio.[34] Since Sumrall had spent a good bit of his enlistments in the Big Bend area, he and Graham must have had at least a nodding acquaintance.

Late in the afternoon, Sumrall observed what he considered a possible liquor sale going on and moved to intervene between a black man selling and several white men buying. Graham joined him, and in a flurry of activity, they arrested four San Angeloans: J. W. Lammey, John Williams, Albert Fairbanks, and Roy McLaughlin. Sumrall and Graham then transported the four to the city jail.[35] Roy French, who had been with the four, discovered that his friends had been arrested and taken to jail. He made one of those decisions which, considered in the light of day, probably should have gone in a different direction. He decided to go get his friends out of jail, and made the mistake of being drunk, or at least giving that impression, when he showed up at the jail. Sumrall promptly arrested him for drunkenness, loaded all five into a cell, and left them for the night.

The biggest mistake the lawmen made happened after the men were jailed. Neither Sumrall nor Graham bothered to file charges on the men or allowed them the fully expected courtesy telephone call to inform their loved ones of how the evening at the Fair had turned out. This action, more than anything else, began to irritate the partiers and that irritation festered for the rest of the evening. The next morning, Roy French, J. W. Lammey, John Williams, Albert Fairbanks, and Roy McLaughlin were filed on and released. Their attitude had progressed from irritated to furious and they wanted the world to know about how badly they had been treated.[36]

Roy French swore that the failure to charge them and release them the previous evening amounted to unlawful imprisonment and that he would sue both officers. The charges went to the grand jury, and in January the grand jury indicted both officers for false imprisonment. Graham furnished a bond in each case, as did Sumrall who by this time was back in Del Rio.[37] If either man thought that this was a serious charge, there were no indications at the time. However, the situation was far from over. Graham returned to Texon and Best and began what would develop into another feud with potentially deadly consequences.

When Graham returned to the oil field he encountered an old friend with a resume as long as his. J. J. "Jack" Allen was a veteran of two wars, had been sheriff of Terrell County, deputy sheriff in Brewster County, as well as city marshal and postmaster in Alpine. At a couple of odd times in his career he had been a schoolteacher. He was as successful at that as he had been in his other ventures. At one point when some of the older students threatened to whip him, he dismissed the class except for the older students, blocked the doors and said, "Well, boys, I'm ready."[38] That matter was settled quickly and the semester continued without problems. When the oil business hit, he had been asked to take over management of the local Alpine Lumber Yard located in Best. The job might have sounded tame based on his previous experiences, but running a business in the oil field called for a man with a particular edge and Jack Allen had that. He also had an encounter with Graham, which Allen related to Brian Montague.[39]

Graham had known Allen from their days on the border and it can be assumed, based on what happened between the two men, that there was a level of respect between them. He and Graham had followed a trail of stolen horses into Mexico years before, and had brought the horses back in a long running gunfight with the temporary owners.[40] Jack Allen was known as an outstanding shot with rifle or pistol and was utterly fearless as evidenced by his career in law enforcement. Allen lived in a small Quonset hut outside of town and had recently rented part of it to Johnny Malone who had a reputation for fighting with his fists equal to Allen's reputation as a gunfighter. In addition to those qualities both men enjoyed taking a drink from time to time and that brought them into contact with Graham Barnett.

He was aware that the pair likely had liquor in their small house and he and a deputy approached them one evening near midnight. It is questionable how well advised a midnight raid was on two men such as Allen and Malone. The officers identified themselves and were met with a startling response. Malone picked up a shotgun and Allen grabbed his Winchester and replied to the request to open the door with, "Come in you sonsuvbitches, you're as welcome as a corpse."[41] The raid was promptly called off. The following day, Graham drove to Stiles, the county seat, and filed a complaint on both men.

Sheriff Rankin called Jack Allen, and told him that he had some paper on him. Jack drove over, made bond, and prepared to leave. In his memoir, Montague described what Jack Allen told him about the next few minutes. Jack told Montague that he and the sheriff were close friends and that Sheriff Rankin was concerned over the possibility of a confrontation between Allen and Graham. Allen and the sheriff sat down and discussed the incident and Sheriff Rankin began to talk about his gun collection. In fact, he opened a trunk and showed the collection to Allen. He then announced that he had to deliver some messages out to a ranch and would be gone for thirty minutes or more and left Allen with the collection. "I took one of the pistols and some shells out of the collection because I knew that was precisely what Mr. Rankin wanted me to do when he left," Allen explained to Brian Montague.[42] If it were true that Sheriff Rankin armed Jack Allen on purpose, he made a strong statement about how he felt about his friend, and how he felt about his deputy.

This may have been the point when Graham's stock began a downturn with the sheriff's department. His behavior showed he had little respect for the use of search warrants, and he continued to attempt to intimidate people with cursing and threats. People who might have supported him at the beginning of his tour began to question if he might not be contributing to problems rather than solving them. The situation with Jack Allen brought all of this to the attention of the sheriff in a manner that he couldn't ignore. If Rankin had to choose between an old friend and a new deputy, there really wasn't any choice.

On the afternoon of the day that Jack Allen picked up a pistol from Sheriff Rankin, Graham showed up at the lumberyard to take up business where he had left it off the night before. Jack and C. E. McCool, the general manager for Alpine Lumber, were out in the yard at work. No one who recorded anything about the meeting stated whether Jack had the pistol with him but a man doesn't survive two wars and a number of informal skirmishes by not being prepared. Graham started the conversation and it quickly turned ugly. Graham began to call out Jack about the previous night. Jack Allen was not a man to back up. He cussed Graham and when he did, Graham began to reach for his pistol. McCool, who witnessed it all, said he was scared to death that there was going to be a shooting and he was going to be in the middle of it. Graham hesitated and Jack told him, "Pull it you son of a bitch and I'll make you swallow it without water."[43]

Something happened: Montague didn't describe it, McCool didn't comment on it, and Jack Allen never mentioned it, but for some reason, Graham's bluff had been called and he didn't respond. The key may have been that he knew Jack Allen. He understood in the clarity of a moment that Jack Allen would not back down, and at that moment, Jack Allen might have been a little tougher than he was. They had worked together, and Allen was the kind of man that other men looked up to. If Jack faced him down, Graham may have experienced that moment of doubt about what he was doing. For someone who is about to pull a gun against another man with a big reputation, it was a sobering moment. For whatever reason, Graham chose that moment to ease off on his rough handed law enforcement ways, and it was probably a good thing that he did. Even Graham Barnett got beaten some of the time.

The tension of the moment was broken and everyone backed up. McCool reported to Montague that he thought the feud was over, that there would be no more problems between the two and as near as can be determined, there never was. If the two had other encounters, no one knew about it. There is nothing in the records to indicate if Jack Allen was ever arrested for illegal booze, but it is clear that Graham saw fit to let that offence go. The friction between the two was typical of Graham's continued inability to understand that his policing had to be done differently with different people.[44]

The year 1925 was momentous for a number of people in the area around Texon and Best. Carroll Bates and Harry Odneal both got into new jobs. Carroll Bates had a somewhat checkered career in law enforcement. Early in his career he had been a policeman in San Angelo, later a Ranger captain and then game warden. When he moved back to San Angelo where he worked in a variety of jobs ranging from being a salesman ended up as police chief by 1926. That job would later bring him back into conflict with Graham in a very forceful way.

Harry Odneal floated around the oil field as special investigator for a number of different offices. In 1925 he was enlisted in the Rangers and served as a private for nearly two years, being discharged in 1927. Neither man could entirely separate themselves from allegations concerning their interaction with bootleggers. The sheriff's office in Reagan County changed hands as well. J. D. Christy was elected sheriff in Reagan County in November and took over January 1. Graham remained with Big Lake Oil but it was only a matter of time before their patience and his job ran out. While his days were numbered, he continued with some slick detective work after the New Year.

Employees of the Kaw Boiler Works were paid on Saturday, January 10, 1925, and what money they had left on Sunday went toward a little gambling action in the warmth and security of one of the Big Lake Oil

Company dormitories. A little after nine in the evening the doors swung open and instead of two new players, two robbers walked in. They stood the oil field gamblers up against the wall and relieved them of nearly $200.00 before locking the men inside the dormitory and heading for the transitory pleasures of the bordellos and beer joints of Best. Before they got there, mindful of how quickly money gets spent when having a good time, they stopped on the road and buried fifty-two dollars on the prairie, including in that cache a ten peso Mexican bill.

The workers back at the dorm handled the locked door issue fairly quickly and contacted the police. Graham and C. F. Sheppard showed up to work the case. The two undoubtedly put the clues together. Pay day weekend, Sunday night, partying not completed but money tapped out, the officers headed for Best, which was the closest local site for sin and vice. By about three in the morning, they had made the arrest of Red Shanahan and C. T. Pritchard. Shanahan confessed to the crime and led the officers out into the brush where the fifty-two dollars was recovered. The two were arraigned in front of Justice of the Peace Arnett and were tucked away in the local jail. The boys from the Kaw Boiler Works, however, decided that they needed to deal more directly with the thieves, and the next day Shanahan and Pritchard were hauled off to a more secure setting where they awaited their trial. Big Lake Oil spokesmen noted that this was the first case of "hi-jacking in the Reagan County oilfield" and hoped that it would be the last.[45] The newspaper was full of more praise for the officers. "Reagan County officers cooperated in every way with the private police, Graham Barnett and C. F. Sheppard, who made the arrests and appreciation of the quick work done marked by unity of action between the various officers, was expressed by officials of the Big Lake Oil Company and other operators."[46] Graham could do good work when he was focused. The problems seem to come when he had less to do.

In the latter part of January 1925, Graham was involved in a stunt that brought an end to his employment in the oil field security business. Had it not been so serious, it could have served as the comedy relief for a western movie. Fueled by some of the bootlegged liquor that he either had confiscated or imported, he pulled up in a wagon in downtown Best. He initiated a memorable party in the downtown area that was capped when he began to shoot whiskey bottles out of other drinkers' hands and generally conduct an activity that had been known in frontier times as "treeing" the town. Treeing a town occurred when an individual or a group decided to take over part of a town by fear or intimidation. It lasts until the drunks quiet down or the citizens take their town back. Graham had to be subdued by the townspeople, his guns collected and then he was tucked away in a room above the Post Office. The night was not over and much of the rest of the evening was spent with Graham yelling from the temporary jail, commenting on the character of his fellow citizens, discussing what he would do to those people who broke up the party, and being a general nuisance.

The next day he returned with two Texas Rangers and the night watchman, a man known as George "Two Gun" Baker. The four patrolled the town and promised all kinds of retaliation to the spoilsports from the evening before. J. T. Mace, an employee of Big Lake Oil, wrote a two-page letter to the adjutant general requesting aid in calming the local law enforcement officials down and describing conditions in a less than humorous light. The nature of the letter was that Graham and his deputy, George Baker, had "held up many citizens on the streets and around the town, have searched them and in most every instance [the citizens] have had to take their abusive language and their threats to kill, the officers in most instance have NOT been armed with search warrants, many houses have been searched under the same conditions."[47] While no formal record has emerged, it is probable that this incident was the final straw for Graham in the law enforcement business. It seems likely that Big Lake Oil decided that they could no longer ignore the complaints from the people in both Best and Texon. Charles N. Hickcox stated later, "Levi Smith fired Graham for making unauthorized arrests and pistol whipping workers in San Angelo."[48] By the end of February, Graham was unemployed again.

There is no record of what the reaction was from his family with regard to leaving Texon. It was a serious blow to them and his career. The place in the community was gone, along with the prestige of having a job with a company who took care of its people. So, as he had done before, he turned to Joe Graham for help.

On February 25, 1925, Graham and Annie moved back to Sterling City.[49] When he left Texon, he had in mind to go back into the sheep business and did, in fact, partner with members of his extended family in Sterling County, but he grew restless in Sterling City. It was hard to adjust to the quiet life of a small town after the excitement of the oil field. He played cards and drank and got into trouble with Vern Davis who sent him home when he could and arrested him when he had to. Davis had known him for years and both liked and respected him but as sheriff he had a responsibility to the rest of the community to help Graham adjust to the slower life he was now a part of.

Needing something more to do, he returned to bootlegging and that eventually brought him back into contact with Carroll Bates. Sterling City was forty miles from San Angelo and with both men smuggling in the same area, some conflict was going to occur. As a result, what Brian Montague called a "bitter enmity" grew up between the two men.[50] Despite the boot legging, Graham remained close to a number of his friends in law enforcement, particularly the attorneys Brian and Joe Montague.

At Brian's urging, Joe Montague had moved to Fort Stockton in 1923 and established his law practice.[51] Graham met Joe and the two became friends. While both attorneys were busy prosecuting cases against bootleggers, at least part of the time, Graham and the brothers kept up their relationship, which proved to be beneficial to all. Despite the three men being friends, they did not always have all the details concerning what each man was doing.

When Brian Montague was district attorney, several people from Big Lake and the surrounding area had come to him to discuss the possibility of bringing outside investigators into the area. The idea was to gather information to determine the extent of crime in the Big Lake area. Montague thought it was a good idea and supported it, but almost immediately after that, in the summer of 1925, he resigned as DA and moved to Del Rio to enter private practice. The plan was not forgotten and subsequently it was acted on. The decision was made to being in someone who had contacts in the area and information gathered later indicates that Graham was brought in Big Lake as the undercover operative.[52]

With a reputation as big as Graham's the question of how "undercover" he could have been remains unclear. It appears that Graham continued with his usual bootlegging and minor extortion activities and didn't disclose to anyone that he was gathering information for the sheriff's office at the same time. This scheme was typical of situations in which Graham worked with local law enforcement and at the same time shut down criminals who might be competing with him for a share of the market.

When Brian resigned to go to Del Rio, his brother Joe was appointed in his place as DA, and it fell to Joe to carry out the plan to disrupt criminal activity in the area. Joe not only went along with the plan but actually went on some of the raids that occurred in Best, Big Lake, and other parts of Reagan County. When he did, he began to see the extent of the activity and how much of it was ignored by several of the law officers in the area. While none of the officers were indicted, a number of other people, including Kirtley "Noisy" Watson, were arrested along with one of the key figures of the bootlegging business, Colonel J. O. Brooks of Big Lake. It isn't known what connection Graham had to these raids, although there are persistent stories that in his role as an undercover operator, he supplied needed information to the DA.

Because of the size of the raids and the number of people arrested, it became apparent that business of crime in the area was going to be disturbed for quite a while. Many of the small criminal networks reacted strongly to the raids, and the word was out that they were going to seek revenge. Judge Claude Sutton took Brian aside and told him that he thought Joe's life might be in danger because of the size and nature of the raids. He revealed that after a trial one afternoon he and Joe were standing outside the courthouse in Big Lake and were approached by Judge W. A. Wright of San Angelo, who was representing several of the bootleggers, and Harry Odneal. Odneal, who was a Ranger with Company A at the time; he later became a special officer in McCamey in 1927.[53]

Wright took this opportunity to attempt to get some of the indictments thrown out by producing an affidavit that alleged the new DA had engaged in some official misconduct during the raid based on statements from Ranger Odneal. Sutton handed it to Joe who read it and said, "Judge Wright, this affidavit is a damn lie and Harry you're a damn liar."[54] Joe's response to the affidavit stunned Wright and Odneal. The awkward attempt to get some indictments thrown out hadn't worked, and Wright and Odneal had made a couple of enemies who would not forget the attempted blackmail. Wright and Odneal turned and left but Sutton was convinced that something was going to happen. That "something" turned out to be a vendetta against Joe Montague. Several months later the two brothers talked and Joe told his brother that the word was out the Harry Odneal was going to kill him. A death threat was not something to be ignored, but Joe Montague was a man who possessed a love for both the law and the .45 automatic. He kept the .45 within arm's reach and also tossed his .30-30 Winchester into the back seat of his car. He was prepared to continue with his prosecution of every bootlegger he could find.[55]

After trying a case in Carlsbad, New Mexico, Joe returned to Fort Stockton to spend the night. Three people that he knew came to him and told him that Harry Odneal was in town and had been telling people that he was going to kill Joe. The next morning, after putting on his .45, Joe drove downtown to get breakfast. He noticed Odneal standing across the street watching the DA as he got out of his car. Joe slowly walked to the Marmon Hotel where he intended to eat breakfast. In the best traditions of the street scenes of later Western movies, he watched Odneal watching him. Joe later described to Brian what had happened. Joe knew that Odneal was left handed and told Brian that if Odneal moved that hand Joe was going to settle the matter before breakfast.[56] It didn't come to that. Odneal continued to watch while Joe entered the hotel for his breakfast and any fireworks were cancelled, for that day at least. Shortly afterwards, Joe visited with Judge James Cornell about the situation. Cornell, who had killed a man in Del Rio a few years before, was aware of the impact of that action on the survivor. The judge urged Joe to resign and move away from the oil fields but the attorney would not budge. He was there, he had a job, and he was not going to be run out of the country by a bunch of bootleggers and their enforcers. The word was out, and there was little doubt that Joe Montague was going to have to face some ugly choices in the future.

That is where the situation was until Graham Barnett showed up in town and listened to the gossip about the lawyer's future. Graham had a deep regard for the brothers, and even though Brian regretted recommending him for the Texon job, the Montagues and Barnett remained friends. When Graham heard of the death threats, he dealt with the matter in a very straight forward manner. He drove to Fort Stockton and confronted Harry Odneal. In one of his now familiar good-bad man roles, he decided to end the problem of the threats against his friend.

There are at least two stories concerning what happened next. Odneal was no fan of Graham and shouldn't have expected a cordial visit, but was probably surprised by the abrupt nature of their conversation. According to Brian Montague, Graham said he would kill the lawman if Harry harmed either Brian or Joe Montague. There was very little discussion of the matter, no arguments, no hollow threats, simply a statement of fact.[57]

The other version involves Graham approaching Odneal and telling him to leave the brothers alone. Then he placed two .45s on the table and told Odneal to pick either one, they were both loaded, and they would settle the matter immediately. Odneal stared at the pistols, considered the offer, and shook his head. At that point, Graham administered his customary cursing, picked both guns up, and left.[58]

Brian was unsure if it was the death threat or if Judge Cornell, or another one of the visiting judges, had cooled the situation with Odneal, but there were no more threats toward the brothers. Brian saw Odneal one more time in Fort Stockton at the beginning of a trial. Odneal approached the lawyer, shook his hand, and inquired about how he was enjoying life in Del Rio.

Odneal remained in law enforcement for the next nine years. He was an ardent supporter of the Democratic Party in Texas and especially of Jim Ferguson and his wife Miriam, both of whom served as governor of the state. When Miriam returned to office in January of 1931, she forced the resignations of most of the Ranger force and replaced them with her own choice of people. Harry Odneal was one of the people rewarded for his support, and he became a Ranger captain in Fort Worth in 1933.[59] That situation did not last long. In 1934, suffering terribly from injuries he sustained in a car wreck, he committed suicide at his home. [60]

Graham chased sheep, drank, and played cards in Sterling County and fretted about a number of things. One was the trial pending in San Angelo for false imprisonment resulting from the arrests at the San Angelo Fair in October. The indictment had been split and he and Bob Sumrall would be tried separately. Graham was a Reagan County officer at the time of the arrest. While he could assist Sumrall, whether he had authority to arrest in Tom Green County would be a factor. The odds on bets were that Sumrall, as a Ranger, would be found not guilty, and Graham would lose the case and perhaps win on appeal. He had told his defense lawyers that there were at least two bootleggers who would be able to explain what had happened when he and Bob Sumrall had arrested the five men. They all agreed that the situation was serious, but probably not devastatingly so. Attitudes toward both bootleggers and law enforcement were changing, but it was impossible to predict what a jury would do. The decision that the jury would make set events into motion that would change Graham's life for the next two years.

Chapter 9

"No, he isn't going to kill me. He hasn't nerve enough"

1925-1928[1]

Part of the spring of 1925 was spent preparing for the false imprisonment trial of Graham and Bob Sumrall. What might have been thought of as a misstep by the officers promised a six month stay in jail if they were found guilty and Graham had made up his mind he would not go to jail. He had hired E. F. Vanderbilt of Big Lake and R. T. Neill to fight the indictment.[2] For a man who had dealt with a number of serious encounters with the law, Graham did not want to take a chance on being found guilty in what was more a case of bad judgment on the part of the officers than any real misconduct.

While he waited for the trial, Graham probably kept up with the ongoing war on liquor that was being waged all around him. Attitudes seemed to be changing towards bootleggers and those people who supported them. Law enforcement was taking a more active role against the bootleggers and raids were going on throughout the area. Hardly a day went by when local newspapers did not have at least one front-page story detailing another arrest for local people for either possession of liquor or distribution. In Best, a massive series of raids had been conducted at the request of those citizens who were offended by the general lack of order and disgusted by the town's reputation. Rangers, accompanied by some of the local law enforcement and Joe Montague, the new district attorney, shut down a number of the gambling parlors and whorehouses. Noisy Watson, the trucker who had fought with Graham a few months before, was arrested and released on bond. A number of other bootleggers had been indicted or run out of the county. If Carroll Bates had been involved, he had covered his trail well because he was not indicted. However, there began to emerge the story of an informal group of smugglers referred to as "the Line" who moved liquor and managed vice in many of the towns from Eastland to Texon. The reports tended to be incomplete but hinted at an organization based in San Angelo that seemed to be managing liquor movement and distribution. As usual, the gossip hinted at "important people" being involved but details were lacking.

There appeared to be more than enough details in the latest Graham Barnett case. On July 24, 1925, the trial for Bob Sumrall on the false imprisonment charge was heard. The jury of six listened to the testimony from Roy French, a butcher, and his fellow fair goers, J. W. Lammey, John Williams, Albert Fairbanks, and Roy McLaughlin. French's statements were terse. No, they had not done anything wrong. They had seen the officers harassing a black man whom the officers had suspected of possessing liquor. Williams, Fairbanks, Lammey, and McLauglin had intervened to support the black man. French was separated from the original group. When his friends were arrested, he decided to go to town and bail them out. When French arrived downtown, he pulled up in front of the Tom Green County Jail and was arrested for being drunk and disorderly. All five men were tucked away in the jail and released the next morning. None of them had been formally charged, nor given the expected single telephone call. The next morning, when they were filed on, they decided that the failure to file on the evening before amounted to false imprisonment and that the officers had exceeded their authority.

The six jurors who heard the case deliberated for five and a half hours and found Sumrall guilty of false imprisonment. The verdict called for imprisonment of five days in the same Tom Green County jail where French and his partners had spent the night. The defense immediately filed an appeal, and Sumrall was released on a $200 bond.[3]

While the appeal was going to go forward for Sumrall, a separate trial for Graham was called for nine o'clock Friday morning. Graham's lawyers asked for a continuance. Graham believed that at last three men had observed what had happened and could be brought in as witnesses on his behalf.[4] Why the witnesses were not made available to Sumrall is unclear, and what exactly they would be able to testify to remains something lost between that Thursday afternoon and the rest of time. The witnesses were not named in the newspaper, but Graham had an idea who they were and where to find them.

Seventy miles west of San Angelo, Big Lake, Texas, was having a rodeo and roping the fourth weekend in July. The town would be full of rodeo fans, cowboys, and bootleggers. For Graham, it would be a chance to find the men who could make a difference in whether he spent some time in jail or went back to chase sheep in Sterling City. Graham told his lawyers that he thought witnesses who could support the contention that the men arrested had been buying liquor would be in Big Lake, and he knew where to start looking: Colonel J. O. Brook's Recreation Hall. The Hall was a gathering place for sporting men of all sorts and on any weekend night the domino parlor and gambling house would be full of people seeking a little entertainment and a drink or two. Graham decided to drive over in the percolating heat of the late afternoon of July 25 to check out the condition of the bootlegging trade in the small town.

Graham was working with the sheriff's department doing investigations of bootlegging in the area and that role had brought him to the rec hall on a couple of occasions and he was well-known there.[5] The possibility to find a witness in his own case and to gather more evidence about bootlegging in Big Lake was too good a deal to pass up, especially on a rodeo weekend.

The rodeo had started on Thursday afternoon, and the tiny town was filled with the smell of barbecue and humming with the excitement of bronc riding and steer roping. It seemed as though the town's population had tripled overnight, and the streets were crowded with cowboys, oil field workers, and people from surrounding towns looking for some entertainment. With all the excitement, the city fathers had thought the out-of-towners might need a little structure and discipline in case they developed too much enthusiasm fueled by illegal hooch. They had hired additional lawmen to control the crowd and to pick up the pieces in case people got out of line.

One of the special deputies hired was Ellison Carroll.[6] It was his first time as deputy, but it wasn't his first rodeo. The sixty-three-year-old Carroll had been considered the best steer roper in the history of the sport. Before he retired to ranch at Big Lake, he would rope anywhere, anytime, against any opponent, and had retired as World's Champion in 1913. He was not the kind of man who would back up from a challenge, and since he knew many of the rodeo cowboys, he was a natural as a temporary lawman. With the end of the day's roping competition, Carroll ambled around the town and watched as the crowds began to break up, and people began to decide what to do in the evening.

As the rodeo wound down, men slipped into Colonel J. O. Brooks' Recreation Hall. J. O. Brooks was a man who was typical of many who followed the oil booms, but he hadn't come to Big Lake, Texas, to be a roughneck. Brooks made serious money providing entertainment and amusements for the men who did the hard work. He was a handsome man in his mid-forties who wore $200 suits from Dallas, San Antonio, or Houston, and usually topped off the suit with a bowtie. He looked like "a Philadelphia lawyer."[7] When he was working, he draped his expensive shirt and pants with an apron that kept both of them clean and identified him as the man in charge. He gave his occupation as "druggist" both when asked and when he was indicted. The reality was that he had contacts all over the oil patch country and was thought to play a major role in bootlegging.[8]

Brooks got along well with his clientele but didn't make a great effort to get along with people who didn't show up at the club. He knew he wasn't going to retire in Big Lake, Texas. He would be there until the oil boom slowed and then he would be off to the next opportunity. He ran a well-disciplined saloon and was big enough and tough enough to settle a dispute that might spring up over a dropped domino or an insult that might slip after a drink or two. Brooks wasn't too fond of lawmen, and he especially did not like Graham Barnett since the two had met professionally during the spring and summer.

There had been trouble at the recreation hall at least twice. In the vernacular of the times, Graham had tried to "take over the place." Apparently both times he had been drinking and had pulled his pistol and lined everyone up against the wall. What exactly he had planned isn't clear; it was another one of the Graham Barnett performances. Both times problems were averted when several of his friends calmed him down and ushered him off the premises and away from Brooks and his customers.[9] It was an incident fresh in the minds of a number of people who had been there when Graham walked into the hall on that hot July afternoon.

The place he walked into was a narrow room with a long bar down the side and tables scattered from the front door to the rear. A series of coolers were jammed in the rear of the hall near the back door that opened into an alley wide enough for people to park their trucks. The alley also served as an informal meeting area, and a place where some gamblers shot craps against the wall of the building. In the evenings, some of the patrons wandered past the coolers in the back, out the door, and sat on the running boards of cars to smoke, drink, and generally carry on the business of the day. There was an outhouse about forty yards to the left across the alley. To the right, the alley led to the back door of a café where a man could get a meal for thirty-five cents. Jim

Brown, the colonel's black porter, kept the interior swept up, the tables bussed, and paid close attention to whatever mischief the customers were getting themselves into. He kept the colonel informed about what was going on in the bar and outside in the alley. Between the two of them, they had a fairly simple system in place to deal with problems: when Jim saw the problem, he called the boss.

It was late in the afternoon when Graham arrived in Big Lake and drove up to the hall. As usual, he had at least two pistols with him, a .45 and probably a .38 as a backup. Vern Davis commented that he had taken a cut down .38 off of Graham on at least one occasion and that one, or one like it, was what Graham had with him in Big Lake.[10] In an unusual turn of events, Graham removed his pistols and left them in the bar. Frequently guns were tucked under the bar or hung behind it while men gambled and drank. While it was a fairly common rule for men to leave the guns with the bartender, it was very unusual for Graham to do something like that. It may have been a rule enforced by Brooks in response to his previous escapades but he did not have the guns on him for the brief period of time immediately after he entered the recreation hall.

He had a couple of drinks, visited with some of the people he knew, and began to look for his witnesses. He walked through the back door and out into the open alley behind the Hall and spotted Noisy Watson and a couple of others sitting on a truck.[11] W. R. McCravey was among the men who were talking to Graham. Apparently remembering that Watson was on the never-ending list of people who had created a problem for him, Graham began to mumble about the bootlegger. McCravey was standing close enough to Graham to hear him say that Watson "... had it in for him and that he [Barnett] was going to 'jump him up about it.'"[12] McCravey, who saw most of the action that night, drifted to the back door after Graham wandered outside. Graham walked up to the truck the men were gathered around and began to talk to "Noisy." The porter, Jim Brown, moved toward the rear of the hall and saw Barnett and Watson talking but recalled later they were "not doing anything" and looked away for a moment.[13] He was too far away to hear what was said.

Since the conversation sounded like it was going to get personal, the men who were with Watson moved away from the pair. Whatever Watson said was lost in the low rumble of noise in the hall. McCravey was close enough that he heard Graham ask Watson if he had said certain things about him (Graham). "Whoever said that is a son of a bitch," Watson responded.[14] Roger Blain, a rancher from Crockett County who knew Graham slightly, looked up and heard Watson say, "You're just full of whiskey and trying to raise hell."[15] Whatever happened next in the sequence remains confusing. Jim Brown swore that Watson then swung and hit Graham.[16] When McCravey looked again, he saw Graham knock Watson back against the wall.[17] As quickly as it started, Colonel Brooks and another man, C. C. Woodward, rushed over to separate the two men, but before they could reach them, Watson bounced off the wall and crouched down and picked up a brick to smash Graham's head with.[18] When he did that, he effectively armed himself against an unarmed man. Brooks told him to throw the brick down, and Watson, after a moment, complied with the request. Graham stepped away from the fight and headed back into the bar. Brooks and Woodward took a few steps away from the site of the fight. Woodward sat down on the truck, Brooks stood and the two talked until they noticed Graham coming back out of the bar.[19]

When Graham started back into the beer joint, several men thought he was in one of the furious moods that he was known for. Among the men was Roger Blain who had known Graham previously. Several of the men joined him and began to warn Watson about the potential problem he was about to have. Blain and several others told Watson it was time for him to leave.[20] Graham was going for his guns and he would kill him if he found the bootlegger in the alley when he returned. In a misjudgment of immense proportions, Watson looked at the group surrounding him and replied, "No, he isn't going to kill me. He hasn't nerve enough."[21]

When Graham rushed off, T. C. Rutledge walked out of the bar looking for a friend named Ross Woods, unaware that Woods was spending time in the outhouse about forty paces away. Rutledge, not knowing he was about to become a witness in a fatal shooting, began to talk with several of the men in the group standing in the alley. Blain, apparently satisfied that he had done all he could, turned his back and walked down the alley and headed for the street.

Graham had rushed back into the hall, past C. B. Karnes who worked for Big Lake Oil and who knew him from the oil fields, past the card players and beer drinkers, and headed for the bar. Technically the fight was over, Graham was out of danger, but he had been threatened again by Watson. The bootlegger had tried to hit him with a brick when Graham had nothing in his hands, insults had been exchanged, and there was the matter of being called a son of a bitch in public. This was not something he could walk away from. He was mumbling to himself, and while none of the witnesses heard his words clearly, it was plain that he was going to settle the matter. Karnes stayed by the back door with some idea that he might be able to stop Graham from going back outside.[22] Graham rushed to the counter and picked up both of his pistols and headed for the back door. Karnes was probably only slightly aware of what had happened in the alley, but he did recognize how angry Graham was.[23] Graham was excited and agitated. As he walked across the floor, an oil field worker named Cliff Denson was standing close enough to hear him say that Noisy Watson had tried to kill him with a brick.

McCravey decided that he might be able to stop Graham when he came back outside. He walked back into the hall. As he got to the door, Graham brushed past him with a pistol in each hand. McCravey must have realized that the fight had just moved to a different level. He stood inside the door and watched as Graham went across the alley toward the group of men who stood around Watson.[24]

As the gunman walked by, Karnes stepped in front of him and grasped at him to prevent him from going back into the alley, but Graham shook him off and kept walking. Outside the crowd was breaking up. It was close to seven in the evening and shadows were lengthening. But in the open alley there was still plenty of light. Sunset would not come for another fifty minutes. Across the open space, R. B. Walton, a cook, had come out of the café to pick chickens for the anticipated supper rush. He settled on a box and glanced up a couple of times at the men in the rear of the rec hall. Watson was still close to the wall where the fight had taken place and looked up to see Graham coming out of the back door with a revolver in each hand. Noisy Watson now had only a matter of seconds to reconsider the thought about Graham having a lack of nerve. According to some of the men, he threw both hands up and yelled for help. Rutledge, still trying to find Ross Woods, had walked up to Watson to question him about his friend. When he did that, he walked into a shooting.

"For God's sake, save my life," Watson pleaded and he tried to get the startled Rutledge between Graham and himself.[25] In a show of either extreme bravery or a complete misunderstanding of Graham's furious nature, Rutledge stayed between the two men. In his panic, Watson grabbed at Rutledge's shirt and tore two buttons off as he wrestled with his human shield.[26] At the corner of the building, Roger Blain turned for a moment and saw the confrontation. Either thinking that Rutledge would be successful, or deciding he didn't want to be involved anymore, he continued around the corner.

Back in the alley the struggle continued for a few desperate seconds. Watson panicked and grasped at Rutledge. "Don't let him kill me," the bootlegger pleaded.[27] Forty yards away, R. B. Walton looked up from his chicken picking but later said he didn't notice that Watson had his hands in the air, and he heard no yelling for help. Ross Wood finally finished his business in the outhouse and stepped out into what in a few microseconds was going to become a crime scene.

Graham stepped forward and fired one shot from the .45. The bullet struck Noisy Watson in the chest, and he staggered a few steps and fell. For a few seconds, there was no sound except that of Graham mumbling through a long monologue of cursing.[28] Rutledge spun and grabbed Graham around the waist, pinning his arms against his sides and keeping him from lifting his gun again. Ellison Carroll, the special deputy, was in the street, and the sound of the shot brought him down the alley and onto the scene. Jim Brown, the porter, and Allen Holder, another bystander, began to struggle to get the guns away from Graham. Rutledge continued to hold him, and finally, the three along with Ellison Carroll were successful in disarming Graham.[29] Ellison had known Graham for years and knew that he was dealing with a dangerous man when he was in one of his killing moods. Carroll backed Graham away from the shooting scene and desperately tried to decide what to do.

Nothing empties a beer joint like a gunshot. Many of those inside wanted to see what happened in the alley, others wanted to be gone, and took the opportunity to leave by the closest exit. The crowd began to swirl around the scene, and the retelling of the shooting began immediately. Graham continued to talk in a loud voice about the late Mr. Watson, and people who knew both of them began the inevitable picking and choosing of sides. Ellison Carroll had a problem. He had a murder, a semi-drunk crowd on his hands, and a belligerent shooter who did not use a lot of discretion in how he was talking about the recently deceased. Graham's actions after the shooting didn't help his case. He was "muttering, cursing, and acting like a wild man," onlookers said.[30] It was a blueprint for a lynching. Ellison grasped Graham and hustled him down the alley and headed for the office of the justice of the peace.

As popular as Graham was with a certain group of people, the bootlegger lying in the alley was equally popular with the folks he had been delivering liquor to, and his partner Colonel Brooks was not entirely pleased about the shooting of one of his transporters. To complicate matters further, there was no jail in Big Lake. The original county seat was in Stiles, but since Stiles had become a ghost town since the discovery of oil in the Big Lake fields, the county seat was in the process of being moved to Big Lake. The jail wasn't finished, and there was no place to put a prisoner. W. D. Risner, the justice of the peace, decided to conduct a quick inquest and designated the lobby of the Cottage Hotel as the best place for the activity. Everyone who had any interest in the shooting and all the witnesses that could be located crowded into the lobby and gave a hurried description of what had happened. Showing the best judgment he had shown since leaving San Angelo, Graham apparently had nothing to say. It is possible that someone had gone to get his lawyer, E. F. Vanderbilt, who lived in Big Lake, who advised him to calm down and be quiet. Feelings were running a little high about the shooting, and the Reagan County sheriff J. D. Christie loaded Graham into his car and drove the seventy miles to San Angelo where he was booked into the Tom Green County jail and tucked in for the night. As it developed, it wasn't just for one night.

The next morning, following the standard practice of the time, the press was allowed to interview Graham. They found him up in the second floor "runaround," a large freestanding cell in the center of the floor of the east wing of the Tom Green County jail.[31] Generally the runaround held four or more prisoners, and this morning it was full. When the reporter from the San Angelo Standard found Graham, he was talking with several people he knew who happened to be spending time in the jail. Among them was Gratton Davenport who had worked on a ranch near Mertzon. Grat had shot and killed a ranch foreman named Sam Rogers who, like Noisy Watson, was also unarmed at the time of his demise. When asked if he would like to make a statement for publication, Graham told the reporter he would have something to say later, but implied that he would plead self-defense.[32] That story was already out on the street.

The next morning, an examining trial and bond hearing was held. Judge W. W. Pittman denied bond, and Graham was taken back to jail while his lawyers began the process of getting him out. His attorneys filed a writ of habeas corpus, and a hearing was held on August 9 in Marfa. His friend, Brian Montague, was one of the district attorneys, and was asked to represent the state. Montague thought he had as open and closed a case as he had ever seen. "I felt that the witnesses we presented made a perfect case of murder with malice aforethought ... for that evidence established that when he was shot and killed, 'Noisy' was facing Graham with both arms extended upright."[33] He couldn't have been more wrong. At the bail hearing, Graham pleaded self-defense, and no one really seemed surprised. Judge Claude Sutton, who probably knew about Noisy's reputation as a tough bootlegger, granted bail, and Graham was loose again.

In an odd turn of events, after the bail hearing, Brian resigned as district attorney to go into private practice in Del Rio, and his brother Joe was appointed in his place. Even though Graham had defended Joe against Harry Odneal earlier, and he and the brothers had been friends for years, no one doubted that when they all walked into the courtroom, friendships would be left at the door. Joe Montague believed the case was a sure thing. Brian Montague recalled, "Joe felt, as I did, that notwithstanding the fact that Graham during the preceding three years had developed a very friendly feeling for him, he would not have a great deal of trouble obtaining a conviction."[34] Joe Montague began to plan a case that could result in the death penalty or a lengthy prison stay, and Graham began to look for a way to avoid both of those possibilities.[35]

CHAPTER 10

"I WANT YOU TO SEND HIM A TELEGRAM AND TELL HIM THAT I AM THE BIGGEST DAMN LIAR...IN THE STATE OF TEXAS"

1925-1928[1]

Things were desperate for the Barnett family. Lawyers, especially good ones, were expensive and the men Graham had retained were first class, but the family had limited resources. The business of day-to-day expenses for the growing family weighed heavily on Graham and Annie. The wool business was still good in 1925, but a rancher couldn't shear and sell anytime he wanted to. Weather and the market still played a huge part in the business, and Graham would have had to sell a lot of wool to fund the two or three lawyers it would take to keep him out of Huntsville. The family was in a bad situation, and the evidence of this can be found in a letter written in August by Annie to Levi Smith. As the head of Big Lake Oil, Smith was probably the most important man that they knew, as well as being the most financially secure.

"Mr. Smith, could you let me have fifty dollars as a loan but under the circumstances couldn't pay it back for some time. You know all this trouble has made it awfully hard on me financially."[2] It is significant that she doesn't mention Graham. Smith had been in San Angelo on the weekend of the shooting and undoubtedly knew about the situation Graham had put himself in. Levi Smith responded with a letter and a check in September when he returned from a business trip. "I most sincerely sympathize with you in your troubles, and will be glad to be of service anytime I can."[3] Adjusted for inflation, the fifty dollars would be equivalent to about six hundred eighty dollars in 2014 dollars. If he was contacted again, there is no record of it.

Graham had conferred with lawyers and together they must have decided to get him out of the public eye for a while. An old friend of Graham's, Sim Weatherby, told his son James that he took Graham down to his ranch at Juno, a tiny ranching community nearly 160 miles south of Sterling City.[4] Boog joined them there for a short time.

Sim Weatherby was no stranger to life in West Texas. His family had ranched in a number of sites and he and Graham had been friends for years. Both men had a high level of respect for each other. San Angelo police chief Sam Haynes had called Sim on one occasion to help the police deal with Graham when he turned up drunk and disorderly in the Roberts Hotel.[5] Graham had been drinking and had hauled a load of guns and liquor up to his hotel room. Haynes knew that if he sent some of his officers to the hotel there was a chance that someone would end up getting shot. Haynes also knew that Weatherby was one of the few people who could reason with Graham after he had gone off on a drinking binge. Sim was called, drove over to the hotel, and walked into Graham's room. He found his friend with two pistols, a rifle, and shotgun, along with a bottle of whiskey. He shook his head and said, "Damn, Graham, if you're not a hell'uva sight. I'd hate for your mama to see you."[6] Graham was stunned by the comment. In a moment that predated some of his future instability when he was drinking, he put his guns down and broke into tears. Sim bundled him off to the Weatherby house in San Angelo and called Boog. Together the pair of them got him out of town.

After the Watson shooting no one was sure what kind of repercussions, legal or not, might be coming down. Weatherby, who had ranches at Juno and Marfa, was a natural to provide Graham a quiet place to stay out of the way while initial appeals were made and continuances were requested. James Weatherby remembered, "We were glad to have him, he was a good cowboy, wasn't lazy, and the most congenial son of a bitch you would ever be around."[7] While Graham stayed with the Weatherby's he impressed them with another habit besides his congeniality. He practiced daily with his pistols. The only time he used a holster was when he was on horseback, the rest of the time he tucked the .45 into his belt on the left side and covered it with a ducking jacket. He kept the .45 close at hand and supplemented it with a doubled barreled Derringer that he had taken off a bootlegger. Graham stayed with the Weatherby's for nearly six months, on and off. He drifted back to Sterling City and the family, but tried to stay out of sight as much as possible. Noisy Watson may have been a bootlegger but he was a popular man who had friends on both sides of the law. Graham couldn't be sure that some of those friends might decide to short circuit the legal processes and handle the penalty phase of the proceedings themselves.

While he was cowboying and practicing his shooting, Graham was dominated by the specter of the murder trial coming up. E. F. Vanderbilt and Robert T. Neill, his lawyers, assured him that they could be successful with the self-defense plea. Self–defense at that time was based on the justification that if a person was threatened, and the individual making the threats had the capacity to carry them out, then the person threatened was justified in using force to avoid the threat. The jury had to be made to understand that this was a long standing problem between the two men and that when it erupted into violence, Graham had to respond and his response was justified. The jury had to understand that a death threat could be carried out in any fashion and a brick could be as deadly as gun if you were close enough.

The lawyers planned to go back into the oil field and find people who were aware of Watson's reputation as a bootlegger and establish him as a man who had the capacity for violence. What the jury would hear was that Noisy was dangerous, and if Graham dealt with him harshly it was something that had to be done because there was the chance that the next time they met Noisy would have a pistol in his hand instead of a brick. The search for witnesses was on.

While the search began, Graham began to look around for a job. Newt Gourley was sheriff of Brewster County and took him on as a deputy, a position he would maintain until 1927.[8] It provided an income and kept him out of the public eye for a time, and it put him back in the Big Bend.

The trial was originally set for October 14, 1925. Twelve of the prosecution witnesses were subpoenaed for the trial but both they and witnesses for the defense were hard to find. Graham pleaded not guilty and the lawyers asked for a change of venue from Big Lake to Marfa. In December, they came back and asked for a continuance for the next session of the court. The lawyers maintained that important court papers had been delayed but more importantly, many of the defense witnesses were "scattered and in distant places as defendant had learned through efforts which he promptly made to locate them."[9] The major witness who could testify to Graham's state of mind of being threatened and fearful was Cliff Denson, the oil field worker who had heard Graham excitedly saying that Noisy was trying to kill him. The problem was that Denson was nowhere to be found, not in Big Lake, not in Fort Stockton, maybe not even in Texas. It was as if he had dropped out of sight.

Witnesses were a problem for both sides. Prosecution witnesses, W. R. McCravey and Allen Holden, both of whom had been in close proximity to the shooting, didn't make the hearing and were fined $500.00 each. A continuance carried the trial over again to July of 1927.[10] In the middle of not being able to find enough witnesses prosecutor Joe Montague suddenly found that a witness that he had counted on was not a witness at all.

Prosser Martin was a very well-known saddle and tack maker from Del Rio. He worked throughout West Texas and was known not just for his exemplary leatherwork, but also his penchant for telling stories about himself that didn't always involve the truth. On the afternoon that Noisy Watson was killed in Big Lake, Prosser was showing some of his saddles at a barbeque and roping in Best. The story of the shooting reached them at the barbecue quickly, and Prosser internalized it and took it back to Del Rio with him. When he got home, someone asked him about it. He later told Brian Montague "I rared [sic] back and told them that I was standing in the pool hall in Big Lake and witnessed the shooting and it was nothing less than cold blooded murder and Noisy had his hands in the air when Graham shot him."[11] There is no way to know how many times Prosser told the story and there is equally no way to know how much bigger it got during the serial retelling.

In July of 1927 a second round of subpoenas for witnesses went out and Prosser Martin found that his story telling ability had bought him trip to Marfa as a witness for the prosecution. The subpoena wasn't the only thing that worried him; the other was a visit he had from Graham Barnett. Earlier in the summer, as Prosser sat in his car in front of his saddle shop, he looked up and saw Graham come out of a restaurant and angle across the street to where the saddle maker was parked. Graham eased up, leaned on the car, looked in and said, "Prosser, I understand that you claim to be an eye witness when I shot Noisy Watson and that you have stated that he had his hands in the air and totally unarmed when I fired."[12] Prosser did the only thing that he could have done at the time. He laughed. "Oh, Graham you know what a damn liar I am. I was in Best, not in Big Lake. I didn't see anything and didn't know anything. But when some of my friends inquired about it, I thought I would entertain them with the story I told but it was all a damn lie."[13] Graham stared at him for a long moment and Prosser said later that he was never more frightened by anything then he was by sitting there watching Graham Barnett.[14] Graham settled the affair by promising Prosser that he would see to it that the saddle maker would be subpoenaed and that he would have to sit on the witness stand and admit the lie.

Graham spoke with ex-sheriff Dudley Barker about the conversation and it is likely that Barker told Joe Montague, in a wonderfully convoluted strategy, that Prosser would be a useful witness.[15] The defense then could face down the errant saddle maker on the stand, get him to admit that he lied, and in doing so, cast doubt on his statement and possibly the statements of other witnesses. Knowing that the variety of confusing statements would make the case look less open and shut, the defense was looking forward to Mister Martin's testimony.

Prosser probably didn't think much about the incident until in the early part of July when he was subpoenaed as a state witness. In a panic, he showed up at Brian Montague's office in Del Rio and told him that he wasn't going to comply with the subpoena. Brian explained that the sheriff would come and collect him, and one way or the other he would be in Marfa, Texas, on July 27. Prosser countered that threat by explaining the Sheep and Goat Raisers Association was having its annual convention in Kerrville to honor Captain Charles Schreiner and that he had arranged for an exhibit of his work there and that he intended to be with it. "I want you to send him a telegram and tell him that I am the biggest damn liar not only in Val Verde County but in the state of Texas. Just make it as strong as possible and you can't go too strong."[16] Montague didn't keep a copy of the telegram he sent his brother but he warned him that once Prosser got on the stand the trial strategy might need some restructuring. The subpoena was dropped, Prosser went to Kerrville, and no deputies showed up looking for him.

Prosser Martin wasn't the only witness that seemed to be having trouble. The defense insisted on calling people who were not in the area any more. Oil field workers moved frequently, and there were some witnesses who didn't want to be involved in the proceedings. The search seemed never ending, eventually the list was ready, subpoenas were issued, and the trial was on. The defense witness list was an unusual mix that included a number of sheriffs in the area, Texas Rangers, district judges, including John Sutton, the brother of the judge hearing the case, as well as county attorneys and district attorneys. Annie and Boog were subpoenaed, supposedly to testify to Graham's family connections, and they were accompanied by his mother and all the children. The list included people who had been involved in the Texon-Best-Big Lake area and also law enforcement from the Eastland area, another oil boomtown that had recently undergone its own massive arrest raids for bootlegging. A change of venue moved the trial to Fort Davis. Court records do not include transcripts of the testimony, and so the record of exact testimony has been lost, but some conclusions can be drawn from newspaper accounts and statements made by some of the principals.

From the beginning the trial was a mixture of the hilarious and the horrifying. The San Angelo newspaper announced that an entourage had left to take part or observe at the trial. Judge John Sutton, whose twin brother Claude would hear the trial, was joined by T. C. Rutledge and Ross Wood (both of whom were witnesses), Judge J. T. Matheson (country judge in Coke county), and ex-Ranger Carroll Bates who might have been a witness, or just had decided to go along for the ride. Since all of the men had had some contact with Graham, the ride would have provided an amazing opportunity for the collector of folklore and lies.[17]

Graham rode to Fort Davis with police chief Sam Haynes. Haynes claimed he smuggled Graham to the trial, taking an around about drive to avoid going through Big Lake and several other small towns that might provide a security problem for both of the men.[18]

The trial got off to a quick start, which illustrated that this was as close to a celebrity trial as West Texas had seen. Selection of the jury was a critical process and with a man as well-known as Graham, the process was potentially the most critical aspect of the trial. Judge Orland Sims told the story later of a young cowboy who must have heard the gunslinger stories of Graham Barnett and was impressed with what he had heard.

"They were examining prospective jurors and called up a typical young, back-county cowpoke who had just made it into town. He was red-headed, freckle-faced, unshaven and unshorn, and still in his well-worn ranch working togs: Levis tucked in his boots and all. After being sworn, he was seated on a raised witness chair with his old, big greasy hat on his gangly, bony knee, obviously a bit awed and self-conscious in the presence of all the dressed up lawyers and city folks. After giving his name address and occupation, the district attorney asked him, "Mr. _____ are you personally acquainted with the defendant in this case, Graham Barnett?" The boy, evidently much impressed to be basking in the aura of such an eminent gunman, rose to his feet, made a sketchy bow, and said "Howdy Mr. Barnett, I'm shore pleased to meetcha." Needless to say he was instantly excused as a juror amid the unrestrained laughter of all present."[19]

Most people thought it would be an open and shut case. It was, in the words of Sheriff Vern Davis, a "bad looking killing."[20] Graham had pleaded not guilty, that he had acted in self-defense. Graham, through his attorneys, stated that "the deceased was about to kill defendant with a brickbat at the time of the fatal shooting."[21] In order to show that Graham had been threatened by a dangerous man, was provoked and in fear of his life at the time of the shooting, the defense had subpoenaed almost everyone in the beer joint. A total of forty-four character and actual witnesses were subpoenaed, but not all testified.

The prosecution was lead by Joe Montague, but the DA had an unlikely assistant whose presence might have surprised many people. At that time, private individuals who had an interest in the case paid for other attorneys to assist the prosecution, and in this case Montague was assisted by Judge W. A. Wright. This was the same Judge Wright who, along with Harry Odneal, had accused Joe of improper behavior when he was leading some of the bootlegging raids in Best and Big Lake in July of

1925 that had resulted in Noisy Watson's arrest. Wright was known as an attorney who had represented a number of bootleggers in local trials. His appearance added another level of drama to the proceeding. Joe had no options other than to accept Wright as co-prosecutor, but the conferences between the two must have been tense.

The defense team had as a goal to weaken the case that seemed to be so open and shut. But they also knew that they could make a couple of other moves that might strengthen their position. They decided to file two motions: one directed toward the prosecution, the other toward the conduct of the trial. First they filed a motion asking that W. A. Wright reveal who had hired him to assist in the prosecution. The consensus was that Wright was funded by bootlegger money and if that could be shown the jury might be led to see a conspiracy of outlaws trying to put an honest lawman in jail. Wright declined to identify the source of his funding, and that action undoubtedly influenced the jury against the prosecution.[22]

The second motion involved the defense hedging their bets slightly on the self-defense plea. Back on July 19, 1926, almost exactly a year previously, they had filed a "suspension of sentence" request with the court. The suspension of sentence allowed that in the case of a first offence felony, that the jury could find the defendant guilty but recommend suspending the sentence in their verdict.[23] Apparently, everyone forgot about the felony aspect of the Babb killing years previously. The request was a critical play because the defense team seemingly was saying that the jury might find Graham guilty but, under the circumstances, the jury could still free him. What was implied was that despite the nature of the case, there were mitigating circumstances even beyond self-defense to be considered.[24]

The stream of witnesses for the prosecution came and went. Jim Brown, the porter, said that Watson struck the first blow.[25] W. R. McCravey contradicted that by saying Barnett swung first. McCravey expanded on what he had seen. Graham had asked Watson about something that he had said about Graham. Graham had responded that he (Watson) had it in for him. Whatever Graham had asked Watson about, Watson's reply included a common three-word response that the newspaper had cleaned up and used only with dashes. He said, "Anyone who said that was a _____" and the fight started.[26]

With the possible exception of McCravey, no one had seen the entire encounter from start to finish. Some of the people had heard the fight, others had gone outside to see it, and a few had heard the mutterings of Graham as he came back into the recreation hall for the pistols he knew were under the bar. They were prepared to testify that they had heard him talking excitedly to himself about the man with the brick trying to kill him.[27] Colonel Brooks' testimony seemed inconclusive. He had seen the fight, he had separated the men but he had not seen the fatal shot fired. Beyond that, like all good bartenders, he kept what he knew to himself.

All of the testimony seemed to flatten out with the statements from Cal Rutledge about how Watson dropped the brick when he saw that Graham had come back with a gun. Rutledge described how the frantic Watson clutched at Rutledge's shirt, tearing buttons away in his panic to get someone between him and the man with the gun. All of it built to the point when the jury heard about the deafening sound of the shot, and the smack of the heavy bullet as it tore into Watson and how he took two or three steps and collapsed at the feet of the two men.

The defense called one witness the first day: the lonely chicken picker R. B. Walton who had sat out the fight and the shooting on a box behind the café. He said he didn't hear Watson call for help, neither did he see the man's hands in the air. The defense seemed positive about the day's work and the outcome of the trial, despite the seemingly overwhelming evidence against Graham.

Even with all the testimony, the events were vague and hard to explain. Two men with reputations and a record of questionable behavior had met on a summer night, and decided to settle an old dispute over something that had been said at another place and time. Whatever was said was lost in an alley behind a beer joint. Whatever evidence Graham was looking for when he drove to Big Lake, he didn't find it with Kirtley Watson. What he did find was a man with a brick who had whipped him before and showed every indication of being prepared to do it again. The testimony for the defense was clear: Graham Barnett feared for his life and he decided to end that threat.

The self-defense argument was not the only one. The self-defense claims were combined with the overwhelming testimony from dozens of witnesses who alleged that Watson had fought with Graham before and had made a number of threats against him. These testimonies must have gone a long way toward changing minds about the nature of the case. An additional quirky piece of information that seemed almost insignificant at an early period of time must have played well to a jury that was hungry for evidence. The plan to bring in an undercover operative to assess the local crime problem that Brian Montague had been part of back in 1925 reemerged to the surprise of many people. Some of the citizens of Big Lake were convinced the criminal situation was getting out of hand. In response to their concern they had developed a plan to gather evidence through the use of an undercover operator. Originally they had floated the idea of private investigators from Dallas being brought in. The information they gathered would be used to make indictments against the outlaws who appeared to be operating at their own discretion in the Big Lake, Rankin, and Best area. Brian Montague had approved the plan but left the DA's office shortly afterwards and lost touch with the progress of the undercover operation. What Joe Montague either didn't know, or overlooked, was that the citizens went forward with their investigation. The only modification was the decision to use local people rather than out of town investigators.

Based on trial testimony it appears that Graham was the man picked to do the undercover work in Big Lake. County sheriff J. D. Christy dropped what might have been considered a bombshell that was repeated later by the defense. In a brief newspaper article announcing the verdict, defense attorney E. R. Simmons quoted the sheriff as saying, "Barnett was a special officer in Big Lake where the killing occurred, having been sent there by the sheriff at the request of several citizens."[28] Apparently the use of a part-time bootlegger with a questionable reputation like Graham had a better chance of infiltrating the outlaws than an out of town operative.

Sheriff Christy's comment seemed to take the case out of a common beer joint dispute and change it to a more law-focused situation. Now it wasn't two drunks fighting. It was a bootlegger and an undercover investigator. It seems impossible that the prosecution would have overlooked the significance of that detail, but for the jury, it might have tipped the case in Graham's favor. It seemed to be a plotline right out of a pulp fiction magazine: undercover man is found out in speakeasy, bootlegger threatens him, good guy has to shoot his way out. It was a storyline that could be believed by everyone who heard it because it was played out nightly on the radio dramas and in the popular fiction of the time.

The issue of Watson's character figured into the case prominently. While many people considered him a local character that had worked hard, ran a trucking business, and did dirt jobs on the side, it could not be ignored that Kirtley Watson was a bootlegger. He was indicted for that activity in the raids that had just occurred in Best. The defense painted him tough, capable, and a man who carried out his threats. Whatever reputation Graham Barnett had, Watson was an accused criminal and even though he was a popular one, he was still the outlaw and Graham was the lawman.

While this may have influenced the jury, none of it was included in Judge Sutton's charge to the jury; it all came down to the issue of self-defense. "If you believe that... Kirtley Watson...had made or was making or was about to make an attack on [Barnett] which from the manner and character of it and the defendant's knowledge of the character and disposition of the deceased...caused him reasonable expectation or fear of death or serious bodily injury...then you will acquit him."[29]

In the end, the jury was out for forty minutes before returning with a stunning decision: not guilty. The defense must have collapsed in their relief. The prosecution could not have believed it: it was supposed to be an easy case. Brian Montague talked with his brother and recalled, "...Graham was represented by a battery of very fine trial lawyers and they simply overwhelmed the prosecution with evidence of the general reputation of Noisy Watson as a violent and dangerous man, and one who was calculated to, if the occasion offered itself, to execute 'alleged' threats to kill Graham and as numerous threats of that nature were testified to, true or false only the Lord know, to his dismay, Joe had to hear the clerk read a verdict of 'not guilty.' When I read of this verdict in the paper, I was shocked and could not account for it until I next saw Joe, and he bitterly complained that he 'had played against a stacked deck.'"[30]

Joe Montague never explained publicly what he meant by a stacked deck or if he did, Brian never recorded it in print. There were numerous guesses about who stacked the deck and how it was stacked. Some were remarkably similar to the accusations made in the Babb case years before. They ranged from the conjecture that the entire jury was Masons and secret hand signals reminding everyone of their brotherhood were passed between defense lawyers and the jurors.[31] For others there was the idea that the law officer was not going to be found guilty in the case of killing a bootlegger, especially when the bootlegger was, moments before, trying very hard to kill the officer. For many people it was simply a case that Graham Barnett was a legend and no jury was going to convict a legend. His prominence as a folk hero could not be ignored.

It was explained about as well as it could be by Judge Orland Sims, who used the case to describe what he saw as a failure on the part of the public for creating a hero from a man who had just killed someone else in a beer joint. Sims identified two aspects of public opinion that impacted the verdict. He said that people had "sneaking admiration and respect... for the criminal and the open hero worship of the gun-slinger."[32]

Criminals were seen as heroes by many people. The man who skirted the law was admired as someone who faced an unpopular police establishment and won. As for the gunfighter, that icon had deep roots in Texas. Graham fit into both categories. It was as Orland Sims had stated earlier, Graham was a hero because he was seen as a gunfighter and the people loved that. He was the cowboy hero who lived the kind of life that many of them admired. He was like a figure out of one of the films they watched on the weekends. He was a throwback to an earlier period of time. How could you find someone guilty who had defended himself? Many people had members of their family who had done the same thing, or claimed to.

Invariably others questioned the entire process. Was Joe Montague too close to Graham Barnett? Did their friendship impact how Joe carried out the prosecution? Was it payback for Graham defending Joe against Harry Odneal? Or was it just the temper of the times? People could understand the need to defend one's self when threatened. The lawyers had made it clear that Watson had threatened Graham and people understood that it was hard to live with a constant threat. The challenge to the jury from the judge made it clear: if Kirtley Watson had threatened Graham and if he had the power to carry out the threat, it was a case of self-defense.

It was a classic "him or me" defense and people in West Texas understood dealing with a problem that had continued for much too long. Kirtley "Noisy" Watson was just one more name on a list of people who were looking for Graham Barnett. Living a life with a threat has a way of wearing on a person's patience. In conducting research for this book, this case was discussed with several long-time West Texas residents. One summed up the consensus of opinions when she said, "Well, he ought not to have shot him, but I imagine he was tired of messing with him."[33]

Illustration 10. Annie and Graham on left, unknown location, and others on right, circa 1925

(Courtesy John T. Barnett)

CHAPTER 11

"AS FREQUENTLY OCCURS, JEALOUSY AND ENMITY BETWEEN RIVAL GANGS DEVELOPED"

1927-1931[1]

While there had been a Graham Barnett legend before the killing of Noisy Watson, it exploded after the acquittal. Everyone seemed to know him or to know a story about him, and they were not reluctant to repeat it. The stories grew with each telling. Whether the story was real or not didn't seem to matter; it was a Graham Barnett story, and Graham was a hot item. Everyday activities became more exciting if Graham Barnett was involved. A barber in San Angelo told that when Graham came in for a haircut and shave, he kept his pistol in his lap under the cloth and insisted on sitting in the back of the shop.[2] People knew why. There was always someone looking for him. Far-fetched stories were told about how, either out of meanness or to protect his uncle's sheep and cattle, Graham had shot Mexicans who were trying to cross the Rio Grande.[3] With each story, the numbers grew. If the speaker was an opponent of Graham the stories got more exaggerated. In a letter offering his services as a prosecutor, an attorney in Del Rio estimated that the number of men that Graham had killed probably would dam the Rio Grande up.[4] One of the basic problems with these accusations of mass murder was that the people had seen him shoot, just not shoot people.

As his reputation grew so did the stories of his marksmanship. It was phenomenal. People swore that they saw him shoot pecans off fence posts at fifty feet.[5] He shot the heads off quail with a German Luger, a pistol that took some getting used to after years of practice with a 1911. Zeb Decie and his brother told of the time when Graham offered to shoot targets at a hundred yards for ten dollars a shot. The Decie's refused.[6] He guided hunts and shot deer with the .45 if his clients were unsuccessful with a rifle. In a part of the world where marksmanship was appreciated, Graham's abilities were considered legendary. It was obvious to the storytellers that no one was better. The reality of the matter was that there were other people just as good, maybe better, but they didn't have a following.

It didn't seem to matter to people whether Graham came off as the winner or loser in the stories. He was going up against someone or something bigger and taking them down a peg. What mattered was that Graham was beating the odds again. There was a story that when he was body guarding a prominent citizen in San Angelo, Graham was poisoned and wound up in his hotel room near death.[7] Only the quick action of the hotel staff in getting him to the hospital where his stomach was pumped saved his life. When the public heard the story the Graham supporters decided that in a short time, someone would pay for underestimating how big a dose of poison it would take to kill a legend. The Graham detractors said it was all about some bad bootleg liquor Graham had drunk instead of pouring out.

The notoriety seemed to be something that he neither sought nor backed away from. It came to him because to the people of the area, he was someone to be admired. He was also someone to be talked about. After the debacle as a deputy, Graham and his cousin Oscar took some work in one of the expanding oil fields. During a lunch break several of the roughnecks told expansive stories about the latest escapades of the well-known Graham Barnett. Later Oscar asked Graham why he didn't tell the men who he was. "I just wanted to catch up on what I had been doing lately," Graham replied and they went back to work.[8] He must have enjoyed the notoriety; he had become the man everyone told stories about. The impact of all of these stories on Graham is hard to determine. People told the tales, his reputation grew, and as he became more famous, people expected that he would continue with his gunfighter-outlaw behavior. It would have been hard to stop acting like Graham Barnett even if he had wanted to.

Despite the reputation, he was a man who needed a job. He began to look into some old contacts within the law enforcement business for some other opportunities and found it in the booming business of body guarding.[9] People needed bodyguards because people with money always attracted the attention of people without it. Most of the jobs were short term but the pay was good. They might involve keeping an oil executive and his family safe from a kidnapping, or a rancher making a cash deal for cattle in Mexico might need someone to ride with him down a lonely, dusty road to make a buy. Occasionally it was an outgrowth of the gambling business. Gambling was illegal, and high dollar games were hijacked from time to time and serious gamblers required serious protection. Gamblers hired *pistoleros* to provide security not only for the game, but for the trip back to a hotel or to the train station when the game was done. Most of the body guarding involved doing something that the boss could not or would not do for himself.

The new business put Graham in situations he had not been in before. He went to fancy hotels, business meetings, and formal dinners. Graham laughingly told about a dinner party he attended with an employer in San Angelo. He had been somewhat nervous about attending the dinner armed and being the only person in the room with a gun. He had developed a habit of slipping his .45 out of his waistband and placing it under his leg so it would be easy to reach during the meal. At some

point he dropped either his fork or his napkin and bent to pick it up, and
when he did he glanced under the table at the other guests. He swore
that each one, man or woman, had a pistol in their laps.[10] There were
advantages to body guarding; the pay was good, he said he could make
$500 a month when he worked, but he did not work all the time.

He didn't just bodyguard. Brian Montague implied that Graham headed
a gang, or some sort of organized criminal enterprise during this period.
While the evidence supporting that view was limited, two letters from
Ranger captain Will Wright indicate that Graham did work with a
group of maverick officers who performed a series of unauthorized
raids on bootleggers and gamblers, arresting some and confiscating
contraband from others. Wright was formally directed by the adjutant
general to investigate the extralegal raids. In addition he had been told
that, despite claims made by both Graham and his partner, neither
had Ranger commissions.[11] Whether the raids were supported by the
local district attorneys or whether they were conducted by the officers
themselves in a series of quasi-official activities isn't clear, but the
evidence seems to support the latter. Wright's investigations uncovered
evidence that Graham and several other officers broke into the hotel
room of a bootlegger in Pyote on November 20, 1927. Fifty-eight pints
of liquor were seized but only six were turned into the local sheriff. A
gambling hall was taken over in Pecos, with $1260.00 taken off the tables
and eighty gamblers arrested. Wright noted that the officers were seen
putting the money into their jackets. The next day, the gamblers were
fined a dollar each by the local authorities. The sheriff commented to
Wright that some other hijacking of gamblers had been taking place
but he was unable to catch the men robbing the outlaws.[12] Wright's
investigations produced a list of names of deputy sheriffs from different
jurisdictions across the area who had taken part in the raids. Graham
was mentioned several times in the report as being prominent. Wright
mentioned only the raids in Pyote and Pecos, but other raids took place.
No arrests of officers were noted, perhaps indicating there was at least
some support from some officials. The investigations by Captain Wright

provide at least some credence to the story that Graham spent a lot of time shaking down bootleggers and gamblers and making life difficult for people who opposed him.

Graham looked to a number of officers for more legal work. One of the officers that he had worked with when he was at Texon, Bill Fowler, had become police chief in McCamey. Fowler and Graham had worked well together and had kept in touch over the past two years. Bill Fowler, or more formally, William Clarence Fowler, had lived a life not unlike Graham's but without the flamboyance. He had been born in Hamilton, Texas, on October 1, 1889, to David and Willie Fowler. The family eventually grew to four sons and a daughter. David was a carpenter, and he may have also farmed some. By 1920 Bill was farming near Lubbock. He had married Clara Elizabeth Sparkman in Roswell, New Mexico, where he had owned or managed a rock quarry.[13] He eased into law enforcement as a deputy in Miami, Arizona, and then in a variety of law enforcement jobs back in Texas. He was a ruddy-faced man, six feet tall with black hair and an angular face set off by piercing eyes. By 1930 he was living in a home that he owned in McCamey with his wife and three children, Kenneth, 16, Eugene, 14, and Margaret, 12. He was city marshal in McCamey and listed his occupation as "peace officer" and "state ranger."[14] After he moved to McCamey he continued to find other ways to make money. He ranched on the side and put together a successful cattle feeding operation.

Graham and Fowler enforced the law together and broke one or two on occasion. Once they went to Juarez and sauntered into one of the famous saloons that lined Juarez Avenue. Fowler noticed that the bartender had stacked shot glasses into a pyramid that decorated the middle of the bar. Graham dragged his hand down the bar and through the glasses, scattering shot glasses amid the shouts and cursing of the bartenders. Getting out of that bar was not as easy as getting in to it. Fowler remembered that incident for a long time. "I thought we were going to have to shoot our way out."[15]

Bill Fowler had his sights set on things other than disturbing the peace in Juarez. He had become police chief in McCamey and wanted to run for sheriff. He thought he had a strong power base, and if he could pick up a few votes, the sheriff's job was his. When he discussed these plans with Graham, he mentioned that there might be a place for Graham in his administration if he could be elected. The "if" was a major factor. Fowler was up against an established power in Upton County, and his election would take some time to achieve. Graham couldn't wait on a job that was dependent on something as hard to predict as an election. He kept looking.

The state legislature provided something to do in 1927. In order to deal with the boom in cars and trucks and the increased traffic on the highways, laws had been passed requiring a number of changes in how people drove. Drivers were required to have licenses, the cars had to have two license plates, which had to be purchased at the rate of $16.70, and each car had to have a tail light.[16] Trucks were regulated as well with regard to load size and commercial applications. The Legislature authorized the establishment of twenty enforcement districts and appointed a license and weight inspector to enforce trucking laws and assist the local law enforcement in each district. The inspectors were to be paid $150.00 per month, used their own cars for which they were paid $60.00 per month, and paid $3.00 per day for food when they were outside their county of residence.[17] They carried portable scales for the trucks and .45 automatics for other issues. It was not an easy job.

West Texas had a bad name for not complying with the new laws and it promised to be a busy place for the inspector. Some newspapers claimed that the county governments failed to support the new laws. "The [Highway Commission] perhaps rashly throws out an accusation that county authorities, in West Texas, are openly permitting the law to be violated," observed a writer for the *El Paso Herald*.[18] The newspapers claimed the cost of the license plates was too high and that was why people did not comply. People were apparently splitting license plates and putting one on one vehicle, one on another, or just not paying the license fee. If the county officials would not chase down the local lawbreakers they observed that the [Highway] Commission would "... send its inspectors, as threatened, to take over the burden to run down impecunious owners of automobiles."[19] The stage was set for a new job for Graham.

Regardless of the lack of popularity of both the law and the inspectors, Graham saw it as a chance to be involved in law enforcement again. It is likely that he was helped in his pursuit of this job by either Judge John Sutton or his old friend, Dudley Barker. Graham took over as the inspector for District 6 in Alpine on October 10, 1927.[20] It wasn't possible to say that he was back in uniform; the Legislature had not provided funding for uniforms. At least he was back in law enforcement. When he was not chasing illegal truckers, he spent time raiding gamblers and taking over illegal liquor shipments. Neither of which were including in his job description, but they paid well.

The job had a number of strong attractions for Graham. He was on his own, he had few guidelines, he had miles of West Texas highways to cover, and he could drive as fast as he wanted. That was probably what he was doing on January 11, 1928, when he hit a horse on the Bankhead highway near Pyote.[21] One of his ears was almost severed and he had additional injuries that were severe enough that he resigned from the Highway Department effective February 29, 1928.[22] After five months, Graham was out of work again, but that condition did not last long.

He returned to the on-again-off-again life of the paid *pistolero*. This time Dudley Barker hired him to help with Barker's administration of the Downie Estate. Barker had been hired by Mrs. Louise Downie to manage the estate, a large ranch of about 150,000 acres. The fabled property had been founded by Charles Downie, a Scottish immigrant and legend in the area. When he died, the everyday management of the place fell to his widow and son. Barker was hired to assist, and he brought Graham in to help with the extensive area. Barker's work as an administrator of the ranch was not without controversy, and when Mrs. Downie died as a result of injuries suffered in a car wreck in Mexico, both he and Graham were out of a job again.

According to the memories of a number of his friends, he went back to bootlegging and backed that up with gambling on the side.[23] He still held to the idea that if he could keep people in a poker game long enough, he would eventually win. As with everything else he did, the stories grew about his card playing. One of the most often repeated ones involved a marathon game in San Angelo. After an extended game that had continued over some time, several of the players decided to leave. Graham had not made the money that he thought he deserved, and he objected to the game ending. His fellow gamblers headed for the door and Graham shot the doorknob off, extending the game by some hours.[24]

When he wasn't gambling he was acting as a bodyguard. He worked briefly for P. D. Anderson of Presidio.[25] Anderson farmed and dealt in real estate, but also was the owner and operator of the international bridge at the border crossing between Presidio and Ojinaga, which had opened in December, 1927. Anderson was an important man and as such had made a few enemies. He and Graham had met professionally after someone had taken a few shots at the real estate man. He decided that he needed more protection, and Graham was back in the bodyguarding business. As in any business, there were good days and bad days. After one of the bad days, the pair of them were seen rumbling around Presidio in a bullet-riddled touring car after a now forgotten dispute. Longevity in the bodyguarding game was hard to predict. Anderson's business and popularity improved, and a need for a bodyguard lessened, Graham headed north again.

Mostly he drifted between jobs and moved between law enforcement and law breaking. It is difficult to say whom exactly he was working for when he was involved in one of his more spectacular and long remembered disputes in San Angelo, which added more luster to his legend.

San Angelo was a typical West Texas town dedicated to rapid growth and not particularly interested in being in total compliance with the laws pertaining to prohibition. The town had attracted business because it was a center for the sheep and goat trade. It was also quickly expanding into oil and banking. The financial activity brought a number of ancillary businesses, and those included hotels and restaurants that filled consistently with area ranchers who had come to town on business and stayed overnight. It was the after-hours diversions that provided additional income for the city and made it a kind of entertainment center for adults. The diversions included not only eating and drinking, but a number of Texans' favorite vices were available.

Liquor seemed to be easily found in the hotel and restaurants. Hotel bellboys ran a bottle-by-bottle business for their guests, and several of the dining clubs had access to whatever the customer wanted.[26] Gambling still attracted men to the San Angelo area referred to as the "Sharp End." Sporting gentlemen came by train several times a year to take part in what seemed to be the regional playoffs of gambling.[27] Additionally, San Angelo still had a reputation as a town that had an active bordello district, and that business was booming as well. All of the entertainment business hinged on selective enforcement of state and federal laws.

The process that had been in place for years, which allowed business to go on relatively free from official harassment, involved the payment of protection money. Certain hotels that featured marathon poker games, the bordellos, and many street criminals paid to be warned when something bad was going to happen to them. For the criminals it was part of the cost of doing business. For the cops it was like a tax paid by the criminals for services provided. The system worked not just in San Angelo but in any community large enough to attract a criminal element with money to spend. The community had access to the liquor it wanted, the cops got paid and enough arrests were made to keep up the image of a crime fighting law enforcement organization. For the system to work properly it required coordinated planning combined with a police department that understood selective enforcement.

This was the situation when one of Graham's old adversaries, Carroll Bates became police chief. The tall, ruddy-faced Bates had a long and quirky background in law enforcement. He had been deputy city marshal in San Angelo from 1907-1909 and city marshal from 1909-1917. He wielded considerable political influence in San Angelo and had close contacts with Senator Claude Hudspeth, a prominent West Texas state senator. It was through Hudspeth's influence that Bates was made a captain in the Texas Rangers in 1917.[28] It was Bates's own shortcomings as a captain that caused him to resign his commission on August 31, 1918. He had purchased a ranch near Marathon which was viewed by the army as a location used by smugglers, although this was denied by Bates. The denial was supported after an investigation by Bureau of Investigation agent Gus Jones, who had worked for Bates earlier in San Angelo. Jones hinted that Bates was working as a double agent to gather information on smugglers.[29] Bates bounced around as a salesman and a game warden before being appointed police chief in San Angelo May 1, 1927. The appointment as police chief indicates that he had considerable support from enough of the power brokers in town that he could step into a locally powerful job that paid unusually well.

As early as 1926, Bates was involved with a large number of people in an organized bootlegging and protection scheme.[30] His exact role prior to his appointment as police chief is unclear but testimony from two bankers indicated that he was making serious deposits of money early as May of 1926.[31] As liquor protection business expanded, the scheme had gotten more sophisticated. Before it was all over, the scheme involved people from the police to the manager of the Drillers Club, and others involved in the dining and entertainment business in San Angelo. The wholesale supply end of the business was controlled by several people but primarily handled by J. A. "Curley" Shields. Shields was the son of Gerome "Rome" Shields who had been sheriff of Tom Green County from

1890 until 1900. Rome remained a formidable figure in county politics and a man who enjoyed a drink from time to time. Subsequent investigations by prohibition agents showed he also maintained a spectacular personal bar with an inventory of liquor whose value exceeded eight thousand dollars.[32]

The liquor came in by train or truck and was stored in a number of places around town, mostly under the protection of some of the San Angelo Police Department. The criminal organization referred to as "the line" then took over supervising storage and delivery. With Carroll Bates firmly established as police chief, the broader criminal organization was settled in as the premier liquor supplier in the area. Bates apparently slipped into the roles of both police chief and protector of bootleggers without a ripple. His new jobs put him directly in conflict with Graham Barnett.

According to Brian Montague, Graham was back in the business of bootlegging and had run into problems with the Shields-Bates organization. Graham may have been trying to expand into new territory or it may have been just the friction that came up between two groups of people involved in the same business, but Graham and Carroll Bates seemed to be ready to continue with the feuding that had developed in the oil fields several years earlier. To Brian Montague what was happening was clear: "The prevailing opinion in West Texas was that Graham was likewise engaged with others in the same avocation [as Bates] and as frequently occurs jealousy and enmity between rival gangs developed."[33] As far as Graham was concerned, the "jealousy and enmity" that Brian Montague observed had to be dealt with.

There was another factor in all of this. Bates still was not happy with the verdict in the Watson murder trial. When the Watson trial was completed, Graham needed a ride to Sterling City. Sim Weatherby and his wife took him and said later that Carroll Bates and a carload of men were armed and waiting outside of Sterling for Graham to drive by. He was unseen in the Weatherby car and missed another shooting.[34] Bates believed that the killing of Watson was nothing less than murder, and he commented to several people that he was going to kill Graham.[35] Word of this situation reached Judge John Sutton. On one occasion the judge was awakened at night by a man who said he had some information that might involve a shooting. When Sutton met with the man, the informer told him that Carroll Bates had been drinking and had said that he was going to kill Graham. The judge listened to the man and then asked, "Is that all you have to tell me?" When the man nodded, the judge replied, "Don't worry about it." Later Sutton commented that Bates was as scared of Graham as he was a "box of rattlesnakes."[36] Whether he was afraid of Graham or not, one thing was certain, Graham Barnett had been a problem to Carroll Bates in the past and was becoming one again.

Bates's threats combined with the business competition caused Graham to respond in what was becoming a standard pattern for him. After stewing over the situation, he decided that he had only one choice—to kill Carroll Bates before Bates had a chance to work himself up to succeed in the murder business. Based on the events that occurred on the day of the encounter, Graham developed a plan. It was relatively simple; he would kill Bates in broad daylight on the main street of the city, in front of witnesses. The approach he decided to take was to set up a situation where self-defense would again play a role in the shooting. The success of the plan hung on the technicality of getting Bates to draw first. That might not have been seen as much of a problem, but, as it turned out, it was a major stumbling block. Despite his days in the Rangers Bates didn't have a reputation as a gunman. Vern Davis, sheriff in Sterling County, commented that "Bates didn't know what it was to shoot someone or be shot at."[37] For the plan to succeed, Bates was going to have to cooperate by either pulling a gun or making a move that could be interpreted as a threat. Shooting the police chief probably was not the best way to deal with the competition, but the plan did have the advantage of being short on details and long on outcomes. The advantage to Graham's plan was that it was simple. The problem with over planning a fight is that the details tend to get confused when the shooting starts.

The plan showed a remarkable confidence on Graham's part in his ability to beat Bates's draw and to equally beat the legal system. It also disregarded how citizens might view a shooting of a city official on the main street of town. While Bates was not popular with Graham, the chief did have a following. Their encounter was remembered for a long time by people who were there, and a number of them who were not, and it contributed a large piece of folklore to the Graham Barnett legend.

Brian Montague wrote of the incident and, although he was not a witness, he provided a good overview of what happened. Graham had a friend drive him to San Angelo from Fort Stockton, where he was living at the time, and he began to wander the streets in search of the police chief.[38] Apparently Bates had made enough comments about Graham that people understood the deadly nature of the situation. The specter of a well-known gunfighter inquiring about the location of the chief of police was quickly seen as an explosive situation. People who knew both men began to telephone one another to try to decide what could be done to head off what could be a shooting scrape in the downtown shopping area.[39] The phone calls did tip off Judge James Cornell who was a friend of both men.[40] Cornell took to the streets to see if he could find his ex-client or the chief of police before they found each other.

There is no indication that Bates was warned about Graham being in town and looking for him, but he knew Graham and he knew how he operated. He had been subpoenaed in the Watson case and certainly had some idea of how Graham worked both to intimidate his target and to make a play that could be seen as self-defense.

Graham found Carroll with a group of followers on Chadbourne Street and Concho at the Arc Light Drug Store, which had been the Arc Light Saloon in better days. According to some reports, the chief was standing by the cash register when Graham strode up.[41] Depending on which witnesses were telling the story, Graham asked Carroll for a cigarette.[42] Carroll Bates had been a Ranger and had been a deputy sheriff and was not a man who was cowed easily, but this day he was up against someone who came with a reputation, a bad attitude, and a .45 in his belt. Bates put together what was happening. He knew Graham didn't just drop by to visit about how the bootlegging business was going, and Bates read the situation and reacted accordingly. Bates wisely didn't move his hands from his coat lapels and told Graham he had quit smoking. He asked the girl behind the counter to give Graham a pack of cigarettes. The pack hit the counter and Graham asked him if he had a match. Carroll swore he didn't have a match either, and he told the girl to give Graham some matches. Carroll kept his hands in plain view and made no move that could be interpreted as a move for a gun. When the demands for smoking supplies didn't work, Graham began to cuss him out. Carroll Bates had seen this technique before and wisely didn't respond to the cursing.[43] Some witnesses said that Graham kicked the ex-Ranger in the shins and slapped him across the face but Bates made no move for a gun.[44]

Finally, Graham seemed to run out of curse words or breath, and stopped cussing for a moment. The plan was not working, there was no movement from Bates, and apparently no amount of cussing or slapping was going to get him to move. Frustration set in. When it became obvious that Bates was not going to do anything that could be interpreted as a move for a gun, Graham did the only thing he could have done; he walked away from the now silent group of men. Bates, in remembering the encounter, later told Sam Haynes, the previous chief of police, how he had not moved for a gun. Haynes, who knew Graham well, commented, "I think you used very good judgment."[45]

Perhaps because of his recent trial, Graham knew that if he was going to shoot someone in public he better have some kind of defense and in this situation, Carroll Bates was not giving him any excuses. No defensible shooting meant jail time, and Graham Barnett was not going to go to jail. He walked back toward the center of town and almost immediately ran into James Cornell, who had finally found the group of erstwhile witnesses. Cornell, who had observed part of the encounter, had decided Graham needed to be off the street. He grasped his old friend by the arm and asked him to come to his office to discuss some things and then they could have lunch. The two left what was almost the scene of a crime.[46]

Cornell brought Graham up to his office, and began to plan to get him out of town to avoid another encounter with Bates. He made up a story about needing to go to Fort Stockton and asked Graham to ride with him. Cornell brought along a local seventeen-year-old named Bascom Sheffield in case an extra driver was needed. Sheffield was treated to an hour in the life of a living legend. When Graham got in the car, he pulled the .45 out of his belt and placed it on the floor of the car where he could get it if it was needed. He then began to ruminate on his failed plan and what he would do to Bates in the future. The discussion over the long drive must have shocked the seventeen-year-old. Cornell said later that he didn't think the boy enjoyed the trip as much as he should have.[47]

The incident in San Angelo was significant for several reasons. Graham had stated that he was going to kill the police chief and he made a determined effort to do so in front of a number of people. The cursing and intimidation should have worked, should have caused a less cautious man to strike back. Carroll Bates didn't intend to die that day, and he kept his hands on his lapels and his pistol in his belt. Graham had faced down his opponent, but he hadn't killed him. That was a problem; people expected a gunfight and instead got a public cussing and humiliation. Neither man won in the encounter but Graham came off as the aggressor, and Bates emerged with nothing more than a damaged reputation. People who heard the story and repeated it must have been disappointed that the clash ended with nothing more than a pack of cigarettes being exchanged and the chief of police maintaining as much of his dignity as he could.

The incident created a stir and became a standard bit of the Graham Barnett lore. No one who actually saw the incident recorded their memories of the experience but that didn't stop people from talking about it for years afterward. The stories include Graham telling Bates to jump up on the counter of the Arc Light Saloon/Drug store and the fearful chief doing so. In other versions, Graham got a lot pushier with Bates, but the chief never responded with movement to justify a shooting. The story of the gunfight that didn't happen was absorbed into San Angelo folklore and even though the names of both men are forgotten in some retellings, the story remains part of the common thread describing wilder days in downtown San Angelo.[48]

Carroll Bates stayed a step ahead of fate that day, but time was running short for the police chief and the organization that he was part of. It all ended with a series of indictments that resulted in his arrest on January 11, 1929, along with Allen W. Brown, night police sergeant, and twenty-nine other men and women.[49] Included in the indictment were J. A. "Curley" Shields, and a collection of some of San Angelo's better-known store managers, salesmen, taxi drivers, and at least one of San Angelo's ladies of the evening. In the best traditions of that time, Bates commented that he looked forward to an opportunity to clear his name, and resigned from the police department two days later.[50]

The indictments were a result of an investigation that was begun by Federal Prohibition Agent John Wright. It wasn't much of an investigation since a lot of the activity took place more or less in the open. Most of what Wright found came from watching activity in town, and also from picking up William H. Hutchison, the accountant for the Bates-Shields organization. Using techniques that should have been familiar to anyone who followed the activities of law enforcement, Hutchison was offered the opportunity to make a deal. He could become the chief witness for the prosecution or plan to move into the federal prison system for an extended stay. Being a good accountant, he made the best deal that he could. He produced documents, testimony, and gave all the information he had to both the agents and the grand jury.

The story that Hutchison told to the Feds enabled them to put together an overview of what was going on in the San Angelo liquor business. Bates and Shields shared "ringleader" status as far as the newspapers were concerned. The pair supplied, controlled, and protected the wholesale liquor business for a vast number of clients.[51] The people who were indicted were not prominent in the sense of possessing a great deal of wealth, but they had connections that reached deeply into the fabric of the community. The entire scheme could not have worked without the support of the local police department.

Liquor flowed into San Angelo via truck and train. It was off-loaded and stored at various sites within the city. From these sites, it was moved by truck to the various clubs and restaurants that continued to serve it illegally to customers. The Bates-Shields organization focused on the wholesale liquor business and did not directly deal with the public.

Bates supplied coordination and protection for what the newspapers called the "rum ring." When raids were scheduled, the organization was notified and Shields picked up the booze from his distributors, hid it until the raids had been conducted, and then returned it. He may have also picked up liquor for other people that he knew, and stored it until the raids were done. There were allegations that some of the liquor that had been stored at the police department had been recycled into the Bates-Shields inventory, although Sergeant Brown denied this.[52] The "line" also organized against other bootleggers coming into town and that is probably what brought Bates and Graham back into conflict.

The investigation found that the police chief was heavily involved, and that Carroll Bates was receiving a cut of the profits amounting to $600 to $800 per month from the organization.[53] Hutchison acted as bagman for the protection money. On Mondays he called the chief, told him he was coming by, and drove to the police station. Chief Bates would join him in the car and they would drive around the block where Hutchison would give Bates $150 to $200 per week, sometimes a little more or less depending on the time of the year. Rodeos and holidays affected the cut. They would drive back to the front and Bates returned to his office. Bates then distributed a part of the money to another partner in the business, Patrolman Allen W. Brown, who was eventually indicted also. Brown presumably passed money on to other members of the department who had connections with the project.[54]

Continuances and delays took the trial well into 1929. The business was further complicated when one of the coconspirators tried to bribe his way out of the indictment, which only made things more difficult for everyone. On April 28, 1929, the trial began in San Angelo. At the trial, Bates denied everything. Not only did he not know anything about the conspiracy, he had never taken any money, and had only spoken to Hutchison one time during the entire time he was in San Angelo.[55] The ever faithful Brown backed him up on all statements.

The problem was the money. Between 1926 and 1929 he managed to bank $54,000 in San Angelo's Central National Bank, all on a $300 per month police chief's salary.[56] His explanation for how he could bank that kind of money was that he was a lucky man. He had sold a farm, probably the ranch he had bought in 1918, which had brought in some funds, but mostly he had bet on the outcomes of elections and the world's series, and he had been incredibly lucky. The prosecution brought in two bankers who testified that Bates had made the deposits and had done so on a regular basis. The jury found that his luck had run out, and on May 3 sentenced him to eighteen months on a road gang in West Virginia and a fine of $7,500.[57]

In an interesting footnote to the entire affair, twelve of the men convicted in the trial were scheduled to leave on the evening train on May 4, 1929, for Fort Leavenworth. According to newspaper reports, a rally of support was held and about a thousand people escorted the prisoners to the train station.[58] They were accompanied by a coronet player from one of the local hotels who serenaded the entire parade and closed with a mournful rendition of "How Dry I Am" as the men boarded the train for prison. To describe the moment as "festive" probably didn't capture the emotion involved but the men laughed and joked with the crowd of supporters and one of them engaged in a long speech from the train window concerning the character and actions of William Hutchison who had provided the state's evidence. Bates made the train on time but had no comment with regard to the send-off or to his conviction. [59]

For years there were unsubstantiated stories being told about Graham's involvement with the investigation.[60] There is no indication that he was involved but there are persistent rumors that when Carroll Bates would not fight, Graham found another way to undermine his bootlegging opposition. Eighteen months on a road gang was hard going but it was better than getting shot by Graham Barnett.

CHAPTER 12

"HE WOULD KILL YOU IN A HOLY SECOND"

1929-1931[1]

When Graham was not bootlegging he worked for his uncle, and any other place he could pick up day work. Some of that work required some skills that were different from the typical stock work. Drilling water wells and installing concrete water tanks required someone with expertise and Graham found a willing worker in Anton Hess. Tony Hess, as he was known in the area, was a tool man, a concrete worker, and pretty good cowboy. He had worked on and off for Graham from as early as 1927. He became not only a friend but an eye witness to the major events of the rest of Graham's life. He was not an average West Texan.

Tony Hess was born August 6, 1904, near Zurich, Switzerland.[2] He completed his education and went on to spend four years as an apprentice in the blacksmithing trade.[3] In the depression that swept Europe after World War I, he could not find a job, so with money borrowed from his uncle he came to the United States in February, 1923.[4] He lived in Cleveland, Ohio, but a combination of the work and homesickness caused him to move again to Goliad, Texas, where he lived with relatives there.

He moved again to Raymondville, Texas, where he began to learn to
be a cowboy; "I got a job on a ranch and I start to learn cowboy [sic],
riding horses, fixing fence, cutting posts."[5] He loved the job, but hated
South Texas. The heat and humidity made life miserable for the Swiss
émigré. Friends told him about West Texas and the mountains around
Alpine. Getting out of the choking humidity and heat of South Texas
was an answer to a prayer, and the chance to work on some of the last
of the large ranches drew Hess westward. "So I come to West Texas,
San Angelo was my first stop. I worked on a ranch maybe eight or ten
months so I could make a hand. Riding, working cattle. I got acquainted
with a fellow, he told me about Alpine and the Big Bend. I always loved
mountains so I got me a horse and a packhorse and I started for Alpine.
I got two or three jobs, day work along the way. I rode into Alpine,
July 1925."[6] He completed the long journey, and went to work on the
Kokernot Ranch. That job led to his meeting a German who was in the
water well drilling business. When the German learned that Anton was
trained as a blacksmith and could dress tools and maintain the equipment,
he offered Hess a job at two dollars a day, more than he was making as
a cowboy. In a couple of years, the German decided to retire, and Anton,
now known as "Tony," bought out the business and went on his own
as well driller.[7] Driller soon expanded to general contracting, and that
job led him to Graham Barnett.

To the 23-year-old well digger, Graham Barnett must have represented
the typical West Texas cowboy. Tony soon found out that the man he
worked with was anything but typical. Graham told the Swiss well digger
about his adventures since Langtry and the killing of Will Babb. After
listening to the tales of the border and adventures in bootlegging and
sheriffing, Hess came to realize that the man he worked with was living
a life completely different from any that Hess could have imagined. He
noted that Graham was a strong family man, loved his wife ("he didn't
flirt"), loved to drink, worked more than one job at a time, and that he
had a pistol close to him at all times.

As their friendship grew, they found that they shared some common goals. They wanted to stay in the Big Bend, continue with their side jobs, and be successful in the ranching business. Graham brought practical experience to the pair, and Hess brought his mechanical expertise combined with the immigrant's desire to succeed. They began to discuss various business ventures from feeding out cattle to gathering horses for the army remount service. There was a problem. All the ventures required money, and that was in short supply for both men. They made great plans, but continued with their regular work. For Hess, that was digging water wells and being a general contractor. For Graham it involved juggling ranch work, a series of jobs with other lawmen, and operating on the edge of being outside the law.

Graham continued to work with Bill Fowler, currently the city marshal in McCamey in Upton County. Just as he and Tony Hess planned for cattle ventures, Fowler and Graham planned for the election of Fowler as sheriff. If the election went as they planned, and Fowler was elected sheriff, Graham expected to be hired as a deputy.[8] Bill Fowler was a man who was amassing a lot of law enforcement experience, and was seen by a number of people as a man who had a future in the business.[9] According to Tony Hess, Graham and Fowler spent a good bit of time discussing how Fowler could win an election for sheriff in Upton County.[10] Fowler would have to run against the current sheriff, John "Bud" Barfield. Bud Barfield had a good deal of support from the county and to defeat him, a man would have to be smart and have a strategy. Barfield might be vulnerable because of a recent shooting that was attracting a good bit of attention across the state. He and two deputies had shot two men suspected of trying to rob the bank. .

The threat of bank robbery had become a problem in Texas. It had grown to the point that the Texas Bankers Association had decided to intervene in what they viewed as an epidemic. The association had promised a five thousand dollar reward for "Dead bank robbers, not one cent for live ones."[11] As a result of the rewards being offered, a number of shootings had taken place, some involving bank robbers, others involving questionable situations near a bank, and one involving an oil scout who had been shot because someone thought he might have robbed a bank.[12] The shootings attracted the attention of Governor Dan Moody who directed Frank Hamer, Captain of Company A, Texas Rangers based in Austin, to look into the situation.

Hamer was not one who would easily side with the bad guys. He was a career officer with a reputation based on surviving gunfights and upholding the law, but there were a number of troubling elements about the current crop of bank-related shootings.[13] Of the four incidents that were to be paid for, three occurred at night with no surviving robbers.[14] In those three, the dead men were transients or vagrants with no previous records as bank robbers. The fourth shooting, at Cisco, involved four known robbers who had experience and long rap sheets. In that situation, one man was killed and three were captured. Because of those circumstances, Hamer was less interested in that shooting. It was the three previous shootings that troubled him. The three all occurred in small towns: Stanton, Odessa, and Rankin and all involved law officers doing the shooting.[15]

Hamer became convinced that the shootings were part of three separate schemes to collect money from an over anxious Banker's Association for dead bank robbers. He believed that someone might be setting up transients, or small town hoodlums, to rob a bank. When they showed up with equipment and bad intentions, they were met by a sheriff and deputies who ended the robbery spree abruptly. The bankers paid the money and the word would go out that it was decidedly unhealthy to rob banks in Texas. Five thousand dollars was a serious amount of money and even divided three or more ways it made a neat payoff for an evening's work. The Rankin shooting fit Hamer's model and he wanted to investigate it further.

In the Rankin shooting, the sheriff had received information that two men were going to break into the bank after hours and rob it. Sheriff

Barfield and two deputies staked out the bank for three nights in January 1928. When two men with welding equipment showed up, they were shot and killed. The Bankers Association proclaimed that this was what they were looking for, and prepared to pay the reward of ten thousand dollars to the three men.

His investigation didn't attract much attention initially. The shootings sounded like good lawmen ridding the world of bad bank robbers. The similarities of the cases, particularly the involvement of transients continued to trouble him. Hamer followed the trail with the determination that made him both feared and famous. When he decided he had found all he could, he made use of a technique that had been used against him in the past: he went to the newspapers.

Throughout the spring of 1928 information flowed to the newspapers, and people began to take notice. Hamer's questioning of the robbery scheme led to the grand jury for Upton County subpoenaing him and a number of other officers to appear and tell what they knew about the potential bank robbery-murder conspiracy.[16] Graham was one of several officers who were subpoenaed.[17] He may have been working as a special officer or investigator at this time, since all of the officers who testified were currently serving in some capacity in the West Texas area, and it is doubtful that the grand jury would subpoena a civilian to provide information in this kind of case.

Hamer and the others testified April 6 and 7, 1928, but his evidence didn't convince the grand jury that anything sinister had taken place. As with grand jury testimony everywhere, the exact nature of the testimony was not revealed; Sheriff Barfield and his deputies were not charged with murder.[18] The evidence presented, oddly enough, was strong enough for the grand jury to indict two other men, J. H. Dumas and Carl Woods.[19] Dumas and Woods were alleged to have set the vagrants up to rob the bank. If there was a connection between them and the sheriff, it was a tenuous one but the grand jury had seen something to make them think an indictment might clear up any questions.[20] Despite the investigation,

Barfield remained a popular sheriff with some of his voters, but at least one citizen decided that his tenure should end. That citizen was Bill Fowler.

While the grand jury might not challenge Sheriff Barfield in the courts, Fowler, who was city marshal in McCamey, decided to challenge him at the voter's booth. Graham supported Fowler in the election because Fowler hinted that if elected, he would find a place for Graham in the sheriff's department. Despite their work, Barfield won in the primary election, but Bill Fowler was not going to walk away. Instead he contested the primary results saying that the Barfield faction had brought in oil field roughnecks to vote illegally, thus packing the ballot boxes.

In August, he filed a writ of mandamus asking Judge Claude Sutton to allow a runoff because of election irregularities. In his request, Fowler contended that there had been "casting of illegal ballots."[21] Fowler was convinced that he had been cheated out of the office that should have been his. Judge Sutton, who by this time must have known most of the gunmen of West Texas by their first name, refused and Barfield coasted to an easy win in November of 1928. Fowler went back to McCamey and chewed on his defeat and swore that next time he would be more ready for a fight.

Secure in the sheriff's office, Barfield decided to ride out the questionable publicity of the shooting and continue with administering law in a quiet county. The county might have been quiet but it was also a bustling center for bootlegging and that made it a target for Graham Barnett. It was only a matter of time before Graham came up against Barfield and Chief Deputy Clarence Shannon

Shannon had a reputation of something of a gunman and had his own method of finding an edge in the fight. He had a habit of wearing a coat with the lining of the pocket cut out so that when he put his hand in his pocket it rested on the grips of his pistol.[22] People who knew this fact were aware that when Clarence Shannon put his hand in his pocket, something was going to happen. That "something" almost happened in the autumn of 1929.

Graham continued to be drawn back to Upton County by the opportunities for bootlegging. The feeling in the county was that there were enough bootleggers operating without adding one more. There were allegations that some of the local bootleggers were members of prominent families in Rankin and they enjoyed protection provided by the current sheriff's department.[23] Undeterred by that, Graham tried to make a deal with Shannon to bring in liquor, but the deputy told him he was out of business. Graham persisted, with the result that he and Shannon had a dispute over his running illegal booze through town.

In a situation strikingly similar to the one in San Angelo with Carroll Bates, Graham met Clarence Shannon on a busy street in Rankin. The two men met and began a conversation that could possibly result in more headlines and a funeral. The discussion got heated and in the middle of the argument, Graham put his hand on his gun and Shannon slipped his hand in his coat pocket for his pistol. Both men froze for a second and then to the surprise of almost all the observers, Graham walked off. For some reason, Graham did not have the edge that he usually needed in a fight. Perhaps it was that Shannon was as ready for a fight as Graham was on this particular day. Years later, Billy Rankin shared an opinion about what had happened. "Barnett turned and walked off and left him because he knew there would be two dead ones [if he had stayed]."[24] For his admirers, walking off from that fight didn't mean Graham was scared, it did mean he had added another name to his list of people he planned to get even with at some point. Rather than seeing Graham as losing face in the fight, Billy Rankin remembered that it had little affect on Graham's reputation. He steadfastly remembered "That Graham was a tough son of a gun. He would kill you in a holy second."[25] Instead of being damaged, the legend of the dangerous gunfighter was enhanced. What they did not know was that Graham might have walked off from that fight, but he had a couple others that he could not walk off from.

It seemed that Graham Barnett, the man, was walking away from fights that Graham Barnett, the legend, never would have. As tough as he was, things were changing for him. First, he was getting older. He was thirty-nine at the time of the Shannon encounter. He had lived a life that was riddled with stress since the killing of Will Babb in 1913. He had had stomach problems since the First World War, and now was also struggling with a smoking problem. He was trying to quit, but when he did, his weight ballooned and to counter that, he would start smoking again. The smoking and weight change had become something that he and Annie talked about, and she worried about.[26] He worried about other things.

He seemed never to have any money. Vern Davis, sheriff in Sterling City, recalled that almost all of the money he had went for lawyers and the expense of a growing family.[27] The family must have worried him the most. How could he take care of them? Expenses were only going to go up. His daughter Maude talked of going to Sul Ross College; if she went the others would have to go also. The cost of raising a family wasn't something you could fund out of the salary of a part-time lawman and itinerant bootlegger.

He must have felt concern for his actions when he drank. Everyone agreed that when he was not drinking he was a pretty even-tempered fellow. When he drank that fellow was replaced with someone who thought of nothing but settling old scores. He loved to drink, but the drinking caused more problems than it solved. The drinking was a habit he could not shake, and perhaps he did not want to.

The drinking magnified another problem. Just as he had a list of people that he planned to get even with, Graham was on a lot of other people's lists as well. He continued to suspect that people intent on killing him were around every corner. He talked with some people, notably Brian Montague. He was convinced that there were attempts on his life. He had lived so close to violence for so long that he saw it everywhere. There were rumors of a bounty on his head in Mexico, whether from years before when he cowboyed there or from something more recent, no one knew, but they talked about it. There were still stories of the bounty put on him by the Babbs and time did nothing to ease that worry. The Babbs didn't forgive and they didn't forget. The stress of living life as both the hunter and the hunted began to tell on him. Vern Davis knew something was going on but couldn't quite pin it down. "After he went so far in life, he was like a keg of powder, you didn't know what would set him off, didn't know what his reaction would be."[28]

There was something more. He had told Annie that his eyes were bothering him. He didn't know what was wrong but he couldn't see like he used to.[29] He never had the problem diagnosed by a doctor but it was an ongoing issue for him. Now when he went out to hunt, shots he could have made easily seemed to elude him. He missed as often as not and no amount of practice seemed to improve that. For a man who seemed to be the embodiment of the West Texas legend, time and age were writing an end to the gunfighter's story. But Graham wasn't ready for that ending yet. He still had plans; he knew people, knew their secrets, and knew their weaknesses. Time might be running short for Graham Barnett the gunfighter, but Graham Barnett the gambler still had a few cards to play.

He worked for Dudley Barker again when the ex-sheriff was investigating cattle thefts in the area. Rustling remained an ongoing problem. The numbers of actual thefts were hard to keep up with, but the losses seemed to drop with Barker and Barnett on the job. While it isn't known if the two actually encountered the rustlers or if their presence led to a temporary slowdown in the business, rustling took a hit with the two on the job. They worked at least one murder case. A prominent member of the Mexican community had turned up missing. His body was found stuffed under a hollowed out river bank. That one was never officially solved.[30]

In December of 1929, Graham was in Austin and received a Special Ranger commission. The exact nature of the work he was doing is not known, but it is significant that the commission had been granted at the request of Judge Sutton, endorsed by Frank Hamer, and sworn in by the adjutant general Robert L. Robertson. The enlistment papers indicate that Graham was sworn in for six months and his address was given as the

Naylor Hotel in San Angelo. He was not assigned to any company. While the enlistment was for six months, it didn't last that long. The warrant was returned to Austin on January 30, 1930, indicating that whatever work he was doing was over in barely a month. Special Rangers worked without compensation from the state, but Graham Barnett did not work without pay. Someone was providing funding. Who that someone was and the nature of the work has been lost. Although he was signed in Austin, giving his address as a hotel in San Angelo indicates that the work would have been done there, but again, no records support this. Speculation is strong that Graham was doing some short term, focused work either for the county or that he was investigating some activities in the area. It is interesting to note that Bill Fowler also received a Special Ranger commission on the same day, at the request of the district attorney for the 112th Judicial District, which included Upton, Sutton, Crockett, Pecos, and Reagan counties.[31] It is tempting to suggest that the two were working on some kind of special investigation, but as of this writing, no hard evidence has emerged.

Whatever he did in San Angelo was over quickly, and Graham began to look for other employment. He heard that the city marshal job was open in Presidio, and decided that it would be a natural fit for him. Despite the fact that it was an area of extreme heat, slow commerce, and was viewed as the end of the world by many people, it seemed to offer promise for Graham. He still had some contacts in the area, and it was on the border, located just across the Rio Grande from Ojinaga, Chihuahua. The legacy of the revolution remained and the area was still a rough one. Bandit activity in Ojinaga had prompted the army to continue to patrol the area, and the cavalry from Camp Marfa wandered along the trails and across the flats until 1928 when the patrols were abandoned. The town had pinned its hopes on the arrival of the railroad, but the anticipated economic boom that would come with its arrival in 1925 was offset by the Depression. By 1930, the small town became the exit point for many Mexicans returning home because of the loss of jobs in the United States due to the Depression. The flow of strangers through the area may have caused concern about general safety for the townspeople, at any rate the town needed more law enforcement than it had, and Graham needed the job.

Graham knew the area well. He had been a bodyguard for P. D. Anderson, the bridge building real estate man.[32] It may have been through Anderson's influence that he was selected for the city marshal job. The offers were made and accepted and Graham took the job, probably in late September or October of 1930. Almost immediately he began to revert to an old pattern of behavior. When he put on the badge, he began to push back against any actual or perceived opposition he found in the town or in the area. A number of stories began to spread about how Graham seemed to be abusing his power again. He seemed to be especially pushy with the Mexican population in the area and, since most of that area was populated by Mexicans, that became a big problem. [33]

While his employment in Presidio would not last very long, the stay did provide for the acquisition of what would become a critical object in the final part of the Graham Barnett legend. Graham decided that he needed more firepower than his trusted 1911 Colt could provide. Perhaps he was inspired by the bank robbing situation he had observed in Rankin, but he decided that he needed something heavier than the 1911 he carried. He knew what he wanted: a Thompson submachine gun. Exactly why he needed a weapon capable of firing 600 rounds in a minute to police a town that was not really overrun with crime is academic. He was on the Border, bandits were supposed to be in the hills, someone had money, and the Thompson was on the market. He had to have one.

While the Thompson had not been especially successful as a military weapon until the late 1920s when it began to be used by the Marine Corps in the Banana Wars, the new era of the automobile and the heavily armed bank robbers left many police and sheriffs needing a little more weaponry than they could carry in their holster. The Thompson seemed to be the answer. Despite a weight of about ten pounds, the gun was easily manipulated in a car or in a house because of its compact size. The barrel was only ten and a half inches long but was made two inches longer with the addition of a Cutts Compensator designed to control recoil in extended fire. It could carry fifty rounds of .45 ACP ammunition in a spring powered, wind up drum fitted under the breech, and was capable of single shots or fully automatic fire when a selector was activated. A new Thompson cost about two hundred dollars with a drum magazine. To put this in some kind of perspective, a new Ford Model A roadster, the entry level vehicle, cost three hundred and eighty-five dollars. A top of the line Ford Fordor would require the prospective owner to lay out five hundred and seventy dollars. The Thompson was a pricy toy. They caught the imagination of the public and the police and served with both criminals and lawmen during the 1920s and 1930s.

While the Thompson is usually associated with the FBI and other urban crime fighters, they were incredibly popular in Texas. Sheriff Val Ennis of Bee County, Texas, mounted one on the hood of his car and rigged it to be fired with a wire.[34] There are no records of the sheriff ever using the rig on a car he was pursuing although one can only imagine the problems encountered on a narrow, bumpy road with a bouncing car and a Thompson submachine gun aimed dead ahead. Sheriff Bill Decker of Dallas County had one, and when he went out at night, assured his wife that she should not worry; "Mr. Thompson" was with him.[35] Ranger Hardy Purvis carried one in the trunk of his car in a fitted case.[36] Captain Will Wright's Ranger Company in South Texas had a pair of them which they used on bootleggers.[37] Graham was in good company with his appreciation of the Thompson.

The Thompson figured prominently in the Graham Barnett legend, but it seems that instead of one, there may have been two of the well-loved weapons in the narrative. One of the guns can be traced fairly simply. Records obtained by the authors show that Graham's gun was purchased through Wolf and Klar Pawn and Jewelry in Fort Worth in October, 1930. Wolf and Klar was a well-known establishment that provided firearms to law enforcement and civilians throughout the Southwest.

Auto Ordinance factory records show that a Thompson, with a ten and a half inch barrel and a Cutts compensator, was shipped to Wolf and Klar in a shipment of one gun for "City Marshall Graham Barnett" on October 17, 1930.[38] Based on the list provided by the FBI, not only county governments purchased the weapons, but some individuals and agencies did also. Since the shipment was made directly to Graham instead of Presidio County Sheriff's Department or some other agency address, this may indicate that the Thompson was a personal purchase. At this period of time individuals could own fully automatic weapons since the National Firearms Act was not passed until June 1934, and thus there was none of the pesky paperwork demanded by later law enforcement regulations. Where he would have gotten the money would be a bigger problem for him. If Graham had purchased or somehow obtained a Thompson in October of 1930, he retained it long enough to carry it and use it briefly before trading it off to a friend. This was the gun that ended up in Rankin a few months later. Although the county requested its return, evidence shows the gun was not turned in at Presidio.

Brian Montague provided another explanation about how Graham got the Thompson and its eventual disposal. "He must have been quite persuasive when he appeared before the commissioners Court of Presidio County... inasmuch as he induced that body to purchase and give him possession of a 'tommy gun.' The court... later regretted what they had done, as evidenced by the fact that several months later, Graham was advised that his services were no longer needed, and his commission as deputy sheriff was revoked, whereupon the court requested graham [sic] to deliver the gun to the sheriff of Presidio County."[39]

It was a good thing that he got the first gun when he did, since the job with the city didn't seem to be working out. At some point the mayor or the city council ran out of patience with him, likely over complaints concerning how he was treating people, both Mexican and Anglo. His job with the city ended, and he was back in the business of picking up jobs where he could find them. Apparently Graham traded the original

Thompson off and by the spring of 1931 had another, this one apparently acquired in El Paso.

In March of 1931 he had a second Thompson, or access to one, when he was acting as a bodyguard for P. D. Anderson and working for the Highland Hereford Association, a cattleman's organization. Based on newspaper reports he must have had a disagreement with some people in town and he showed up with the Thompson. "According to reports from Presidio, Graham Barnett entered the Oly Flyer Café. 'Just to show you I mean business, watch this,' Presidio citizens quoted Graham Barnett as saying. He fired several shots and a dog across the street howled as the bullets struck him in the hind quarters."[40] The café clientele "waited for no more demonstrations" and Graham, secure that he had made believers of them, wandered off.[41] The newspaper accounts do not identify him as "city marshal," which indicates that he was no longer in that office at that time. However, he was identified as a bodyguard for Anderson in the story. Firing off the occasional burst of full automatic fire in front of a café could have only made the employment situation worse for Graham, but he was getting a name for making the wrong decisions at the wrong time anyway.

The story of the second gun turned out to be a bit more convoluted than the first. In March of 1931, Harry Barnett, owner of Barnett Loan and Jewelry Company of El Paso, wrote the mayor of Presidio to inform him that Graham Barnett and P. D. Anderson had purchased a Thompson from him the previous year for the price of $206 and he had not been paid. The two had purchased the gun and told the pawnshop owner that he would be paid "when the spring taxes were paid."[42] The mayor responded that the city had not purchased any submachine gun, and that Graham was not city marshall.[43] While it is only conjecture, it seems that the pair may have decided they needed at least one more gun and went to El Paso and purchased one using an involved, but dubious method of payment. Since pawnbrokers rarely allow guns to leave the premises without some kind of money exchange or a note being signed, how the transfer was accomplished remains in question. The matter eventually went to the grand jury in August to determine exactly what had happened but apparently no indictments were handed down.[44] Who finally paid for the gun is a mystery. There were no follow up stories in the newspapers. It is likely that the El Paso gun had remained in Presidio and was picked up by the irate pawnbroker Harry Barnett.

What happened to the Wolf and Klar gun was much simpler. It ended up in the possession of Bill Fowler. Graham and Bill Fowler both admired good firearms and Fowler had been bitten by the Thompson bug as well. Graham and Fowler made a deal and Fowler bought the gun. Joel Starnes, assistant county clerk and friend of Bill Fowler, claimed that he had written Graham a check for payment of the gun.[45] If it was paid for with county funds as Starnes stated, the transfer would have taken place after January 1931 when Fowler took over as county sheriff.[46] At any rate, the Thompson moved to Rankin with Bill Fowler. It is possible that Graham sold the gun to Fowler and paid Presidio County the $206.00 owed for the second gun, but that is conjecture. What was clear was that Bill Fowler became the owner of a Thompson submachine gun that had been owned by Graham Barnett. That transaction was one of the last of the friendly deals between the two of them. With the gun in Fowler's possession, the end of the Graham Barnett story was being constructed. The penultimate piece involved the destruction of the friendship of the two men.

The two were still working closely enough that when Bill Fowler was ready to run for sheriff again in the fall of 1930, Graham was ready to help him. Graham told Tony Hess that this time he had a plan. If election fraud worked for one side, it just might work for the other. Apparently Graham and Fowler decided to engage in one of the oldest and most dearly loved of Texas political schemes: rigging an election. Years later Tony Hess explained, "Since nobody but me knows, I let you in on a secret: Graham told me he put Fowler in office. When election was held he went over to Crane and hauled carload of [roughnecks] to McCamey to vote for Fowler. Fowler promised him a position if he won the election. But after he backed out."[47]

Fowler won the election and with a new sheriff in town, Upton County began to look to the future. Graham Barnett began to look to the future also, but if the story Tony Hess told was correct, Bill Fowler didn't hold up his end of the deal. Graham had planned on getting back into the law enforcement business, but that wasn't going to happen. Whether the election was rigged or not made no difference now, Fowler was sheriff and Graham was not going to be the deputy. In retrospect, not hiring Graham showed remarkably good judgment on the part of the new sheriff.

Fowler probably made his decision based on the increasingly erratic behavior he was seeing with Graham. The incidents in Presidio and in a later fight in Fort Stockton must have caused Fowler to decide to back off from his decision to hire Graham. If he was brought in as chief deputy and began the aggressive behavior he had shown before, Fowler would be forced to confront him and that would create a huge problem for both of them. What is certain is that what had begun as a friendship between the two men had begun to slowly turn to a relationship of fear and hatred. Graham did not forget that he had been promised a job, and that it had not developed. The friendship between the two men began to unravel, and it finally came unwound in a violent encounter between the two.

The exact date for the problem is difficult to nail down. It was after November 1930 when the election took place and before January 1931 when Bill Fowler would take office in Rankin. Graham was working on the Elsinore Cattle and Land Company ranch south of Fort Stockton, probably as a guard in the newly developing oil field.[48] Both Bill Fowler and Graham were involved along with two other men who may have had a misunderstanding to begin with.

Mack Adams had cowboyed all over West Texas and in 1915 had become superintendent of the 329-section Elsinore Land and Cattle Company.[49] Adams was also chief deputy for Joe Bunton, sheriff of Presidio County. It seems likely that Adams gave Graham the job on the Elsinore after the debacle in Presidio. It was a dual role, guard for the oil field and guard for Mack Adams who had some difficulties with people in the business. Boog Barnett recalled that "he was body guarding Mack Adams at the time."[50] Part of the Graham Barnett method of body guarding was not just providing protection but taking an active role in eliminating the opposition. In this case part of the opposition was a relatively mild mannered man named Raymond McKay.

McKay was the grandson of Annie Riggs who was a well-known pioneer woman in the area. He was a rodeo promoter although, at this time, he operated a filling station in Fort Stockton.[51] McKay and the following incident was the spark that ignited the feud between Graham and Bill Fowler. Exactly why Fowler and Graham went to see Raymond McKay isn't clear, except that there was some kind of difficulty between Mack Adams and a number of people working on the oil lease or on the ranch. Perhaps Graham had decided that the problems could be fixed by a preemptive strike instead of waiting for something to happen.

Accompanied by Bill Fowler, Graham walked into the Rooney Hotel in Fort Stockton and located McKay's room. Without a lot of preliminaries, Graham walked into the room, grabbed McKay around the neck, pulled his pistol from under his coat, and began to pound McKay in the side with it. McKay was taken by surprise and was unable to make much of a defense. Graham established why he was there by yelling, "I'm doing Mack Adams fighting."[52] The fight was short and brutal enough that Fowler, who had been watching from the hall, came into the room and pulled Graham away from the stunned McKay.

Graham was furious at being interrupted. He had come to fight McKay, but now he would fight Fowler. He swung at Fowler and the scuffle in the room exploded into a full-fledged fight in the hall. The two were swinging, connecting, and slamming into walls. The noise drew other men out of their rooms and the two were eventually separated, but Graham was still in his fighting mood. He was wide eyed with fury; he cussed Fowler and told him he would kill him. Fowler tried to calm

Graham down, but it did no good. Graham swore and shouted that he would kill Fowler, that he would fight him, and give him the first three shots. There was no doubt in the minds of the men who witnessed the fight that Graham was serious with his threats.[53]

The relationship between the two men was changed completely after the incident. Before the fight, they had worked together, drank together in Mexico, and had shared the kind of fear and excitement that came from taking down a bootlegger. Now things had changed and nothing was the same any more. Old friendships were forgotten and old secrets were no longer kept.

The anger that Graham exhibited in Fort Stockton resulted in another name being added to the long list of people that Graham was going to get even with. While he might have wanted to kill Fowler, Graham had another reason to keep him alive. The one big secret that tied the men together concerned the alleged fixing of the election.

Graham may have made this point to Bill Fowler between January of 1930 when Fowler took office and December 7, 1931. Graham made several trips to Rankin and on at least two occasions he received money from Fowler to leave town.[54] While testimony at the later trial explained the money was given to encourage him to leave the county, had Graham's ongoing financial problems that had existed for years finally caught up to him? Or was it something more sinister? Was he now blackmailing his old comrade?

Brian Montague believed that both men were still involved in bootlegging. "I do not know whether, as many suspected, Bill afforded Graham protection in bootlegging, or other activities, or that it was nothing more than a renewal of an acquaintance made years previously."[55] Whether the money was payoff for threats or loans to a friend, it is impossible to say. The difference was very thin. The money did buy him some time to make plans, to determine what he would do next.

Typically, after the problems he had been dealing with, Graham retreated back into the Big Bend. He split his time between the small ranch the family called the Wade Place and Alpine. The family stayed in Alpine during the school year so the older children could go to school. In Alpine, they lived in a house they referred to as the Rock House because it was one of the few made of stone. In the summer the family moved to the Big Bend and spent their time at the Wade Place. It seemed like an adventure out of *The Swiss Family Robinson*. The house had no glass in the windows and food was kept cool by placing it in the creek. The kids could ride horses and Conger, known as Bill, the youngest, got lost one day. He had been told to ride around the corral but strayed off, and never forgot the joy of seeing his father walking out to find him and leading him back to the house.[56] If Graham said anything to the boy, Bill didn't remember it. He just remembered the joy he felt when he saw his father coming to rescue him. Graham was still a hero to the family.

Graham kept up his practice with the .45, shooting at birds in the air to the astonishment of the family. Some he hit, some he missed. There were five children now, Maude, the eldest who took after her dad in her ability to shoot, Joe Junior (known as Bud), Conger (known as Billy), Jerry, and Mary Anne.[57] They were a tight group. They spent as much time together as they could. At the end of the summer the family headed back to Alpine and a return to school. Graham stayed in the Big Bend. He was taking care of a ranch for a doctor who lived in Wingate, and he and Tony Hess had returned to their planning. He concentrated on plans for the future and plans for the family.

Illustration 11. Rock House in Alpine where Ann and Jerry were born.

(Courtesy John T. Barnett)

CHAPTER 13

"I WASN'T SURPRISED WHEN THEY TOLD ME"

RANKIN, TEXAS, DECEMBER 7, 1931[1]

Having a plan was one thing; having a plan that would work was another. The planning still bounced between feeding out cattle, and capturing horses in the Big Bend and selling them as remounts to the army. Both deals promised some profits in exchange for a great deal of hard work. The plan hinged on one factor: they needed money to get started. Graham began to slowly develop a scheme to get enough cash together to push the two of them over the line from cowboy to cowman.

Graham continued to work at whatever he could find to do, and he juggled several jobs at a time. He continued to live on the Rosillos Ranch and he and Hess started a small cow camp a few miles away at Dripping Springs.[2] They gathered horses and broke them at that camp. He managed ranches for people, although at times his reputation created a problem for him. When Jack Mosley and his wife moved onto a place near a ranch Graham was taking care of, Mosley was warned by other neighbors that Graham was "an outlaw" and he needed to be careful. A short time after that Graham showed up to visit his new neighbor. Graham asked for a drink of water. Mosley showed him the well and they talked for a while. Mosley and his wife got along well with Graham but Mosley couldn't get the outlaw comment out of his head. The man might be a neighbor, but he was still an outlaw.[3]

Graham began to go back to his old job of troubleshooter for people who faced some uncomfortable personal situations. The jobs he was getting were a little different now, fewer jobs with cattlemen's associations, more with individuals. It was his reputation that seemed to be carrying him. Brian Montague followed the career change as best he could from a distance. "Judge Cornell told me he had reason to believe that Graham had become a hired killer but no details were stated and I made no inquiry concerning this statement."[4] The stories of Graham being a hired killer had existed for years but no one had ever taken anything to a grand jury. While the lack of evidence doesn't prove he was innocent, neither does it prove that he was guilty. The people who might have hired him knew that the mark of a good contract man is that he does his job, doesn't leave loose ends, and doesn't talk about his work. Someone who did talk about his work was Det Walker.

Walker was a Big Bend rancher who was involved in a feud with the Francisco Villalba family. Walker claimed that he wanted Graham to protect him from the eldest son, Jacobo, who was well-known throughout the area as a man who was not to be trifled with. Villalba and Walker had feuded for months and the two were obviously on a collision course. When Jacobo Villalba confronted Walker at Walker's house November 19, 1931, he was shot to death. Det Walker and a friend claimed they shot him, but that he had drawn first and is was a case of self-defense. E. E. Townsend was sheriff, and after taking the confession he waited for the grand jury to meet to decide on an indictment. A few weeks later, Walker changed his story. He had been willing to plead self-defense in November, but after Graham was killed in Rankin a few weeks later, he apparently decided that he could play a different card. Walker recanted his confession, and swore that Graham had done the killing.[5] No proof ever emerged that Graham had done anything except provide some bodyguarding for Walker.[6] The grand jury decided not to indict Walker, but the incident shows that Graham's reputation as a man killer was still strong enough that people believed he might have done it, even without proof. The bodyguarding job with Det Walker was the last documented job of that sort that Graham took.

He scrambled for other jobs and his reputation was strong enough to attract all kinds of attention. People still wanted to hunt with Graham Barnett. Near the end of November, he guided a deer hunt for three men who wanted to hunt in the Big Bend. The four rattled off into the desert in an old work truck, and probably another vehicle, and accounted for at least four deer. One of the men brought a camera, and his handiwork froze a moment in Graham's life. The photographic evidence provides a stark contrast between Graham and his more affluent clients.

Two of the hunters and Graham stood behind the truck while the third snapped the usual trophy shot. The hunters are well turned out in engineer boots, jodhpurs, and short jackets that reflect that they have good income and know how to spend it. Their hats look like something that would have been seen in *Outdoor Life* magazine; they are the field version of a trendy fedora. They are displaying an 1895 Winchester and an army surplus .30-40 Krag rifle, both good choices for deer hunting. Graham is wearing what looks like bleached, baggy khaki pants, a non-descript shirt, and what must have been his second-best boots. His hat is creased fore and aft and battered by wind and by its use to fan campfire coals into flame. He holds his custom Springfield .30-'06, a trusted friend on more than one trip in the desert. There were not many problems that could not be solved with a .30-'06. He had a cigarette cupped in his hand and at the moment the camera clicked something had drawn his attention off to his right. The picture was the last taken of him.

Illustration 12. Graham guiding a hunt, November 1931

(Courtesy Russell M. Drake)

While he was protecting Det Walker and guiding, Graham and Tony Hess began to move slowly toward their goal of becoming well off. They decided to start with collecting and breaking horses for the Army Remount Service. Hess recalled, "We rode together, running wild horses down here in the Big Bend. I worked for him breaking horses. We had a camp at Willow Springs up until the time Barnett was killed."[7] The work during the day was slow and hard. The evenings that were spent in the camp left little to do but drink and talk. Tony Hess began to learn some secrets about the man he was partnered with. On some occasions, the drinking was enough that Graham began to review his life, and instead of a furious outburst, Hess observed the gunfighter crying. Hess thought that he had regrets over the kind of life he had led, and when he drank the regrets came back to sit with him. "We spent the nights alone in camp. He would start drinking and then he would start talking about his life, which was a sad story. He went to crying many times. Maybe it was his conscience bothering him; he said people made him what he was."[8] Hess never confirmed exactly what part of Graham's life was the "sad life" part of the story. All he knew was that Graham looked back over his life through an alcohol fog and regretted some of the things he had done.

He may have come to regret being the man who fixed things for other people. He never named the people who he thought had driven him into depression. But at night when he drank those people were there, along with the men he had killed, and he could not get away from their images. It seems that the past was catching up with Graham Barnett, but he was still focused on the future.

The planning continued with Graham and Hess, and they began to expand their thinking on what they should do. The horse business might be a starter, but both men knew the cattle business, and it seemed to be a natural fit for them. According to Tony Hess, they planned a cattle feeder business.[9] It was the same model that Joe Graham had used for years. Graham had seen it work for his uncle; now he decided that it would work for him. Again, the odds seemed to be against him. The cattle business was getting ready to suffer another of its famous declines in 1930. Despite the recent rains, the weather was also turning against the ranching business with a prolonged drought coming up. Not knowing any of this, Graham pressed on.

His usual source of funds and support was his uncle, Joe Graham, but there is no indication that Graham approached him for money. Joe was having problems of his own and couldn't help this time. Any sort of loan was going to be hard to get. 1930 was not a good time to go into the horse and cattle business, but with the enthusiasm that came from desperation, Graham continued with his search for funds. He decided that he would do what he had done before and turn to the people that he knew. He had worked with bankers, with law enforcement, and with people who had any number of jobs. Perhaps his friends would be good for a loan. He reasoned that he knew people, he had done things for people, and now it was time for them to do something for him. If he couldn't borrow the money from family, he would get it from people he knew. This aspect of the plan had a down side: the Depression had finally come to Texas and everyone seemed to be struggling with finances.

Davis Hinson, who was a banker in Alpine, had lent him money before, not so much out of a desire to help an old friend, but more out of concern about what would happen if he didn't.[10] This time, even fear could not push Hinson into a loan; he recalled later that he just didn't have the money. His wife, who worked for the telephone company, did have some money put back and she agreed to invest in the cattle project. "I told her she could depend on what Barnett said and that he would pay her back when he said he would."[11] While he was putting that deal together he put a few other people's names on the list to ask for help.

A number of the sheriffs he had worked with were still in office. They had held onto their jobs and jobs meant money; he would visit several of them in an effort to find some investment funds. It isn't clear if he was going to ask for the funds based on friendship or on some kind of veiled threat. He did have a special plan for Bill Fowler. He was confident that Fowler would be good for some money. In addition to being the sheriff, Bill Fowler ran a cow and calf feeding operation and he was getting money off a small oil royalty.[12] He wasn't rich, but in the eyes of a man who was getting ready to chase wild horses in the Big Bend, he had enough disposable income that he could separate from some of it. If Fowler would not do it voluntarily, he might react to a little pressure.

Graham had a plan to motivate Fowler into giving him a loan. If the money wasn't forth coming, he could revert to some of the intimidation tactics he had used in the past. This time instead of the threat of a gunfight, it was the threat of disclosure. Graham believed that he had at least two incidents he could use to hold over Fowler's head. One of them was the rigging of the sheriff's election. Tony Hess had heard the stories enough that he believed them. "Graham told me he put Fowler in office. When the election was held he went over to Crane and hauled a carload of [roughneck] oil field workers to McCamey to vote for Fowler. Fowler promised him a position if he won the election, but after he backed out. So

Graham decided he owed him something."[13] What Graham decided was
that Bill Fowler owed him a stake to get started in a new business. There
was no way to prove it or to disprove the election story. It had become
part of the Barnett legend. It had been told and told often enough that it
had an aura of truth to it. Irregularities had been alleged in the previous
election and it seemed that the only thing normal about the elections
were that anything could happen. Graham was ready to go beyond the
election fraud issue. He had more information. Graham was convinced
that Fowler was shaking down criminals and he thought he could prove it.

Graham told Hess that "he collected all the evidence he could get from
places that paid Fowler to stay in business. Like gambling, bootleggers,
fancy houses every mont [*sic*]. He got cancelled checks and promises
to help him."[14] There was no question that Graham intended to use the
information to get money or get Bill Fowler out of the sheriff's office.
"Graham never say [*sic*] he was going to kill Fowler, he said he going to
put him in the penitentiary."[15] Despite what Hess maintained, the idea of
someone giving the county sheriff a check to protect an illegal business
seems a little far-fetched, but according to Hess, checks were included
among the proof of the payoffs.

On at least two occasions Fowler had given Graham money to get out
of the county and "to avoid trouble."[16] Maybe he would be good for one
more loan to balance out the election help he had received, and to avoid
any trouble that might come out of an embarrassing and illegal allegation
that he was on the take from the local bootleggers and madams. In their
talks around the fire at night in the Big Bend, the story came back again
and again, Graham put Fowler in the job, and he could take him out of it.
The story would remain in Tony Hess's memory for the rest of his life.
Like a number of Graham's plans it had the advantage of being simple
and, if it worked, it promised a big payoff. In response to the threat that
might undo a career, Graham would offer to make a deal: silence for a
certain sum of money. Fowler had given him money before, perhaps it had
been the same sort of threat, but this time there was more proof behind

it. It was a plan that was born out of desperation. The cattle business was waiting, there were horses to be caught, and he needed the cash.

On the way to Rankin he planned to visit with several sheriffs he had worked for, and backed up in tense situations. He was confident that they would remember what he had done, and they might come up with some investment money for the cattle operation. If he had information on some of the other sheriffs he was going to visit, and planned to use it, Tony Hess didn't say. Vern Davis believed that Graham had bought off several sheriffs in connection with his bootlegging.[17] Perhaps a hint to them that somehow that information was going to be out in the open might help them to invest in the cattle and horse business. Graham was ready for a new life and he had to have the money to make the move.

Another source for funds was his brother-in-law, Joe Conger. Joe was Annie's brother and was an agent for an oil company. He was married with two children and had a good enough job that allowed him to have a live in maid to assist with the housekeeping. That kind of an arrangement indicated that Joe might have some discretionary funds that Graham could access. While Joe might not be able to invest, the Conger house might provide a central location if he needed to be out of sight for a while. Tony Hess never mentioned that Joe Conger was a potential donor, but Graham spent time at Joe's house twice during the short trip.

If anything drove him at this point, it very well could have been desperation. While he was worried about money, he was also worried about his past catching up to his present. It was a story he had lived with for years, and it was one that kept him looking over his shoulder. He swore people were trying to kill him, and as often as not, he tied the anonymous attempts to either the Babb family or people in Mexico that he had gotten crosswise with over the years. He told Tony about the attempt to poison him one time in San Angelo, and other attempts that were no more successful than that had been.[18] If he ever named anyone other than the Babbs who wanted him dead, no one remembered. What people did remember was the Graham was serious about someone wanting to kill him. Now that he was older, the fear made him exercise a little more caution than he had in the past. That caution seemed to disappear when he drank, and he was drinking more than before.

Brian Montague had a memorable meeting with him late in September of 1931. Montague had tried a case and decided to spend the night in Fort Stockton at the Marmon Hotel. At about eight o'clock, a knock at the door interrupted his evening. When he opened it, he found Graham standing in the hall. The two old friends spent the next four hours revisiting what had happened in each other's life over the past ten years. After the talk had run out, Brian asked Graham where he was going to spend the night. Montague offered to have a cot pulled into the room, but Graham's response must have shaken Montague. "You think I want you killed? If those S.O.B.'s find out I'm here they'd kill both of us for certain."[19] Montague must have been somewhat alarmed by that response, and he asked Graham where he would stay for the rest of the night. "Down yonder in that mesquite *vega*. The last time I stayed there I made a mistake and slept under my car as they shot it up; tonight I'll fool 'em for I'll take my bed roll about thirty feet away from the car, and if those birds try to kill me, I'll be able to get every one of them."[20]

If Montague knew who the potential assassins were, he didn't include it in his memoirs, but he did have a parting exchange with his old friend. "'Graham, that's a hell of a way to have to live. Why don't you get out of the country and start somewhere else?' He smiled and shook his head and that was the last time I saw him."[21] Clearly, the cost of being a legend was beginning to take a toll on the man.

Graham stayed busy during October and November of 1931. He guided hunts, and spent time between ranching and chasing horses in the Big Bend with trips to Alpine as often as he could manage. He also collected information. Finally, by the beginning of December 1931, he believed he had all the communications he needed on Fowler and, perhaps, others as well. He was ready to try to talk to his old friends again about money.

Graham and Tony Hess left the Dripping Springs area of the Big Bend early on December 2, 1931. Graham took his stock of evidence with him. Just in case they might need some support on the trip, Graham loaded up the trunk of the car with everything he thought he might need: a sawed off shotgun with six rounds of buckshot, two Winchesters in .30-40 Krag, a couple of decks of cards, and he tossed in a bottle of iodine. A man couldn't tell when he might need some iodine. Graham stuffed his ever-present .45 into the waistband of his pants on the left side and pulled his leather jacket on over it. Because of the warm weather he probably didn't button the coat. Because of the way he wore the pistol, concealment was an important thing. If the coat was buttoned, Graham couldn't draw the pistol. That hadn't been a problem. Graham had always been able to read a situation and prepare himself for the fight or at least begin his intimidation to distract his opponent long enough for him to get his coat undone. Once in the car, he laid the pistol either on the floorboard or in the seat. Graham was as prepared as he had ever been. If Hess was armed, he never mentioned it in later interviews.

Hess drove Graham's black Model A Ford. The road that took them out of the area was familiar. It had been graded but still dusty and rough and the condition of it slowed their drive. Graham was in a good mood, and as they drove along the highway, he rolled up a Bull Durham cigarette from time to time while he began to playfully blast away at the insulators on the telephone poles with the .45.[22] Hess had a good feeling about the trip. It seemed that everything was going to go according to plan, and this might be the first step in a bigger play. Tony navigated them to Alpine where they spent the night with Annie and the kids at the Rock House.

Graham didn't tell Annie much about the trip other than that he was going to see Bill Fowler about some money Fowler owed him. If he said anything about the specifics of the trip, she didn't mention it in later interviews. What she did remember was that Graham was distracted. He seemed distant and to Annie Laura he was more like a visitor in the house rather than her husband.[23] The next morning everyone went about their business with Tony and Graham heading for Rankin.

Somewhere on the road they picked up Romeo Shivley, probably in Alpine. Tony Hess never mentioned him as being with them on the drive out of the Big Bend. Shivley was one of the mysterious characters who lived on the edge of Graham Barnett's world. What he did for a living, where he lived, and where he went after Rankin is a mystery. Even his name was a mystery. It was given variously in later newspaper accounts as Romeo Shively, Rhome Shivers, or Romo Chaves.[24] Tony Hess remembered him years later; "He was Anglo...He was a tall, slender person. No question he was an American."[25] Shivley was around the area enough that Hess knew him and did not like him. "I think he was a pimp. He know [sic] all the shady places around the country. He was an Englo [sic]. He kept Graham informed so Graham know what was going on."[26] If, as Hess believed, Shivley was a criminal and an informant, he could possibly have been the source of information that Graham was planning to use against Bill Fowler. While Hess made no comment about Graham having information on other sheriffs in the area, the presence of Shively may have indicated that the two planned shakedowns on other lawmen in the area.

When they left Alpine, they drove the hundred or so miles to Fort Stockton and then north to Crain. Bud Blair was sheriff of Crane County. Blair was new to the sheriff business but he was an older friend of Graham's. Blair recalled later that Graham asked him for a loan, which Blair later claimed he refused. If there was any animosity felt between the two, Blair didn't mention it, and apparently Graham said nothing to Tony Hess about it. [27]

Illustration 13. The courthouse and jail in Rankin, Texas, circa 1930

(Photo used with permission of Rankin Museum, Rankin, Texas)

On December 3, they rolled into Rankin and headed for the sheriff's office in the courthouse. The courthouse was a two-story brick building that had been built in 1926 in the modern style that characterized Texas courthouses built in the early twentieth century. A series of eighteen windows paraded across the front of the building and a series of steps led up to an arched double door. The jail was a squatty, two-story building next door with a narrow covered portico that sheltered the front door. The sheriff's office was on the first floor of the courthouse. The three visitors found that Fowler was not in the office, but the assistant county clerk and sometime jailer, Joel Starnes, was. Starnes knew Graham from previous visits, and he may have decided he had a responsibility to act as a buffer between the two men.

Graham made it clear that this wasn't merely a social call. "Where's ole Bill?" he asked.[28] Starnes said that he was out of the office, perhaps in McCamey. In Texas in the fall there were only three things to talk about: football (McCamey had beaten Marfa, 32-14), rain fall (17 inches in Midland), and the deer season. Graham and Starnes talked about hunting. Perhaps recalling his recent hunt, Graham told him that there were still some good sized bucks in the Big Bend, and invited Starnes out to hunt. Starnes said he would think about it. Despite the small talk, time started to drag, and Graham began to nervously wander around the office. He strode by the sheriff's desk and absently opened one of the desk drawers and found a box of .45 shells. Perhaps thinking about the ammo he had shot up on the drive from the Big Bend, or in an attempt to show he was in charge of the situation, he picked up the box and dropped it into his coat pocket. When it became clear that Fowler wasn't coming into the office, the three left.[29]

For years, part of the Graham Barnett legend involved the quirky story that he had gone to Rankin to get money for the Thompson submachine gun now owned by Fowler. It made a great story but there is little evidence that it was true. If Graham discussed the supposedly disputed ownership of the Thompson, Starnes never mentioned it in his later interviews other than to say that it had been paid for by the county.[30] It is significant that the only thing that Starnes recalled later about the Thompson was that Fowler had it, not that Graham had asked about it, or mentioned money in connection with it. No mention of the gun was made by any of the witnesses other than Joel Starnes, who stated that he had written a check for the gun. The lone survivor, Tony Hess, never mentioned the gun in any of his letters or correspondence with Russell Drake or when Drake was interviewing him. The absence of this information would seem to support Tony Hess's story that they had gone to Rankin to lean on Fowler about the election, not settle a gun trade. The simplest explanation is sometimes the best, and it appears that no one discussed the gun trade because it wasn't a factor in the attempted extortion.

The morning of December 4, Graham decided to visit the sheriff again. He headed for the Fowler house alone. Mrs. Fowler was cooking breakfast when he knocked on the door. When she answered Graham asked her,

"Where is Bill Fowler?" Fowler had elected to sleep late that morning and was still in bed. She knew Graham from earlier times and she answered that she didn't know where her husband was or when he would be back. The two talked casually for a few minutes, but she noticed the .45 in his belt, with the hammer cocked. She also noticed that he kept his left hand in his pocket, apparently ready to shift the pistol into action. "Tell Fowler that I was here looking for him and that I'll be back,"[31] he said, and then added, "When you see your boss, tell him you might have a new boss. I might just take over."[32] It isn't clear if he meant that as a threat, but Mrs. Fowler took it as one. She went to wake up her husband.

The idea of "taking over the town" was mentioned not only in the conversation with Mrs. Fowler but also by Joel Starnes. Starnes said later that "[Graham] got drunk, got mad and decided to take the town over."[33] What he actually meant by this is open to speculation. Perhaps Graham began to see himself controlling vice and bootlegging in the county, or he might have had something else in mind. There were a number of towns in the oil country of West Texas that were more or less controlled by a syndicate of crime bosses. Best, the neighboring town from Texon, was one and the infamous Borger in the panhandle was another. Small towns in the middle of an oil boom had a way of getting out of hand when they were taken over by outside elements.

Graham must have begun to believe that the trip was not going to work out like he had planned. To begin with, Fowler appeared to be ignoring him. It's hard to threaten someone who won't talk to you. Grasping at straws, he, Tony Hess, and Shively drove to Big Lake and dropped by the office of Ellison Carroll. The world champion steer roper had become sheriff in 1931. Graham had known Ellison for 20 years and he hoped to turn that friendship into some cash, but Carroll refused or was unable to provide any funds for the ranching venture. After they left the sheriff's office, they uncorked a bottle of liquor, and Graham began to drink.[34]

By about 4:00 p.m. they were back in Rankin. W. D. Riser, the former Big Lake newspaper editor and justice of the peace during the Noisy

Watson affair, was in the sheriff's office.[35] He had moved to Rankin and taken the job as tax assessor and worked closely with Bill Fowler. Graham came into the office, and when he asked if Bill Fowler was in, it became obvious that he had been drinking. Fowler, who was in his office, came out, and they spoke to one another. Graham asked if they could meet privately. Fowler said, "Let's get out of here," and they went upstairs to one of the courtrooms.[36]

What was said and who said it is unknown. Presumably, Graham made his pitch: Fowler had been taking money from the bootleggers and madams of the area and Graham had the proof. Whatever threats were made, whatever proof was offered, it apparently wasn't enough for Fowler.

Fowler had been down this trail before with Graham. Twice that year, he had asked Fowler for money and had gotten it.[37] This time something was different. This time there was no money forthcoming, and for some reason Fowler wasn't too concerned about the nature of the proof Graham had. Perhaps he was tired of the shake down, perhaps he didn't think anyone would believe the nature of the evidence that Graham had. Maybe he didn't think anyone would care. This was West Texas. There was a cost to doing all kinds of business, and payoffs to the local law were not a new thing. Whatever reason it was that Bill Fowler refused to give Graham any more money was the secret of the two men in the room, and that secret was never made public. Fowler told Joel Starnes that Graham had asked for a loan of a thousand or two thousand dollars, but he hadn't given it to him because he knew he wouldn't get the money back.[38] One thing was sure, Bill Fowler was not coughing up any money, and things were beginning to look very bad for Graham Barnett.

The discussion lasted longer than W. D. Riser thought it should. Although he didn't hear raised voices, he was concerned about leaving the two men alone in the courtroom. He went upstairs, knocked at the door, peered in, and asked Fowler a question that required the sheriff to come back downstairs. He noticed that the sheriff was pale, showing signs that something was terribly wrong. Graham was red-faced and visibly angry. Downstairs, Riser asked Fowler what the trouble was and Fowler, still with a strained look on his face, said, "I am afraid I am going to have trouble with Barnett."[39] Riser recalled the look on Graham's face moments before, and he remembered seeing Graham in Big Lake and thought of the Noisy Watson shooting. It probably wasn't the best time to tell Fowler, but Riser said that he had seen Graham in this kind of mood before, and it wasn't a good one.[40] If Fowler and Graham had any other words, they weren't recorded. Graham left the courthouse wearing "the killer look" that Riser remembered from Big Lake. Both the sheriff and the former newspaper editor knew the situation was far from over.[41]

Graham, Tony Hess, and Romeo Shively piled in the car. Someone suggested that they find a place to spend the night, and they drove the nineteen miles to McCamey. Once there, they checked into the Bender Hotel.[42] Small town people tend to notice strangers, and in this case either the behavior of the three or the celebrity that followed Graham caused a lot of people to pay attention. Graham was especially loud, rambling on about Bill Fowler and the plans he had for him. E. A. Grattis, one of the porters, overheard Graham ranting about Fowler and heard him say that he would bet fifty dollars that he would kill Fowler before nightfall.[43] The threat worked its way across the county. Grattis reported it to C. C. Gerding, the hotel owner, who got on the telephone and called the chief of police, Fred Senter, and informed him of the threat. Senter called Bill Fowler and told him.[44] Since Graham had been drinking earlier, Fowler had no reason to believe that he would have stopped now. Probably thinking that if left alone, Graham would drink himself out of one of his moods, Fowler elected not to do anything. He told Senter he would be over on Saturday morning and look into the situation. If Graham was in one of his killing moods, approaching him on Friday night when he was armed with his .45 and a bottle of booze didn't seem like a wise choice. Fowler reasoned that most people in McCamey would leave Graham alone, and after supper and a couple more rounds with the bottle, Graham would go back to the hotel, and that would end the crisis.

The evening didn't end as quickly as it should have. Graham and Tony Hess went out to eat and the café manager, Tom Bargasar, overheard part of the conversation. He testified later that Graham had said that he had been trying to get a loan from Fowler: "Bill refused me and I'll give him until 4 o'clock Saturday or I'll put him in a black box."[45] His comments were loud enough that it wasn't only Bargasar who heard him; several others in the café heard the threat as well. By the time the trio had decided it was time to end the evening, word of the threats had spread across town.

Saturday morning, Bill Fowler drove to McCamey, but neither he nor Graham saw each other. Fowler talked with Bargasar and Chief Senter, but he didn't seem to take the situation very seriously. He had seen Graham work himself up into his fighting moods before, and he knew that time was his friend in this situation. Given enough time, Graham would cool down. Fowler talked to as many witnesses as he could find concerning comments made the previous night, and then drove out of town to look at a place he was considering to lease to graze cattle. Fowler checked the lease and drove back to Rankin.[46]

Where Graham and his friends spent the day isn't clear. At some point the three made their way back to Rankin. Graham might have taken this time to call on Joe Conger, his brother-in-law, to see if he could find some investment money. What happened between the two is unknown, but since Graham didn't mention any money to Tony, Joe Conger probably turned him down. What is clear is that as night began to fall, and the wind turned colder with the promise of a norther blowing down from the Panhandle, Graham, Tony Hess, and Romeo Shively drove around town and ended up at the jail, and, not surprisingly, didn't find Bill Fowler there. They did find Albert Franks.

Franks, a black man, was a trustee who served as jail cook and answered the door when the sheriff wasn't there. According to Hess, Graham got out of the car and walked to the jailhouse with his .45 in his belt and a bottle of bootlegged whiskey in his pocket.[47] The main door was locked and Graham knocked until Franks came to ask him what the problem was. Graham said he wanted to see Bill Fowler, but Franks told him that Fowler was not there. Slipping the bottle out of his pocket, he began to talk to Franks through the door, hoping that he could intimidate the black man into unwittingly helping him ambush Fowler. He asked him if he thought Fowler was a "pretty tough man."[48] Franks replied that he didn't think he was. Graham leaned on the door and said that he thought Fowler was a tough guy.

He seemed intent on creating a situation that would lead him to a confrontation with Bill Fowler. He asked Franks how many prisoners were in the jail. Franks told him and Graham said, "Well, I believe I will go up and turn them all out."[49] Franks told him that he didn't think that would work because he didn't have a key.

Graham went back to the car and pulled the sawed off shotgun he packed in the Big Bend out of the trunk. Franks, who must have been wondering what was worse, staying by the door and talking, or backing off and seeing if Graham would break it down, elected to stand by the door. "This will get me in there won't it?" Graham asked, showing him the shotgun. Franks nodded, yes he thought it might, but he still didn't open the jailhouse door.[50]

Graham continued to try to intimidate the trustee. He offered Franks a drink and told Franks he should come out of the jail and ride around with Graham and his friends. Franks shook his head and told Graham it wouldn't look right for him to leave the jail without the sheriff knowing about it. Graham told him, "That's all right, come on with me and let Fowler come looking for you."[51] Franks realized that Graham was trying to put a plan into play that would lead to a confrontation between the two men. He told Graham no, at which point Graham tried to get into the jail. The door was locked and, knowing the reputation of the man on the other side of the door, Albert Franks wasn't about to open it. Graham continued to try to intimidate the trustee but nothing seemed to work.

Graham might have a shotgun, but there was a door between the two, and that balanced the issue out some.

Tony Hess was seated in the car when Graham had retrieved the twelve gauge moments before. He was convinced that his friend was about to start something that none of them would be able to walk away from. When Graham went back to the jail and began to harangue Franks, Hess knew he had to do something. Tony walked up to Graham and told him it was time to go before some kind of trouble started.[52] His words must have hung in the cold, night air for a moment as Graham weighed his options a realized there was nothing to be gained by busting into jail and letting the prisoners loose, or by taking Albert Franks on some kind of drunken joy ride in hopes of getting Bill Fowler out on a wintery December night. He left Franks with a final message for the sheriff: "Tell Mr. Fowler I will see him in the morning."[53] There was no mention of money, or friendship, only the veiled threat that something was going to happen in the morning. He went back to the car with Hess, and they drove to the Key Hotel to stew over the real and perceived insults of the day, get something to eat, and finish out the evening.[54] For his part, Albert Franks checked the doors and went to bed.

People noticed when the three checked into the Key Hotel. Not only were they from out of town, they were loud, and there was evidence that they had been drinking. Joe "Doc" Robinson, a local man who lived at the hotel, noticed when Tony Hess carried the two rifles and the shotgun up the stairs to the room. Not much was made of the weaponry, it was hunting season after all, but the drinking was noticed. The men muttered to one another and continued to talk back and forth about something Robinson couldn't quite hear.

The reports of the threats from Friday and Saturday began to mount up. Joel Starnes recalled later that he told Bill Fowler about being aware of the loud talk on Saturday night, and that Fowler went to look for Graham that night but couldn't find him. In a town as small as Rankin, it seems unlikely that three strangers in an out of town car couldn't be found, but Starnes remembered it that way. Fowler probably cruised the town, spotted Graham's Ford buttoned up against the weather, and decided that the crisis was going to be slept off in the hotel. He went home and went to bed.

During the night the norther hit, and temperatures dropped sharply. Doc Robinson went down for breakfast and saw Graham, Tony Hess, and Shively again. This time he noticed that the men were in a different mood. Graham seemed to be in good spirits. The men had breakfast, and went out to load the car. Then they ran into a problem; the car wouldn't start. They sought out Robinson and asked him if he could push their car with his, which he did several times. Someone suggested that they needed to take the Model A to the service station, and the closest one was the Yoacham station on Eighth Street. With a little effort the Ford was pushed to the station and lodged in front of the wash and lubrication bays.

Illustration 14. Yoacham Filling Station, Rankin, Texas, circa 1930

(Photo used with permission of the Rankin Museum, Rankin, Texas)
Note the two bays on the left side of the station. This is thought to be the area where Tony Hess and Graham Barnett were working on the car the morning of December 7, 1931

Yoacham's station was a modern looking station of light colored stucco. It had three gasoline pumps across its front and an extended portico providing shade for the gas pumps. The bay area provided space for Tony Hess, and whoever was in the station, to try to determine what had happened with the Ford. While they began to work on the car, Graham decided he would make another attempt to find Fowler. Leaving the men at the station, Graham bummed a ride to Joe Conger's house where he called Bill Fowler. The telephone operator noticed that the call didn't go through.[55] Graham went back to Yoacham's station where the men had decided that the problem might have been a clogged sediment bowl for the carburetor and problems with the radiator because of the freezing temperature.

Bill Fowler, in the meantime, had slept late but was awakened around nine by his wife. Albert Franks came by and told him about the confrontation at the jail on Saturday night. While Fowler was taking all of that in, his sons rushed into the house to tell him that they had seen Graham Barnett at Yoacham's service station. He was still in town. Frank Lane, a rancher and oil field owner, also saw Graham and got the information to the sheriff.[56] Graham Barnett had become the bad penny that kept turning up. Fowler had tried to avoid any kind of contact with him but now it seemed that he would have to go talk to the man again. He must have sensed that the talking might not go any better than it had previously, because as he left the house he picked up the Thompson submachine gun, and checked the fifty round magazine. He laid it in the front seat of his 1931 Ford coupe and headed for the service station. If something was going to happen, Bill Fowler was going to be ready for it. Bill Fowler was a cautious man, but he wasn't of afraid of Graham. Years later, Joel Starnes recalled that he didn't think that Fowler was afraid of anybody.[57] However, he needed a backup. After he left, Mrs. Fowler called Joel Starnes. The message was brief, "Go to town. Bill's in trouble."[58]

At Yoacham's, Graham and Robinson had driven off in the light rain to the Marathon station to check for a sediment bowl, but they were no more successful there than they had been earlier. What they talked about on the short trip wasn't memorable, and it wasn't about shooting Bill Fowler. They drove back to Yoacham's and Graham got out and went into the station to warm up. His coat was buttoned against the cold and the rain, which had increased slightly. He went into the station for a moment. Tony Hess was the only mechanic in the group, and he started working on the car in an attempt to get it started and head for home. The engine in the little Ford coughed into life and Hess struggled with keeping it running. He drove it a few feet, stopped, and resumed work. In the next few seconds, everything changed for all of the people in the service station and on the street.

Bill Fowler drove up across the street, and Tony Hess was the first person to notice him. Hess looked up and Fowler beckoned to him to come to the car. Fowler's car was about twenty paces from the filling station. Across the street, O. L. Dickenson, a friend of Bill Fowler's, recognized his car and watched the entire scene unfold. Hess started across the street. Graham came out of the bay area and was walking toward the office. At that point, Fowler must have noticed Graham in the station. Hess believed that Fowler said, "There's the son a bitch I'm looking for," although in trial testimony, defense lawyers suggested what he heard was, "There's the son of bitch that's looking for me."[59] The difference was slight but significant.

When Fowler saw Graham, he yelled to Hess to "stand aside."[60] Graham glanced at the car and probably recognized who was in it. Tony Hess didn't, and he was either unfamiliar with the phrase in English or didn't hear it correctly, and he continued to walk toward the car. Fowler repeated, "Stand aside."[61] Hess then heard Graham tell him to get out of the way.[62] Graham began to walk across the filling station driveway, his coat buttoned and his left hand in his coat pocket. Dickenson swore that from his position across the street, he saw Graham's right hand move across his body.[63] It was the position of his hands that dictated what happened next.

Graham carried his 1911 .45 cocked, with the safety on, tucked into his belt on the left side with the pistol grip facing forward. People who knew Graham knew that the position was only part of the story. They also knew the speed of his draw was accented by his reaching into his coat pocket and pushing the muzzle of the pistol upward so that it began to fall forward, allowing him to reach across and grasp it. The difference between the push and reaching all the way across was a matter of milliseconds but in a gunfight, milliseconds were sometimes all a man had. There was no question that Graham had his hand in his coat pocket when he stepped into the street. The more important question was the condition of his coat. If it were buttoned there would have been no way he could have reached the pistol, fancy draw or not. If it were buttoned he couldn't have drawn the pistol in a conventional manner. If the coat was buttoned, Graham had no intention of drawing a gun at all. As he walked he swung his right hand across his body.

Tony Hess was still standing in the street facing Fowler's car. He saw the sheriff roll down his window, and then saw the odd muzzle of the Thompson with the Cutts Compensator on it creep over the edge of the door.[64] In the next instant the Sunday morning quiet was ripped apart by the blast of the Thompson. Fowler fired fifteen shots, six or seven hit Graham, and the rest rocketed off into the parked Model A and into the front of the service station.[65] Comments from the undertaker suggest that Graham was hit, and probably spun around by the impact. C. W. Northcutt, the undertaker who examined the body and later testified at the Fowler trial, stated that he was hit four times on the left side about three inches apart, one at the corner of the nose and one under the right shoulder blade.[66] The effect was immediate. Graham was probably dead by the time he fell to the ground. In the silence that followed the shooting, Fowler threw open his car door and rushed across to Tony Hess. The noise and blast of the Thompson was disorienting. Hess had dropped to his knees when the shooting began and was still there when Fowler got out of the car and rushed to him. In the excitement of the moment, Hess was convinced that Fowler was going to kill him too. Hess stared at the

Thompson and in a moment of clarity realized the gun had jammed.[67] Years later he described the moment in a letter that was written in the mix of German, English, and Spanish that he spoke for the rest of his life. "Fowler tried to kill me to [sic] he kussed [sic] my out after he killed Graham and put the gun right on my chest but I think the Guardian Engle [sic] protected me. I never forget, looking on the gun, and it was jammed, a shell jammed half in and half out. Thank the Lord for my life to be left to tell the truth."[68]

Fowler didn't see the guardian angel, but he did look around and see the several men who had been drawn to the site by the shooting. Shivley had remained in the office of the filling station and Fowler ordered him to come outside.[69] He hurriedly deputized Jap Taylor and Bill Nix to hustle Hess and Shivley to jail where they were charged with disturbing the peace, vagrancy, possession of liquor, and theft of a firearm.[70]

In the shocked silence that fell on the street as Hess and Shivley were being hauled away, a number of people gathered around the body. Dr. Homer Powers checked the body and knew immediately that there was no hope for any kind of first aid. Observers noted that Graham's left hand was still in his coat pocket. Beab Northcutt, the justice of the peace, pronounced him dead, and as he checked the body, he noticed that Graham's coat was buttoned, as did several people in the crowd. The condition of the coat wasn't the only thing most noticed; they also saw that Graham was armed.[71] When Northcutt opened the coat and lifted the .45 out of Graham's belt, he observed that it was cocked with the safety on. He took it for evidence. After some discussion, the body was moved to the funeral home. Joe Conger, Graham's brother-in-law, was called, and the body was taken to the funeral home in McCamey. Almost immediately, at Fowler's request, a Court of Inquiry was called that was headed by District Attorney Roy Priest of Rankin with fellow attorney Weaver Baker of Junction sitting in. Bill Fowler's comments were limited but centered on, "I had to do it, it was either him or me. He made a move for a gun."[72] The findings of the court were hurried, and not officially released until the following February. Based on what was common knowledge of Graham's behavior around town for the past couple of days the court was unanimous that Bill Fowler was justified in his actions. However, following the practices of the day, Fowler was indicted for murder, and placed under $10,000 bond, which he made and was released immediately.

Joe Conger must have called Joe Graham because later in the evening, two men knocked at the door of the Rock House in Alpine. Annie received the news that she feared, but had known must be coming. Years later she recalled, "I really wasn't surprised at Graham's killing. I always felt uneasy when he was away. But I certainly didn't expect Mr. Fowler."[73] The family seemed to move in a haze, knowing that there was nothing to be done and yet hoping that there was a mistake somewhere. Maybe he wasn't dead, maybe the stories were wrong, maybe Joe Conger was mistaken somehow. Then reality set in and people began to be notified. Boog, Graham's brother, was called, other members of the family were notified, and they began to make arrangements for the funeral.

Graham's body was returned to Alpine where, in the Rock House, it was placed in the living room and the family and friends gathered for the visitation. The next day, December 8, he was buried in Alpine. The pallbearers read like a roster of law enforcement and business leaders in the Big Bend country: Dudley Barker, former Ranger and sheriff of Pecos County, E. E. Townsend, former Ranger and former sheriff of Brewster County, Creed Taylor, former Ranger and customs officer, Forest Robinson, secretary of the Alpine Chamber of Commerce, and Ed Davidson, Brewster County rancher.[74] Almost as soon as the funeral was over, stories began to circulate concerning what had happened in Rankin. There were stories that Graham must have been shot in the back, that no one could have taken him otherwise. As widespread as the stories were, most were put away quickly. As impossible as it seemed, Graham had died in the way most of his friends feared he would, facing down someone in the street with his gun in his belt.

Tony Hess remained in jail in Rankin. Nearly a week after the shooting, he was freed and had no way to get back to Alpine. He wanted to get out of Rankin as quickly as possible so he bummed a ride on a train and finally made it back home. The mysterious Mr. Shively disappeared and, although he was subpoenaed for the trial, never appeared again. Whether he changed his name, slipped into Mexico, or left Texas for someplace else isn't known.

One of the ongoing traditions of the border country is that of the *corrido* or ballad, which usually is fashioned to explain someone's view of a controversial event. The *corrido* is not unlike the old Scots-Irish murder ballads that told the stories of outlaws and heroes. As befitting a slain hero, a group of cowboys created their own ballad of Graham Barnett and after some time it was collected by Joe S. Graham of Texas A & M University.[75] The story it told stayed pretty close to the actual events.

> "Well some of you have heard of Graham Barnett,
> And some of you knew him well;
> And those of you who knew him,
> You have your story to tell
>
> Well Graham was raised in Sterling City
> It was his native land
> But in his early manhood
> He rode to the Rio Grand
>
> In that rough and rugged country
> Amongst those desperate men
> His youth and graceful manhood
> Soon made him many a friend
>
> Well it was while punching cattle
> Along the Rio Grand
> That Graham first met William Babb
> A fearless fighting man."

The song goes on for nineteen stanzas, but two briefly describe the shooting and imply that it was done under somewhat questionable circumstances.

> "Then the Sheriff took his machine gun
> And tucked it underneath his wing
> And drove down the streets of Rankin
> And did this awful thing
>
> He drove up to Graham
> As pleasant as you please
> And burned him down with his machine gun
> Before a cat could sneeze."

The last verse, however, makes a significant statement concerning Graham and the admiration that people still had for him.

> "Now many a man backed Graham down
> And you have heard what they said
> But boys they didn't say it
> Until after he was dead." [76]

For the cowboys who wrote the song, as well as many of the people who admired Graham in his lifetime, the story was clear and told well. Graham was the doomed hero, killed by his friend, in a treacherous manner. In death he was still the hero, and no amount of stories from beer joint toughs who said they had bluffed him was going to change that. The song captured the legendary life in verse, and told the story the way his friends wanted to hear it. For everyone else, the matter would be re-told in a courtroom in Sonora, Texas, during the early spring of the next year.

Illustration 15. Elm Grove Cemetery in Alpine. Grave sites of Graham and Boog Barnett

(Courtesy John T. Barnett).

CHAPTER 14

"IT WAS ALL TOO TRUE"

MARCH 1932-PRESENT[1]

By February 1932, some movement had been made concerning the trial of Bill Fowler. The indictment had been made, and both sides were picking lawyers to assist with the defense and the prosecution. It appeared to be a clear case of self-defense based on the stories of witnesses from the night before the shooting. Graham had made threats, he was capable of carrying them out, and certainly gave the impression that he had every intention of doing so. Still, neither side considered the case open and shut. What was clear from the beginning was that Graham's reputation was going to be the factor the entire case hinged on. While recognizing that the legend of Graham Barnett as an old style *pistolero* would be working against them, the prosecution began to build the best case it could.

The state's case would be brought by Weaver Baker and Bascom Stevenson, both of Junction. Tom Garrard of Lubbock would represent Bill Fowler along with Walter Woodward, the general attorney for the Sheriff's Association.[2] Bryan Montague recalled that even with that level of defense Fowler had asked Montague to assist the defense team. Bryan declined because of his friendship with Graham. A few days later, Graham's older brother, Boog, came by the law office in Del Rio and tried to engage Bryan to assist with the prosecution. Again, he declined because Fowler had been a client of his in an earlier case.[3] Bryan Montague was faced with one of the most difficult decisions that a lawyer could have to make. He knew both men, liked them both, and now one was dead at the hands of the other. Who do you represent? He made the best decision that he could and opted out of both sides. In an odd twist, his brother Joe didn't have that option.

Joe Montague had been appointed judge of the 112th District Court that had jurisdiction in a number of counties, including both Upton County, the site of the murder, and Sutton County, the site of the trial. Even though Joe had been friends with Graham, and the wandering gunfighter had defended the judge against a possible assassination attempt a few years previously, Joe did not recuse himself. Joe Montague had a reputation as an impartial judge, and he had enough character that people knew he would rule on the merits of the case. Still, the temptation to remove himself must have been tremendous.

Sonora, Texas, was not prepared for the impact of legal talent and the 135 witnesses that descended on the small town on March 22 and 23 of 1932. Hotels filled and people sought what other lodging they could find. The local cafes stood to make some money from the crowd, and the school hinted that they might turn out classes for some of the students so they could watch justice being served. At 10:00 a.m. Joe Montague strolled into the courtroom and the race was on. He had decided to work through the trial quickly and did not want to put up with a lot of stalling on anyone's part. The jury was quickly selected from a pool of sixty. That number dropped to twenty-five and, after a few challenges, it went even lower. By the lunch recess, twelve were finally selected. As might be expected from the location, nine were ranchers while the remaining three were a mechanic, a civil engineer for Humble Oil, and the manager of the telephone exchange.[4] When the trial began in earnest at 1:30 in the afternoon, Otto Graham and Boog had joined the prosecutors at their table. Everyone was ready.

The state presented six witnesses. Jack Yoacham told the story as he saw it from the front of his service station. He described the men as being in his station for an hour and a half, finally getting the Ford started and driving it up and down the street, then he spoke of seeing Bill Fowler drive up, and watching the shooting start. Little if anything he said would have condemned either Fowler or Graham.[5]

The spectators must have been excited to hear from the next man. Tony Hess was closer to the shooting than anyone. He was nearly a victim, and he was the only person to see the entire weekend's activity from beginning to end. He was likely the most important witness for the state. What seemed to attract most of the attention about him was not his heavy Swiss-German accent, but rather his clothes. He took the stand wearing a bright red shirt, which was commented on by all the newspaper accounts.[6] Hess explained it later: "I had the red shirt in my wardrob [sic] the only good shirt dad [sic] I had so naturally I put it on to go to the trial. I really had it for hunting season."[7] So the man who was closest to the actual killing sat in the court room in his hunting shirt, and with his heavily accented English tried to respond to the questions he was asked. Hess was ready to tell all that he knew, but he wasn't going to get the chance.

The details of Graham's plan to use blackmail to get a loan were not going to be a story that the jury was going to hear. Hess could hardly have helped the situation with his story of a fixed election and an attempt to force money out of the taciturn sheriff. The prosecution team apparently decided that that information was better left unshared. Claiming that your late client was killed while trying to extort money from a public official was not going to strengthen a case that seemed doomed from the beginning.

Almost fifty years later, Hess remarked that the defense team didn't ask him the right questions. "This trial was a joke to my idea. They not asked me the truth."[8] For years afterward Hess maintained that Graham never went to Rankin with the intent of killing Fowler. "Graham never say [*sic*] that he was going to kill Fowler, he said he was going to put him in the penitentiary."[9] He never was able to make that clear at the trial because the question was not asked. What he did say under cross-examination was that Graham was a nice enough fellow until he was drinking, and that he had been drinking the night before his death. He probably did the defense a favor when he confirmed that Graham was quick on the draw and a very good shot.[10] The rest of the witnesses hardly helped the prosecution. Joe Robinson, who had seen the men in the Key Hotel, testified that Graham was not drinking the morning of the shooting. I. C. Elliott had spent some time in the office of the filling station and presumably talked with Graham and Tony Hess but had little to contribute. Finally Dr. Homer Powers confirmed that Graham had been shot, and C. W. Livingston the undertaker confirmed what Dr. Powers had said and testified to the nature of the wounds.[11] About the only thing the prosecution established was that Graham was a dangerous man and that Bill Fowler killed him.

One final key issue that might have been brought to light was Graham's unusual method of carrying a pistol. The prosecution initially approached this carefully. He tucked it in his waistband on the left side and when he was ready to draw, he would put his hand in coat pocket and push the pistol upward. As the gun moved forward, he would reach across his body and grasp the stocks and pull it forward. A critical point was that he had to have his coat unbuttoned to complete the draw. If the coat was not unbuttoned he could not have drawn the gun. Part of the prosecution's case stemmed from the coat being buttoned, which implied that Graham had no plans of shooting anyone that December morning.[12] As the trial progressed, the question of Graham's coat being buttoned or unbuttoned was never settled. Beab Northcutt, who was the justice of the peace that pronounced him dead, stated the coat was buttoned.[13] Others disputed this statement, claiming it was open. The confusion was due to the timing. The people who saw the body first saw a different crime scene than others who came after a preliminary investigation of the wounds left the jacket unbuttoned.[14] Why the state's attorneys didn't pursue this aspect of the trial remains unclear. Either they did not see it as important, or did not understand that Graham couldn't have drawn his pistol with the coat buttoned. The point that was made was that Graham was armed, and was advancing on Bill Fowler when the shooting occurred.

If the prosecution's case was built on buttons, the defense's case was based on reputation and fear. They decided to show that Graham's contemporaries and associates knew him as unstable, a man to be feared and a man who would carry out a threat. The witnesses to his past behavior were a number of sheriffs and other lawmen who had worked with him in the past twenty years.

Bob Miller, a former Texas Ranger, county sheriff in Concho County, and the current deputy in Littlefield, set the tone for the prosecution. He testified that Graham was "a dangerous and violent man who would carry out a threat when drunk but a different man when sober."[15] This testimony was confirmed by Sheriff M. L. Whistler of Val Verde County, who had known Graham for twenty-seven years. He characterized him as "dangerous when intoxicated."[16] Officers who had previously been Graham's friends testified in a similar fashion, but several added a slight twist that might have been missed by some of the jury. That twist involved the issue of Graham seeking loans from men he had previously worked for. Bud Blair, sheriff of Crane County, said that Graham had asked him for money and that he had refused to give him any.[17] The same story was repeated by Ellison Carroll, who had arrested Graham in Big Lake after the Noisy Watson shooting. He confirmed that Graham had visited with him before he went to Rankin, and had asked him for money which he refused to give.[18] The picture the testimony painted was of an unstable man who was dangerous and who needed money. If the defense was trying to set up a pattern of asking for money and not getting it, they appeared to be successful.

The consensus of the testimony from the various sheriffs was that Graham had changed over the years. He had developed a reputation that caused them to be cautious when they dealt with him. The reputation was of a man who was dangerous not only when he was drinking, but as equally dangerous when he got over it. The term "fear" was not used but Graham's death meant one less person for them to look out for. Joel Starnes commented, "Officers in West Texas got the best sleep they had had in twenty years (if they had been sheriff that long) that Sunday night after Fowler killed Graham."[19]

Establishing that he was looking for money, and not finding it, the defense sought to show that when he got to Rankin, Graham Barnett was running out of time and patience. The testimony from the people who had had contact with him before and during the weekend nailed the door shut.

Raymond McKay sat the scene for Bill Fowler when he described the frightening encounter in Fort Stockton when he was pistol whipped by Graham, and when Fowler intervened, Graham threatened to kill him. That testimony was followed by other witnesses, including Fowler's wife, who described the tense early morning meeting when Graham had come to the Fowler house to find her husband and his comment that he might take things over. If there was any doubt that Graham was emerging as his own worst enemy, the testimony that focused on his last few hours confirmed it. Graham's words from the Saturday night were repeated by the voices of the witnesses, and the words condemned him. McCamey police chief Fred Senter reported Graham was observed outside a restaurant in McCamey. He was very angry and had said that Fowler was avoiding him and that he would "shoot his navel out and throw him in the Pecos."[20] The porter at the hotel, E. A. Grattis, said he heard Graham say, "I'll bet you fifty dollars I'll kill Fowler before sundown."[21] Tom Bergasser, who owned the café, told how he remembered Graham saying, "Bill refused me and I give him until 8 o'clock Saturday or I'll put him in a black box."[22] What all of the witnesses agreed on was that Graham stated that he had asked Fowler for money, and if he didn't get it, he would kill the sheriff. All of the bravado of that cold Saturday night came back and hung in the warm March sunshine. His own words convicted Graham as surely as if he had been there himself.

The testimony from Bill Fowler seemed to put a cap on the proceedings. Fowler described how he had been friends with Graham for four or five years. He talked about the Raymond McKay fight in Fort Stockton, and the Carroll Bates problem in San Angelo. He admitted how he had responded to Graham's request for loans on two occasions since January, and how he had decided that this time would be different. This time there was no money for his former friend, and as a result, Graham was furious. Fowler thought he was going to have problems because of this, and finally on Sunday morning he decided to look Graham up and see if he could settle the situation amicably.[23] He had been informed by several people in town that Graham was at the Yoacham's service station. When he pulled up and Graham walked out of the station, Fowler said that he noticed the look on his face. For Fowler it was a look he had seen before. At that point, Bill Fowler decided that he had to shoot Graham Barnett "to save [his] own life."[24]

Over the years, people often contrasted the two different Graham Barnett's that they knew. One was the friend that helped other ranchers and lawmen, the other was the gunman who seemed focused on being the man in charge, the man who was going to take things over. There were people who could still remember the attempts to take over Brook's recreation hall in Big Lake, the drunken escapade in Best, and Graham's attempt to shut down Carroll Bates's bootlegging operation in San Angelo. Some of these people didn't see the easy-going cowboy; they saw the hot-tempered gunfighter, and that legendary character terrified them. The single factor that ran through the entire trial was that Graham Barnett was a man who was feared by almost everyone and apparently feared no one. The consensus of opinion from all of the officers who gave testimony was that he was truly a dangerous man when he was drinking. They might not have said they were afraid of him, but they left little doubt that he was not to be trifled with. The legendary Graham Barnett, the man the stories said was the deadliest gunfighter in Texas, had come to town, and he could not be avoided and he could not be ignored. The fact that he had been friends with all the officers who testified, and that he and Bill Fowler had been especially close, was noted but not a lot was made of it. In the end, Bill Fowler had taken the only action he could have taken.

Joel Starnes had given testimony and years later recalled the entire weekend. It was brief and very focused: "Everybody was afraid of Graham Barnett. When he was full of liquor he was an altogether different man... He got mad and got drunk and decided to take the town over."[25] He may have decided to take over the town but by mid-morning on Sunday, Graham knew that plan was not going to work. Even Starnes conceded that on Sunday morning, "I think Graham was leaving town."[26] Graham knew that he wasn't going to find the money he needed. If he had a plan to somehow take control of all the vice in the small town by intimidation, with the assistance of a Swiss well digger and a part-time pimp, that plan was destroyed in the cold mist of Sunday morning and the rattle of a Thompson.

The trial sped on throughout the day and, in what was an unusual decision, Joe Montague decided to keep the session going into Thursday evening. By 8 p m., closing arguments were made, and Weaver Baker responded to the unwavering attack on Graham's character when he cautioned the jury to recall that they were not trying Graham Barnett but were instead trying Bill Fowler.[27]

When defense attorney Walter Woodward addressed the jury, he was contending with attacking a legend as much as he was defending a sheriff. The legend said the Graham was the most dangerous man in Texas, that he was so much of a killer that a long line of peace officers could not get a good night's sleep until he was gone. What could Bill Fowler have done against someone who was that deadly a gunman? Fowler was only a sheriff; Graham Barnett was a legend. After stating his case, Woodward leaned forward and stared at the jury. He made the whole thing personal. "Gentlemen, let me ask you, put yourself in Fowler's place. What would you have done?" One of the ranchers in the jury box was caught up in the moment, leaned forward and said, "By God, I'd a killed 'im too." Judge Montague was not going to let the laughter get out of hand; he gaveled the courtroom back in silence.[28]

When the lawyers had finished, Judge Montague was left to address the twelve men in the jury box. The charge to the jury was one he had made before; self-defense was the only option that would keep Bill Fowler out of jail. The judge defined it for the jury: a person was justified in using force against another when the actor reasonably believes that force was immediately necessary to protect the actor against the other's use or attempted use of unlawful force. The defense team had worked that angle again and again. Graham was desperate, he was angry, he had made the threats and he was capable of carrying them out. Fowler himself had summed it up when he said, "It was him or me."

The jury filed out and the spectators settled down for a long wait. The families stayed in the courtroom, as did the high school students and what must have seemed like most of the town. No one wanted to leave and hear about the verdict later from someone who had stayed. It didn't take as long as they had anticipated. In fifty minutes, the jury announced that they had reached a verdict. The bailiff brought them back, and in the silence of the crisp spring evening, the jury announced that on the charge of murder of Graham Barnett, the accused, Bill Fowler, was not guilty.

The verdict wasn't unexpected, but it still must have been a heart-breaking moment for the Barnetts when the estimated 500 people in the audience burst into applause, and many rushed forward to congratulate Fowler.[29] In the same fashion that Graham had faced murder trials and won, the self-defense plea protected Bill Fowler. As much as it was the law that protected him, it was the attitudes of another time that protected Fowler. For the people who watched, it was a story that they had heard all their lives. It was him or me.

While Brian Montague didn't take part in the case as a lawyer, he did witness the final moments of the trial. He had been in San Angelo for a series of meetings, which ended early. He had started on the long drive back to Del Rio and stopped for supper in Sonora. When he heard that final arguments were going to be made in the evening, he decided to stay and see what happened. When he slipped into the courtroom to observe, he was impressed with the number of peace officers in the crowd. It also seemed that everyone was armed. He believed that there could only be one verdict: not guilty. But he knew that the verdict would dramatically impact two families and a number of the officers in the courtroom. When his brother, Joe, announced the verdict and the courtroom exploded with applause, Brian could not help but feel that justice was done, but it was a sad moment.

After the trial, he left the courthouse with his brother and the pair headed off to a late supper. The two walked down the long sidewalk toward the main street of town and discussed the case and their old friend. Joe was struck by a strange double standard that was shown by most of the officers who had testified for the defense. Joe admitted that Graham had become notorious for his behavior both drunk and sober. Despite that, the judge commented that "it was depressing during the trial to listen to one officer after another testify to Graham's general reputation as a violent and dangerous man, when he [Joe] well knew that on more than one occasion, Graham had assisted each of these officers in law enforcement duties."[30] At some point Graham had changed and had "later incurred the enmity of all of them."[31] How he had earned their enmity was not discussed. It was undoubtedly Graham's dogged persistence in working both sides of the law in order to make money. It did not go just one way. Joe summed up the paradox of Graham Barnett when he told his brother, "Brian, you know as well as I do that Graham was just as likely as not to change and hate his best friends." Brian thought it over for a moment and commented, "It was all too true."[32]

The Montague brothers had dinner, and they were approached by Joe Graham, who met with them briefly to ask for Graham's guns. Joe Montague picked up a piece of stationery with the Hotel McDonald logo on it and wrote a request that the guns, which had been sealed in a case for the trial, be returned to Joe Graham. With the return of the guns, the trial was finally over.[33]

The lawyers went home, the Fowlers went to Rankin, Brian Montague went back to Del Rio, and that left only the Barnett family to find some place to go. During all of Graham's absences, Annie had always taken over and made sure the family stayed on track. This time it was no different. The family bundled up and moved out of Alpine to Sterling City, moved in with her parents, enrolled the kids in school, and tried to adjust to a life without Graham. It wasn't the same.

Bill Fowler never got the famed ten-thousand-dollar bounty from the Babb family. That was probably more myth than fact, although one member of the family sent him a box of cigars after the trial.[34] He received an engraved Smith and Wesson .44 Special from an admirer, and wore it on occasion. He apparently enjoyed the support and admiration of the community as he was elected to the sheriff's office three times and served until January 1, 1939.

He never got away from the killing. Some in the community wouldn't let that happen. Joel Starnes claimed that a number of people in town wanted to get in good with the sheriff, so they warned him constantly that someone was going to try to kill him. No one ever accused the Barnett family, although there were references to them from time to time, just that a phantom "someone" was out for revenge. How much good this did for the sheriff's peace of mind is difficult to assess. Starnes recalled, "I had to chauffeur him around all the time. He had the machine gun with him all the time. He was afraid of reprisal."[35] Although the phantom never showed up, Fowler was haunted by the shooting. He told Starnes, "Unless it's absolutely essential, never kill a man, don't unless forced, you never get over it."[36] He never did get over it. Upton County had enough crime over the next eight years to keep him busy. He investigated murders, chased swindlers, and once served twenty-four hours in jail for contempt of court when he moved the school superintendent out of his house on the advice of the county attorney over a hotly disputed football game. He caught a couple of wool thieves who specialized in shooting sheep and taking "dead wool." Fowler was involved in a ground and airplane chase of a robbery suspect named Houston Baker who shot it out with officers on at least three occasions during a two-day chase before being captured. Baker, incidentally, was using a Thompson submachine gun.[37] He was still working, but by the winter of 1938, it was obvious that Fowler was ill; he had contracted stomach cancer and ended his career as sheriff in January 1939. He died in San Angelo, August 1, 1939.

Tony Hess went back to Alpine. He lived in the area for the rest of his life. He worked in Texas and in Mexico and was out of the country when World War II started. At the border crossing as he was coming home, he was mistaken for an enemy alien with his heavy German accent and was interned for a short time. He joined the Navy during the war and afterwards returned home to continue with his business of well digging and ranching. He died in Alpine, February 26, 2000. He was survived by five children and four grandchildren.

Annie did not want to stay in Texas. She was concerned that Maude or Bud might want to settle the score with Bill Fowler. No one ever said anything; it was just a feeling she had.[38] She thought it would be best if there were some distance between the family and Texas. In the spring of 1933, she loaded everyone into the car and had her brother J. T. Conger drive them to San Diego. Polly, Graham's sister, had lived in San Diego for the past ten years and encouraged them to move, to get away from a past that seemed to choke them at times.

Now the entire family, Annie, 36, Maude, 16, Bud, 14, Bill, 9, Jerry, 6, and Ann, 3, were faced with not just a new neighborhood, but an entirely new life. San Diego, California, must have seemed as foreign as any European capital to the family from Sterling City. The transfer of a family of six might have seemed difficult in the midst of the Depression but the Barnetts were not just any family. It also turned out that Graham had not left them without the wherewithal to make a move.

Perhaps fearing the worst over his health concerns, or an honest assessment of the threats on his life, he had taken out a life insurance policy in the amount of ten thousand dollars, payable to Annie.[39] In the midst of the Depression that was a staggering amount, equal to about one hundred fifteen thousand in 2015 dollars. The lawyers got part of it, some of it went to settling debts, but the rest became the nest egg for the family. After she adjusted to San Diego, Annie bought a house and the family began to find their way. Annie had not worked at a commercial job before, but now, in 1933, she took a job as a WPA seamstress in order to have an income for the family.

Illustration 16. WPA Seamstress Group, San Diego, 1933. Annie Barnett, fifth from right, seated front row.

(Courtesy John T. Barnett)

Time doesn't heal anything; all it does is provide some distance, and distance was what the Barnett family needed. As the kids grew older they found jobs. Bill and Bud delivered newspapers, and Bill had an unusually large route and made nineteen dollars a month. He gave ten of it to Annie. All of the children found jobs, but the one constant was that they took care of their mother.[40]

Illustration 17. Bud (Joe Graham Barnett Jr.) on left, Bill on the right, in San Diego, circa 1957

(Courtesy John T. Barnett)

World War II came and went and in 1952 Bill and Bud founded Sterling Plumbing and Heating Company in San Diego, named for Sterling City. They also expanded in 1961 into a booming town in Nevada named Las Vegas. They were destined to do well there. The family stayed close; Boog would visit from Texas and Annie and the grown kids would go back when there was a reason. In the late 1950s they built Annie another house where she lived until her death in 1971. She never remarried.

It is hard to imagine what life would have been for Annie and kids if they had stayed in Texas. The opportunities they found in California dramatically changed her life and the lives of her children. The kids raised families and the story of the gunfighter from the Big Bend slowly faded from the family's collection of stories. The older members of the family didn't forget everything; they just didn't talk much about it. Graham had left the family on a December morning in Alpine with the idea of finding a way to make a new life for them. In an odd twist he did just that. In the 1930s the chances of being successful in Texas were tied to oil. In California, there were a variety of jobs available to a family that wasn't afraid of work and wouldn't quit. What they found there changed their lives totally. Maybe Graham wasn't too far off with the gamble that he made by going to Rankin. He had a plan to find some kind of success for himself and his family. He didn't find the success he wanted, but the people most important to him did.

Graham's brother, Boog, who had sided with him as often as he could, stayed in the Rangers until 1919. Afterwards, he cowboyed all over the southwest and when Annie Laura moved to California he visited the family when money and circumstances would allow. When he got too old to cowboy, he cooked, and then he retired. He never married and had no close family. Jeff Graham took care of him in his final days, and he did not die alone. He passed away in Alpine on December 9, 1982. He was buried beside his brother.

Graham had lived out his life on a stage named Texas. And while all the actors on that stage changed, the stage itself changed very little. The Mexican Revolution ended with the abortive Escobar Rebellion in 1929, and while the ruling PRI (Partido Revolutionario Institucional) Party controlled the country until the elections of 2000, the question of whether the revolution ever really ended is open for discussion.

The oil boom that brought money and jobs to West Texas ebbed and flowed again with changes in technology and the economy. People made fortunes overnight and lost them by the afternoon the next day.

It impacted the Depression era economy, and began to change Texas from a rural state to an urban one. Oil continues to be a major feature of the Texas economy and it continues to drive dreams. Prohibition, which influenced much of Graham's life, ended with the repeal of the Eighteenth Amendment in 1933. Across the state, several counties decided to remain dry, and usually they were bordered by several that elected to go wet. This arrangement generally resulted in heavy traffic to the county line for liquor runs on the occasion of holidays and critical football games. Texans never seemed to get along well with prohibition and it remains so today with other substances. People always want what they can't have.

The frontier mentality changed. Attitudes toward minority populations improved as the minorities became majorities. Law enforcement conducts itself according to more accepted codes of behavior, and the sheriff is not the power he once was in the community. But the frontier is not all gone; some aspects of the old ways are still found. The cowboy still exists, although his role is changing. For many, horses have been replaced by four-wheelers and the pickup has become the indispensable tool for the man or woman working in the country. The dreams of the land remain with many people. The old dreams of having a place consisting of fifty to a hundred sections of land is out of reach for most of the dreamers these days. The romance with the land continues. Every year many suburban yards are converted into gardens where the great-grandchildren of the first groundbreakers plant five or six tomato plants and anxiously scan the sky and wait for the rains. The mentality has changed very little. Only the scope of the dreaming has changed.

Illustration 18. Left to right: Maude, Bill, Jerry, and Ann after Bud's funeral, circa1993

(Courtesy John T. Barnett)

Post Script

"Death steals everything except our stories"

People who grew up in the first decades of the twentieth century grew up with stories of the old time Texans.[1] They admired men who struggled against the odds and fought everyday of their lives for what they thought was right that day. Graham lived that kind of life. There is no puzzlement on why Graham became a legend. In the new twentieth century, he lived like men had on the frontier. In a world that was changing daily, Graham Barnett stuck to the old ways: he drank, he shot people, he dreamed extravagantly, and he fought with just about everyone that he didn't like. He was a traditionalist, a retro, a throwback. People couldn't help but respect that.

Graham Barnett died while he was still a legend, which was probably a good thing. He never had to go through the distressing process of not living up to his narrative, and over time becoming just another regular person. People knew who he was; he didn't hide from being notorious. For the people who lived in his time and place, he was someone to be known and talked about. His adventures and activities provided stories to be told in beer joints, Sunday Schools, and on courthouse lawns. After a while, the stories became bigger than he was and they lived a life separate from Graham. People who knew him knew that he was different from the stories, but many of them didn't care.

He became famous because of his use of a gun, and not just any gun, but a handgun. It was a weapon seen frequently, but mastered seldom. He practiced with them, he gunsmithed them, he collected them, and he carried one almost everyday of his life. It was part of his outfit and the pistol both defined and destroyed him. Being able to use a gun, either for hunting or defense, was considered one of the skills a man needed to survive on the frontier, and Graham was one of many who brought that idea into the twentieth century. He was supposed to be one of the handiest men with a gun in Texas, which covered a lot of territory. Many people think that the gunfighter days ended with the closing of the frontier, but they ignored the later men who made history with a gun. People knew he was good because he showed them and demonstrated the draw and the shoot. It was a skill that gained him both a reputation and served to protect him from some of his enemies. People were reluctant to go up against the handiest man with a gun in Texas.

To his admirers, he was more like the fellow down the street who had gotten in and out of scrapes and had survived them, and that meant something to the other people who lived on that street. The stories claimed that he killed untold men and buried them in hidden graves or dropped them in the Rio Grande River. Some of that happened, most of it didn't. It became easy to explain disappearances of bad men or a decrease in cattle thefts by attributing that to an unseen killer. The conjecture could end with "I bet Ole Graham got 'em." That was good enough for a lot of people. Graham may have been a legend, but he was a hometown legend. People knew who he was.

Graham lived out his life in a manner similar to a number of people in West Texas and on both sides of the Rio Grande. He was neither completely good nor completely bad. People looking for those kind of heroes are often disappointed when they find that the man or woman they have chosen to emulate do not fit the pattern all of the time. It is hard to be consistent about something when bullets are flying or bills are due. He lived life on a day-to-day basis, doing what he needed to do to get by and to provide for his family. The moral code he lived up to was that his priority was to take of care of his family, his people. Family went beyond just wife and children; it included brothers and sisters, uncles and cousins. The things he did, good and bad, he did because he needed to provide for his people, and keep them relatively removed from the kind of life he led. He wanted things to be different for his wife and children than they had been for him.

He had some very bad habits and some behaviors that, in the modern world, would get him sent to anger management classes or have him tossed into the local jailhouse. In reality, many of his attitudes were the same as the people around him. He acted on them, many of his contemporaries did not, and that was why he was a legend. He did things that other people wished they could have done. They didn't want to be Graham Barnett, but they wanted people to think that they were.

Graham made a series of bad choices from the time he began to shoot at people and to take up the business of solving problems for others who didn't want to get their hands dirty. In doing this, he got a reputation both as a lawman and an outlaw, and the outlaw image outlived the other. Judge Orland Sims said that people admired the gunfighter image, and that is likely the reason why Graham was a legend. Sims was there and saw most of it happen, so he is probably accurate in his judgment. What Sims saw as a fault in the society was really a reflection of the society itself. People admired the tough guy with a good heart and Graham was that for a lot of people. Annie Laura Barnett didn't want people to write about Graham because she feared that the writers would make him look like an outlaw.[2] What she didn't understand was that Texans love outlaws, or the image of them, and that is another reason people admired Graham Barnett. They loved the concept of Graham Barnett, the modern gunfighter, brawler, and gambler, but most would agree the real man was hard to get along with. Despite all of that, certain behaviors were expected of a man in West Texas, and Graham Barnett didn't get any mileage out of not doing what was expected of him.

In the end, it came down to a man doing what he was supposed to do and doing what his pride told him he had to do. It was pride that put Graham Barnett in the street in Rankin, Texas, on a cold, wet morning. The legend wouldn't let the man walk off. He could have just left town with Bill Fowler sitting and watching him. The whole town was watching, hell, the whole world might have been watching, as far as he knew. A man couldn't walk away from something like that.

Gaynor Armstrong cowboyed on the Bar N ranch in the Big Bend, and wrote most of the "Ballad of Graham Barnett," the *corrido*-like story of Graham's life and ultimate fall. What he had to say about Graham in 1963 caught up all the emotion and admiration Texans had, even for a bad man. "All of us cowboys thought a lot of ole Graham... We all admired him for his nerve and because of what he could do. He was an all-around man. He wasn't no coward. He just come out and done what he done and, by golly, he didn't back up for nothing."[3] People in West Texas couldn't help but love a man who wouldn't back up for nothing.

Illustration 19. Bill Barnett holding the machine gun that killed his father.

(Courtesy Barnett Family Collection)
The picture was taken inside the Upton County Armory in Rankin, Texas, on November 9, 2006.

Acknowledgments

This work relies heavily on research done by Russell Drake between 1955 and 2001. Russell became fascinated with the Graham Barnett legend and during the time he was a staff writer for *the San Angelo Standard Times* and *the Livestock Weekly* he interviewed many people who knew Graham. After he moved on to other endeavors in writing he continued to collect and to search for people who might have information concerning Graham and the final encounter in Rankin with Bill Fowler. Russell kept all of his notes, some on envelopes, some on scraps of paper, some on carbonless copy paper. All of the information was categorized by the name of the person being interviewed. He kept every scrap of paper. Often he was so focused on the story and on what the people were saying that he did not record other information such as dates of the interview and locations. What was important was the information itself.

He met with Graham's widow and all of the children who were still alive when he began the work. He also interviewed Boog Barnett several times and Joe Graham, the uncle who was so influential in Graham's upbringing. All of these people were able to recreate the life and times of a twentieth-century gunman.

Official records were more difficult to obtain. Since much of the research was done before the easy availability of copy machines, he had to laboriously hand copy newspaper stories and legal documents that he found all over West Texas. Some of these sources have since been deleted from the sites he originally found them. Court records, for example, are nonexistent in a number of counties.

He developed a lively letter writing campaign with people who were hard to contact in person. He kept copies of both his letters and the replies. Tony Hess was one of these people and Hess's communication forms a large part of the chapter on the final days of Graham in the Big Bend and the trip to Rankin. Hess was perhaps the last living witness to Graham's trip to Rankin. Russell and Jeff Graham were able to interview Hess who, at the time of the interview, was in his 80s. Hess was almost deaf and spoke with a strong German/Swiss accent combined with some Spanish that characterized his long stay on the border. Listening to the recording is an adventure in translation and interpretation.

During the late 1950s, Russell became convinced that there was a market for the story and wrote a thirty-four-page treatment aimed at one of the men's adventure magazines of the time. Whether he actually submitted the story or not is not clear. He did correspond with Elton Miles, a prominent folklorist at Sul Ross University. Miles took some of Russell's material and incorporated it into a long story he wrote called "Hell in the Oil Patch." Miles's versions of some of the early adventures were more folklore than fact. He identifies Graham as a border patrolman who tames towns and quick draws Texas Rangers while sticking up for the poor and downtrodden. The story was not published.

Much of Russell's work remained unused until John Barnett (Graham's grandson) and I wrote an article on Graham in the *Chronicle of the Big Bend* published by Sul Ross. I had been collecting information on Graham since the early 1980s with less success than Russell because most of the people were dead by that time. John had many family photographs and had documented much of what happened to the family in California. We put the article together and that caught Russell's attention, and he contacted John and offered all of his material if we would write it. John was working at several projects at that point and was out of the country a great deal. He agreed to digitize all of the notes and collections Russell had put together and provide them to me. I took Russell's research, combined it with mine, tried to find some kind of third party account such as newspapers or legal papers to supplement forty- or fifty-year-old memories, and put it all together. I think we produced a pretty fair likeness of Graham and his time. All of Russell's research is referred to as the Russell Drake Collection or "RDC" in the notes and in the bibliography.

One final point, the Thompson Submachine gun, which figured so prominently in the end of the Graham Barnett story, remains in the custody of the Upton County sheriff's department.

ENDNOTES

NOTES TO INTRODUCTION

1. Orland Sims, *Gun-Toters I Have Known* (Austin: The Encino Press, 1967) 33. Orland Sims knew Noisy Watson well enough that he called him friend. He also knew, or knew of, Graham Barnett, and did not consider him a leading citizen. Sims always thought it was a miscarriage of justice that Graham was not found guilty after the Watson trial. He was a well-known observer of the West Texas scene and his views of the admiration that people had for Graham were fairly accurate. Graham was a hero to people because he carried a pistol, came and went as he wanted, and people admired that. Judge Sims did not.

2. James Weatherby, interview by Russell Drake, 1995, Russell Drake Collection.

3. Jim Coffey and John T. Barnett, "Graham Barnett, A Big Bend Shootist," *Journal of Big Bend Studies* 19 (2007).

NOTES TO OVERVIEW

1. "Graham Barnett Slain with Machine Gun," *San Angelo Standard*, December 7, 1931.

2. Ibid., 1.

3. Ibid., 1.

4. Lee Graham, interview by Jim Coffey, Mason, Texas, July 2005. Otto Graham was Graham Barnett's cousin. Lee was Otto Graham's son and remembered his dad telling him stories about Graham Barnett during an afternoon visit shortly before Otto's death. Otto remembered his cousin

like an older brother who introduced Otto to cowboying and probably other activities.

5. "Graham Barnett slain with machine gun," *San Angelo Standard*, December 7, 1931.

6. Ibid., 1.

7. Ibid., 1.

8. Van "Ripp" Martin, interview by Jim Coffey, Junction, Texas, December 1970. Ripp was sheriff of Kimble County and had an unusual way of dealing with bad guys and people who wanted to be bad but didn't know how to do it. Since he knew most of the people in the county he could talk to them on a personal basis. I recall sitting in his office while he talked to several people that had broken some kind of law, but he didn't talk everyone in. He stopped, fought with, and arrested a number of people that he couldn't talk into coming in. He carried a gun everyday and if he ever pulled it, he never mentioned it.

9. Sarah Massey, ed., *Texas Women on the Cattle Trails* (College Station: Texas A&M University Press, 2006). This collection of essays views women in a different light than either the traditional historians or twenty-first-century feminists prefer to see them. They did whatever was needed to be done to take care of the family and the property. They could work stock, cook supper, and go to the dance that weekend. Much of our view of country women has been influenced by movies and books written by people who did not know ranch women. That is a pity and does not do justice to the women who could, in the words of Jack Kennedy, "bear any burden, meet any hardship." They were people who did what was needed to deal with the issues that they faced individually or as part of a family.

10. E. C. Abbott, *We Pointed Them North* (Norman: University of Oklahoma Press, 1939). "Teddy Blue" cowboyed, drank, and partied from Texas to Wyoming. His description of how cowboys got along with women is enlightening. He tells of occasions where cowboys stayed around a whorehouse after doing their business to have the girls read

to them and teach new dance steps. For some of the cowboys the parlor houses became a sort of lower grade gentleman's club.

11. In San Angelo there is still a story about one of the ladies who got out of the business, invested well in real estate and other properties, and when she died, three local bankers were among her pall bearers not only because of her financial business, but because they thought a lot of her.

NOTES TO CHAPTER 1

1. Boog Barnett, interview by Russell Drake, San Diego, California, 1958, Russell Drake Collection afterwards "RDC."

2. James Weatherby (1919-2001), interview by Russell Drake, Big Lake, Texas, July 1957. James was Sim's son. James's recollections must have been family stories related to him by his father and brother since he would have been a child when Graham was killed. Sim Weatherby was a close friend of Graham's and provided direction, employment, and refuge for him on a number of occasions at ranches he owned at Juno and Big Lake. Sim's wife was Cressie Counts who had gone to school with Graham and Boog "on the Divide in Sterling County." The Weatherbys had provided a place for Graham to go after the Watson slaying. James thought that Graham was working undercover for Judge Sutton when he had the run-in with Carroll Bates. RDC.

3. Family stories related to Russell Drake included the story. Several family members told the story. A similar story is told about Boog when he became a cook later in life. Boog supposedly pulled his six-shooter and forced a man who had griped about his beans to eat them off a rock. RDC.

4. Jeff Graham to Russell Drake, February 24, 1986. (Jeff Moore Graham May 2, 1914- September 17, 2004) Jeff Graham was the youngest son of Joe Graham and was seventeen when his cousin Graham Barnett was killed. His letters provided a genteel view of life growing up in the Graham house. He also accompanied Russell during his visit with Anton

"Tony" Hess. In his letters he provides a balanced account of what he could recall about his cousin. RDC.

5. Joe Graham, "Autobiography of Joe Martin Graham," Manuscript published online. Undated. https://familysearch.org/patron/v2/TH-303-43701-736-99/. Accessed February 10, 2015. P 24 (Joseph Martin Graham June 11, 1872-July 4, 1963) If there was a single figure who Graham turned to again and again for help and direction, that man was Joe M. Graham. Joe was Graham's uncle and as such took care of him for his entire life by providing money for bail, jobs, and direction. Joe was an entrepreneur in West Texas and if he had not gotten overextended with bank loans and bad debts, he would be remembered today as one of the major forces in the agricultural development of the area. Joe Graham wrote a brief autobiography which, while lacking in many details concerning his family, provided a great deal of information about how he worked to bring in enough capital to buy ranches later in his career. He was a businessman who built a reputation on keeping his word and delivering a good product. He was well thought of by the people he dealt with.

6. Ibid., 25.

7. Ibid., 25.

8. Boog Barnett, interview by Russell Drake, 1957. Russell Drake interviewed a number of the Barnett children as well as Annie Laura and Boog. Boog's recollections put him at the center of almost every adventure that his brother had with the exception of the gunfight in Rankin. RDC.

9. Boog Barnett, interview, RDC.

10. Vern Davis (1890- August 12, 1974), interview by Russell Drake, Sterling City, n.d. Davis was sheriff of Sterling County from 1924 until 1947. He was later deputy sheriff in Reagan County from 1956-1974. He was the longest serving Sterling City sheriff. RDC.

11. James Weatherby, interview, RDC.

12. R. P. Brown (1883-1969), interview by Russell Drake. Sterling City, n.d. A longtime resident of Sterling City. Brown worked for Texaco and knew Graham, on and off, for several years. He was a cousin of Graham's. RDC.

NOTES TO CHAPTER 2

1. The author worked for a short time for a man who punctuated his orders by throwing rocks at the apprentice cowboy who happened to have the misfortune of getting caught doing something wrong. On one occasion the rock cracked a board in a gate. You tend to work harder to avoid another correction of that velocity.

2. There are at least two variations of this story, both of them told about Boog. Tony Hess recounts one in a letter to Russell Drake. This time Boog was cooking beans and when one man complained and the bean pot got turned over, Boog pulled a pistol and made him eat the beans off the ground. Both stories are typical of the open range stories told in which a cowboy gets some kind of revenge on a bullying associate. Truth or legend, all of the stories followed the Barnett bothers for the rest of their lives.

3. Graham, Autobiography.

4. Ibid.

5. It is unusual that years later, Joe Graham wrote a brief autobiography but nowhere in it does he refer to Graham, Boog, or the Graham family. He was interviewed late in life by Russell Drake and spoke about Graham easily and candidly. It is possible that the autobiography was written for a later generation of his family, perhaps grandchildren, and he didn't want them to know about their relative. A lifelong West Texas resident commented, "Sometimes you just decide not to tell some things." Apparently Joe Graham decided not to write some things.

6. Brian Montague, "Memoirs of Brian Montague—Graham Barnett," Unpublished document, RDC. (Brian Montague March 26, 1892-October 5, 1972) Brian Montague was born in Bandera and grew up to be a lawyer, district attorney, and finally district judge presiding in Del Rio. He was also a keen student of history and made notes on a variety of subjects. He wrote on such varied topics as the Del Rio Bank and Trust and the system of irrigation canals in Del Rio. He also wrote a short 12 page essay on Graham Barnett, who he knew for the final fifteen years of Graham's life. This document provides much legal background and includes other information that fills in sections of Graham's life that might have been overlooked. Despite his close association with Graham he still makes some mistakes with regard to incidents he was not a personal witness to. Despite this, his is the best contemporary account of Graham's life. His notes on the Babb family form part of the research for this section. RDC.

7. Graham letter to Drake, February 24, 1986. RDC.

8. Graham, Autobiography, 31.

9. Graham, Autobiography, 31. The nature of Joe's health problems are not stated in his autobiography. He found a doctor in San Antonio who gave him some medicine. Based on problems many cowboys faced, it might have been that bane of all horsemen: hemorrhoids.

10. "Ammunition is found in Mexican Houses in Del Rio," *San Antonio Express*, July 8, 1908.

11. Jack Skiles, *Judge Roy Bean Country*. (Lubbock: Texas Tech University Press, 1996.) 154.

12. Joe Graham, interview by Russell Drake, Midland, n.d.

13. "Wild animals killing sheep," *El Paso Herald*, October 13, 1913.

14. Ibid.

15. "Big Movement of Mexican Cattle," *El Paso Herald*, June 26, 1911.

16. Ibid.

17. Jeff Graham, letter to Russell Drake, RDC.

18. Ibid.

19. Ibid.

20. Boog Barnett, interview by Russell Drake, RDC.

21. Jeff Graham, letter to Russell Drake, RDC.

22. "Wild animals killing sheep," *El Paso Herald,* October 13, 1913.

23. Boog Barnett, interview by Russell Drake, RDC.

24. "Graham Barnett Slain by Sheriff," *San Angelo Standard,* December 7, 1931.

25. Rick Smith, "Texas Morning," *San Angelo Standard Times,* October 3, 1976. Smith quotes Joe Graham, grandson of Barnett's uncle, as identifying Coots as being an "old retired, redheaded Irishman." Far from being retired Coots was still a very active cowboy. He was born in 1872. He apparently ran a small place on his own as evidenced by a short note that said on October 9, 1911, he shipped 200 Angora goats to a ranch near Uvalde. "Langtry Has Wind and Rain Storm," *El Paso Herald,* October 9, 1911, 8. He was neighbors with the Burdwell and the Billings families, both whom would become witnesses to Bill Ike Babb's shooting.

26. Ibid.

27. In order to be successful with this activity a horse has to get accustomed to the sound of a gun being fired very close to its ears; otherwise their reaction tends to be abrupt and immediate. The author had occasion to observe a Colt 357 being fired from the back of a horse that was not prepared for it. The results made anything seen in a professional rodeo pale by comparison. As he got older, Graham moved up the ladder of target practice and graduated to telephone poles and insulators. Vern Davis described Graham shooting at telephone poles and Tony Hess mentioned the same thing happening on the drive to Rankin in 1931. It must have been an activity that was practiced often.

28. Tony Hess, interview by Russell Drake, RDC.

29. Skeeter Skelton, *Skeeter Skelton on Handguns* (Peoria, PA: PJS Publications, 1980). "Second Guns Come First," 48. Skelton was a Border Patrol agent and DEA officer during the 1970s and 80s. He wrote that he carried a Model 60 Smith and Wesson tucked in his belt for a cross draw and commented that he had observed this carry on a number of occasions.

30. "Fowler case goes to jury," *Devil's River News,* March 25, 1932.

31. No one ever put a clock on Graham Barnett but the question of how fast is fast comes up from time to time. There are so many variables that there can be no firm answer. The weapon used, the conditions under which it is used, and the experience of the user all affect the outcome. That being said, drawing from a concealed carry and getting a 1911 Model 45 in position and delivering a hit can be done in about one and a half seconds. Your results may vary.

NOTES TO CHAPTER 3

1. Boog Barnett, interview by Russell Drake, 1958, San Diego, California, RDC.

2. Montague, "Memoirs," 2.

3. Dr. J. B. Cranfill, *Chronicle: A Story of Life in Texas* (New York: Fleming H. Revell and Company, 1916). Cranfill was a minister and part-time stringer for newspapers in Central Texas. He reported on the Babb family for several years to local newspapers and they figured prominently in his book. Cranfill and Cherokee Bill remained friends in spite of Cherokee Bill's stunts and Cranfill's reporting of them.

4. Brian Montague, "Narrative on the Babbs," Unpublished document, RDC.

5. Cranfill, *Chronicle,* 235.

6. Cranfill, *Chronicle,* 235.

7. Montague, "Narrative on the Babbs," RDC.

8. Ibid.

9. Ibid.

10. A section of land is 640 acres or roughly one square mile. It might be useful to think of an acre as about the size of a football field without the end zones.

11. Joe Graham interview by Russell Drake, 1958, RDC.

12. Victor P. Tippett (21 May 1877-13 Jan. 1971) did well for a young man who started out ranching on public land. By the 1940s he had cashed in on the oil booms and become a millionaire several times over.

13. Mildred Babb Adams, *From Darkness into Light* (Seagraves, TX: Pioneer Book Publishers, 1978), 12.

14. Tippett, interview by Russell Drake, RDC.

15. Ibid.

16. Ibid.

17. Ibid.

18. Mildred Babb Adams's family history entitled *From Darkness to Light* gives an extended view of her family's position on the land conflicts. Based on later interviews with her conducted by Russell Drake, her views may have moderated slightly with regard to people manipulating deeds in the Land Office. RDC.

19. "Big Movement in Mexican Cattle," *El Paso Herald,* June 26, 1911.

20. "Ranges in Fair Shape at Langtry," *El Paso Herald*, October 2, 1911.

21. "Graham Buys Sheep and Big Land Tract," *El Paso Herald*, March 18, 1912.

22. "To Stock Ranch with 17,000 Sheep," *El Paso Herald*, September 30, 1912.

23. Joe Graham, interview, RDC.

24. Vern Davis, interview, RDC.

25. Victor Tippett, interview, RDC.

26. Ruth Babb Sprott, interview by Russell Drake, Sanderson, n.d. RDC.

27. Adams, *From Darkness,* 13.

28. Russell Drake Collection. Russell interviewed a number of people who could remember Will both fondly and less so. Several recalled the blinking. RDC.

29. A *morral* was a fiber, cotton, or leather bag designed to carry horse feed but which was co-opted into a general tote bag for ammunition, food, or whatever a person needed to carry. It was usually hung from the saddle horn.

30. Boog Barnett, interview by Russell Drake, San Diego, California, 1958. RDC.

31. Ibid.

32. Joe Graham, interview, RDC.

33. Boog Barnett was involved in a situation that was investigated by the Texas Legislature involving him and another Ranger about a shooting that occurred after they were followed by two vaqueros. Boog was not charged in the affair, perhaps indicating how important the idea of stopping and identifying one's self was viewed by the authorities of the time.

34. Jeff Graham letter to Russell Drake, February 24, 1986. Letter in the possession of the authors. RDC.

35. Montague, "Memoir," 4, RDC.

36. Bud Barnett, interview by Russell Drake, RDC.

37. Jeff Graham letter to Russell Drake, February 24, 1986, RDC.

38. Ibid.

39. Joe M Graham, interview by Russell Drake, RDC.

40. Adams, *From Darkness*, 7.

41. Interview conducted with unnamed resident of Langtry. The story is included in Drake's original treatment. RDC.

42. Skiles, *Judge Roy Bean*, 176.

43. Ibid.

44. Doug Braudaway, "W.H. Dodd, Frontier Rancher, Businessman and Justice of the Peace," Val Verde County Historical Commission. http://vvchc.net/marker/Dodd%20narrative.html.

45. Skiles, *Judge Roy Bean*, 177.

46. Boog Barnett, interview by Russell Drake. Boog's exact quote was, "He shot him with a Savage .32 automatic," RDC.

47. Ibid., RDC.

48. Boog Barnett, interview by Russell Drake, RDC.

49. Skiles, *Judge Roy Bean*, 177. Witnesses mentioned the knife and it was addressed in the court papers transcribed by Russell Drake.

50. Skiles, *Judge Roy Bean*, 177.

51. Tippett, interview by Russell Drake.

52. Court Records of *State of Texas vs. Graham Barnett*, transcribed by Russell Drake.

53. Ibid.

54. Ibid.

55. Ibid.

56. Ibid.

57. Skiles, *Judge Roy Bean,* 177.

58. Adams, *From Darkness,* 14.

59. Skiles, *Judge Roy Bean,* 177.

60. Ibid.

61. Adams, *From Darkness,* 14.

62. Skiles, *Judge Roy Bean,* 177.

63. Court records recorded by Russell Drake, RDC.

64. Adams interview by Russell Drake, RDC.

65. Ibid.

66. Vern Davis, interview, RDC.

67. Pat Patterson Papers, Sul Ross University, RDC.

NOTES TO CHAPTER 4

1. Joyce Means, *Pancho Villa Days at Pilares* (Tucson: Privately Printed, 1988), 12.

2. "Cattle Are Being Crossed at Langtry," *El Paso Herald,* February 2, 1914.

3. "Langtry Man Sells Many Sheep and Goats," *El Paso,* February 16, 1914.

4. Martin, *Autobiography,* 42.

5. Martin, *Autobiography,* 42. Joe Graham's comments about the bridge crossing illustrates the kind of man he was: "we got on the track and followed on after the train and the bridge guard Mike Moore who followed the train to the east side of river Mike had gotten to his house at east

end I drove across the bridge got off the track in front of his house I knew him well so he came out and I says Mike you can cuss me out but you cant [*sic*]make me go back he says you tell them I told you, you could cross, of coarse [*sic*]."

6. Court records accessed by Russell Drake, RDC.

7. Montague, "Memoirs," 1.

8. *Fort Stockton Pioneer*, October 2, 1914. Originally collected by Russell Drake. In the early 1950s Russell was conducting original research with people who had known Graham. When he got to Pecos, some of the information concerning the trial was still available in the library and in the courthouse. Much of the information concerning the trial is from his research. RDC.

9. Ibid.

10. *Fort Stockton Pioneer*, October 2, 1914. Originally collected by Russell Drake.

11. Bud Barnett, interview by Russell Drake, RDC.

12. Bud Barnett, interview by Russell Drake, RDC.

13. Tony Hess interview by Russell Drake, RDC.

14. "Bendele Asks for Liberty," *El Paso Herald,* June 5, 1905, 1. On June 6, 1905, Bendele was freed. The court found that Texas had no jurisdiction in the case and Bendele had been tried previously.

15. "John H. Hicks Marries Frisco Girl," *El Paso Herald,* January 3, 1906, 1. Hicks stayed with the T.O. until 1908 when he and the school marm left to ranch in Arizona.

16. "$700,000 for Mexican Ranch," *New York Times,* February 5, 1910.

17. "Kingsberry's Story of the Battle," *El Paso Herald,* August 1, 1911.

18. "All Quiet on the T.O. Ranch," *El Paso Herald,* February 13, 1912.

19. "The T.O. Ranch Is Looted: Orozco Reported near Bandaras," *El Paso Herald,* August 29, 1912.

20. "Raid by Salazar's Men on the T.O. Ranch," *Yuma Examiner,* January 14, 1914.

21. "Invading Mexicans Believed to be from Ojinaga Are Held Back by Men of Villa's Force," *El Paso Herald,* January 27, 1914.

22. "Cowboys Battle with Mexicans," *El Paso Herald,* September 14, 1914.

23. C. H Harris III and Louis R. Sadler. *The Texas Rangers the Bloodiest Decade* (Albuquerque: University of New Mexico Press, 2004), 456.

24. Glenn Justice, "The Murder Trial and Killing of Hod Roberson." http://www.rimrockpress.com/blog/index.php?entry=entry080731-195204 Accessed July 21, 2008. Details on Roberson's career as a Ranger and later as a brand inspector are available from a number of sources but many are colored by his ambush killing in 1923 when he was a brand inspector. Although he was supposed to have killed as many as thirty-eight men, proof of that is lacking in some cases, not all.

25. Ibid.

26. Ibid.

27. "Thirty Cowboys Held by Mexicans," *El Paso Herald,* November 19, 1914.

28. Means, *Pancho Villa Days,* 67.

29. Means, *Pancho Villa Days,* 12.

30. In conversations with Annie Laura Barnett in the 1950s by Drake and in conversation with Graham's son in 2006 conducted by the author, both stated unequivocally that Graham had not been shot and in fact never was wounded until his final fight. His quote used by Joyce Means may have been a slight exaggeration to describe the seriousness of the fight.

31. Justice, "Hod Roberson."

32. Means, *Pancho Villa Days,* 79.

33. Joel Starnes, interview. Joel Starnes knew Graham during the old days in Big Lake and spent a good bit of Friday afternoon, December 5, 1931, talking with him while they waited for Bill Fowler to return to the courthouse. This comment was made during that time.

Notes to Chapter 5

1. Annie Laura Barnett, interview by Russell Drake, RDC.

2. Ibid.

3. Ibid.

4. Ibid.

5. Ibid.

6. Ibid.

7. Ibid.

8. County Records Sterling County, Marriage license.

9. Joe Graham, interview, RDC.

10. Drake, handwritten copy of newspaper article included in original Drake treatment, unpublished. RDC.

11. Ibid.

12. Ibid.

13. Texas Penal Code –Section 9.31 Self Defense. http://law.onecle.com/texas/penal/9.31.00.html Accessed March, 2014.

14. "Graham Barnett a Free Man Again," *Sterling City Record,* October 15, 1915.

15. Skiles, *Judge Roy Bean,* 79.

16. Adams, interview, RDC.

17. Bud Barnett, interview, RDC.

18. Adams, *From Darkness into Light*, 15.

19. "Graham Barnett a free man again," *Sterling City Record* October 15, 1915, 1.

20. Bud Barnett, interview, RDC.

NOTES TO CHAPTER 6

1. Texas Adjutant General Service Records 1836-1935. Barnett, J. Organization: Regular Rangers Call Number: 401-51. https://www.tsl.texas.gov/apps/arc/service/viewdetails.php?id=1081&view=http://www/arc/service/data/RR/view_bar1081i002.jpg#regImg Accessed March 21, 2015.

2. John P. Schmal, "Mexican Immigration in the Early Years." http://www.hispanicvista.com/hvc/Columnist/jschmal/020705jschmal.htm Accessed August 21, 2013.

3. Douglas W. Richmond and Sam W. Laynes, eds., *The Mexican Revolution-Conflict and Consolidation 1910-1940* (College Station: Texas A&M University Press, 2013), "A Decade of Disorder," Nicolas Villanueva Jr., 14.

4. Ibid., 14.

5. Harris and Sadler, *The Texas Rangers* (2004), 256-257. Ransom was one of four men hired by Houston mayor Horace Rice to address an epidemic of concealed weapons on the street. Seven months later the Houston night police chief, William Murphy, was killed by a recently fired policeman named Earl McFarlane. McFarlane's attorney was James Brockman, a well-known and respected lawyer. On October 25, 1910, Harry Ransom shot Brockman three times on a downtown street in Houston. His defense was that Brockman had drawn a pistol first. He was acquitted on that charge and appointed police chief. He brought in

a number of ex-Rangers as special officers and they proved to be as big a problem as the criminals they were tasked with controlling. Ransom and another officer beat up not only criminals, but civilians as well, and most unfortunately, members of the press. He was eventually fired after beating up another reporter and shooting a policeman in the neck that tried to arrest him and was finally urged to leave town.

6. Robert M. Utley, *Lone Star Lawmen* (New York: Oxford University Press, 2007), 28.

7. Harris and Sadler, *The Plan of San Diego* (Lincoln: University of Nebraska Press, 2013), 1.

8. Harris and Sadler (2004), 252. Sadler and Harris provide extensive detail on the political background of the border incursions. Their research indicates that the Carranza government was aware of or at least supported the activities in an effort to manipulate US foreign policy toward Mexico.

9. Ibid., 302.

10. Harris and Sadler (2004), Appendix, 507-575. The appendix lists all Rangers enlisted during the period of the Revolution and includes the dates of service. This was used to develop a list of which Rangers had been hired in May and then checked against their discharge information to determine who had terminated on what dates. Based on this listing, Graham was one of the Rangers of this group who had remained with the service the longest.

11. "Organization of the Texas Rangers 1911," Texas Ranger Hall of Fame http://www.texasranger.org/ReCenter/org1911.htm.

12. Sadler and Harris (2004), 313-14. The controversy is discussed at length in Sadler and Harris. The Rangers seemed to be not only catching outlaws but also running off political opposition. Much of the political opposition was an extension of the war in Mexico with loyalists and revolutionists fighting each other in Texas. It was a mess. Both the Rangers and the Alderete family had a number of altercations. The

movement of the Ranger camp is an indication of how seriously the state government was beginning to take the complaints.

13. Although Company B was later involved in the massacre at Porvenir in December of 1918, while Graham was in the Rangers there were no recorded cases of such extreme behavior.

14. Texas Adjutant General Service Records 1836-1935. Barnett, J. Organization: Regular Rangers Call Number: 401-51, https://www.tsl.texas.gov/apps/arc/service/viewdetails.php?id=1081&view=http://www/arc/service/data/RR/view_bar1081i002.jpg#regImg Accessed March 21, 2015.

15. Enlistment papers for Joe Graham Barnett. Texas Adjutant General's Service Records 1836-1935. https://www.tsl.texas.gov/apps/arc/service/.

16. Monty Waters, "More on 1917 Presidio Shootout," Glenn's Texas History Blog, http://www.rimrockpress.com/blog/index.php?entry=entry090404-184548.

A. G. Beard led a colorful career. He became city marshal of Marfa, and was later suspected in the robbery of a Mexican payroll officer. Beard later moved to Mexico to work with J. Monroe Fox who handled security for an oil concern. Although Beard was suspected of a variety of activities that teetered on the illegal, he was never indicted or convicted of anything. He died in Austin in 1941.

17. Monty Waters, "More on Nathan Fuller," Glenn's Texas History Blog. http://www.rimrockpress.com/blog/index.php?entry=entry081121-095548

Nathan Fuller was a typical Ranger of the period and a good man. He ran afoul of his captain, Jerry Gray, when Gray put a less qualified man over Fuller. The man had also recently lost a prisoner. Fuller's comments are classic, "I told Gray I wouldn't work under Dyches. I will not work under no man who let a few Mexicans come to this side and shoot him loose from a prisoner, in broad open daylight, and the prisoner handcuffed." Fuller became a railroad detective and died in 1969.

18. Darren L. Ivey, *The Texas Rangers: A Registry and History* (Jefferson, NC: MacFarland and Company, 2010), 223, "Battle Record."

19. Mike Cox, *Time of the Rangers* (New York: Tom Doherty Books, 2009), 58.

20. A friend of the author used a '95 briefly for his yearly deer hunt and described the recoil of the rifle as being serious enough to "get meat on both ends." The '95 was a favorite of many Rangers who followed the accepted Ranger policy of cutting the barrel down to fifteen or sixteen inches. While this made it much more portable, the recoil and blast is impressive with that short a barrel. The comment about it being branded "O2" is from the James Weatherby interview. In the only photograph of Graham and this rifle it appears to be a military Krag that had not been cut down as were the ones carried by some of his colleagues.

21. The O2 ranch was a Hereford operation that was one of the largest ranches in the area in the 1920s. It was about forty-five miles south of Alpine. If Graham worked for the ranch it was during the period of time after the Babb killing. The comments from some of his colleagues mention the O2-branded rifle and one of the Weatherbys remembered the gun in Graham's hands. RDC.

22. Texas Adjutant General Records, "Texas Ranger Records," Company B, Captain J. M. Fox, December 31, 1916. Copies of these entries were provided to John Barnett who made the copies available to the author.

23. Ibid.

24. Ibid.

25. "Says Wife Was Slain by Butler," *Huntington Press,* January 26, 1917.

26. "Army Asserts Murder Was Planned," *El Paso Times,* July 21, 1916.

27. "Spannell Gets a Hearing," *New York Times,* July 28, 1916.

28. "Butler Murder Inquiry," *New York Times,* July 22, 1916.

29. "State Rests in Spannel Case," *Sweetwater Weekly Reporter,* January 26, 1917.

30. "Says Wife Was Slain by Butler," *Huntington Press,* January 26, 1917.

31. Ibid., 6.

32. Ibid., 6.

33. Ibid., 6.

Notes to Chapter 7

1. Enlistment papers for Joe Graham Barnett, Texas Adjutant General's Service Records 1836-1935, https://www.tsl.texas.gov/apps/arc/service/ The comment quoted is handwritten on the bottom of the second page, apparently a statement added by someone with access to the decision making process.

2. Louis F. Aulbach, *The Great Unknown of the Rio Grande* (Houston: privately published, 2007), 28.

3. Annie Laura Barnett, interview by Russell Drake, 1958, RDC.

4. Ibid.

5. Ibid.

6. Ibid.

7. Ibid.

8. Juan Manuel Casas, *Francisco Villalba's Texas* (Houston: Iron Mountain Press, 2008), 28.

9. Ibid.

10. "Military Classifications for Draftees," Compiled by Anne Yoder. http://www.swarthmore.edu/library/peace/conscientiousobjection/MilitaryClassifications.htm Accessed March 2, 2015.

11. Harris and Sadler (2004), 329.

12. Enlistment papers for Joe Graham Barnett, Texas Adjutant General's Service Records 1836-1935. https://www.tsl.texas.gov/apps/arc/service/.

13. Texas Adjutant Generals General Service Records 1836-1835, "J.G. Barnett," Call Number 401-51.

14. Joe Graham, interview by Russell Drake, 1957.

15. County Records Brewster County.

16. Conger Barnett, interview by John Barnett, December 2011, in the collection of the authors.

17. Annie Laura Barnett, interview by Russell Drake, 1958.

18. Ibid.

19. "Republican chosen for post in Pecos County," *El Paso Herald,* November 8, 1922.

20. Montague, "Memoirs," 1.

21. A copy of the letter is in the possession of John Barnett, Graham's grandson.

22. Ibid.

23. Not to excuse the practice but it happened often enough that it was not a total surprise to people who lived in the area. The story about shooting at someone from one side of the river to the other was commonly heard up until the 1960s. While a lot of it fell into the range of legal hearsay, it was common enough that when the author heard the stories in the 1960s they were not accompanied by any kind of feigned surprise or shock but rather a "well it happened again today, someone took a shot at someone." The River Riders enforcing the cattle dipping of the 1940s were subject to it. Ranger Joaquin Jackson investigated a case of sniping from Mexico that resulted in the death of one person and the

wounding of two others in 1988 in the Big Bend, not far from some of Graham's old stomping grounds. Such sniping still takes place.

24. At that time most of the men who worked stock in the brush wore leather chaps, short for *chaperajos*, over their trousers as protection from brush and thorns. Most Texans called them "leggings" or more colloquially, "leggins." The leggins had a pocket on each thigh and it was not unusual for a cowboy to slip a short pistol into it rather than try to deal with a belt and holster while working stock.

25. "One Arm Miller," Sergeant Lee Young, Texas Ranger Dispatch, Issue Eight, Fall 2002. http://texasranger.org/dispatch/Backissues/Dispatch_Issue_08.pdf Young grew up in Brackettville and learned many of the stories about Miller and the bootleggers from the people who had been arrested. He based his story on how Miller lost his arm from an interview he had with Tol Dawson, a former Texas Ranger who worked with Miller. With regard to the story about Miller losing his arm in a knife fight in Mexico, Dawson replied, "Well, now that doctor in San Antonio could have been a Mexican and he had a knife and I'm mighty sure Miller put up a fight to keep his arm."

26. Willie Warrior, interview by Jim Coffey, September 1996. Willie Warrior was a deputy sheriff in Val Verde County and a proud member of the Seminole Community. He remembered Miller as one of the Rangers who enforced the prohibition laws. He commented that Miller would walk around in the black sections of the town at night, by himself, searching for bootleggers. Not only was he not afraid, the informant described him as "the meanest one-armed man I had ever seen."

27. Ross Phares, "Colorful Nicknames—Texan Parade," *Waco News Tribune,* July 12, 1954.

28. Montague, "Memoirs," 2, RDC.

29. Rick Smith, "Texas Morning," *San Angelo Standard Times,* 1983.

30. Ibid.

31. Everett Ewing Townsend (October 20,1871-November 19, 1948) was a Texas Ranger, sheriff in Brewster County, a state senator, and the man, more than any other, who envisioned a national park in the Big Bend. He loved the land and wanted to keep it as it was when he first saw it. He supported better relations with Mexico and was a lawman who enforced the law impartially.

32. Montague, "Memoirs," 3. The Caulder case must have impressed Montague because he provided tremendous detail concerning the murder and the aftermath of it. He was clearly impressed that no one was tried for the murder. Ed Caulder appeared to be one of the Big Bend's most memorable characters. Montague uncharacteristically misspelled Caulder's name as "Calder" in his Memoirs document, making it difficult to verify the story. RDC.

33. Year: 1920; Census Place: Justice Precinct 2, Brewster, Texas; Roll: T625_1781; Page: 3B; Enumeration District: 13; Image: 1024.

34. "Brewster County Precinct One 1920." http:// www.rootsweb.ancestry.com/~txbcgs/brew20p1.html. Accessed August 3, 2016.

35. Ibid., 3.

36. Ibid., 3.

37. Ibid., 3.

38. Ibid., 3.

39. Ibid., 3.

40. This story is typical of the stories that fed the legend of Graham Barnett. There is some truth to it and perhaps some fiction in it. In trying to verify the story, the author was unable to find any death certificate for "Ed Harris" in Brewster County during the period 1920-1923. Records do not show any "Ed Harris" in the county in the 1920 Census. This doesn't mean that the story might not be true with another person besides

Caulder. There were several murders during this period and one of those might have involved Graham and his activities with the posse.

41. Ibid., 4.

42. Ibid., 3.

43. Sam Haynes interview by Russell Drake, RDC.

44. Weatherby interview, RDC.

45. Charles Hickcox, interview by Russell Drake, RDC.

46. Vern Davis, interview by Russell Drake, RDC.

47. Ibid.

48. Ibid.

49. Ibid.

50. Vern Davis, interview by Russell Drake.

51. Ibid.

52. Jeff Graham Letter to Russell Drake, February 24, 1986. Jeff Graham, Joe Graham's son, goes on for some length about bootlegging in West Texas, and makes it very clear that the offense was not considered too serious until someone got caught. The adventure with the Sul Ross professors ended up in one of Joe Graham's cotton fields. RDC.

53. Montague, "Memoirs," 4, RDC.

54. Ibid.

55. Ibid.

Notes to Chapter 8

1. Montague, "Memoirs," 5, RDC.

2. Thad Sitton, *Lord of the County Line* (Norman: University of Oklahoma Press, 2000), xii.

3. Thad Sitton, *Texas High Sheriffs* (Austin: Texas Monthly Press, 1988), 11.

4. David C. Humphrey, "PROSTITUTION," Handbook of Texas Online (http://www.tshaonline.org/handbook/online/articles/jbp01), accessed June 8, 2015. Uploaded on June 15, 2010. Published by the Texas State Historical Association.

5. Walter F. Pilcher, "CHICKEN RANCH," Handbook of Texas Online (http://www.tshaonline.org/handbook/online/articles/ysc01), accessed August 13, 2015. Uploaded on June 12, 2010. Published by the Texas State Historical Association. The Chicken Ranch operated in several different locations during its 129-year run. The location off of Highway 71 was established in 1905. It was referred to as the Chicken Ranch because during the Depression money was scarce so Miss Jesse went to the poultry standard and accepted one chicken per transaction. Soon she was able to get into the butter and egg business, which provided some much-needed cash flow.

6. The national Prohibition Act, Title 2 Section 3, The Federal Judicial Center, http://www.fjc.gov/history/home.nsf/page/tu_olmstead_doc_5.html.

7. Gary Sleeper, *I'll Do My Own Damn Killing* (Fort Lee, NJ: Barricade Books, 2006). Benny Binion was a hero to a lot of people both in Texas and eventually in Las Vegas. His misadventures provided amusement for the populace and headlines for newspapers for years. See Gary Sleeper.

8. T. Nicole Boatman, Scott H. Belshaw and Richard B. McCaslin, *Galveston's Maceo Family Empire* (Charleston, SC: The History Press, 2014).

9. *The Miami News*, "Gambler Jakie Freedman was the highest player ever," 9.

10. Jane Wilson, *Texon: Legacy of an Oil Town* (Mount Pleasant, SC: Arcadia Publishing, 2013), 13-14.

11. Jane Spraggins Wilson, "BEST, TX," Handbook of Texas Online (http://www.tshaonline.org/handbook/online/articles/hnb32), accessed June 9, 2015. Uploaded on June 12, 2010. Published by the Texas State Historical Association.

12. Leo Bishop, interview by Jim Ward, James Ward Collection, Angelo State University, San Angelo, Texas.

13. Ibid.

14. Wilson Papers, Jane Wilson collected a tremendous amount of data about Texon and much of it she used in her book of the same name. She provided several pieces of Levi Smith's personal papers to John Barnett and those were included in this work.

15. Montague, "Memoirs ," 6, RDC.

16. Wilson, "Texon," 20.

17. Wilson Papers.

18. Wilson Papers.

19. Conger Barnett, interview by John Barnett, December 2014, John Barnett Collection.

20. Bud Barnett, interview, RDC.

21. Ibid.

22. *San Angelo Standard Times*, Rick Smith, Texas Morning October 5, 1976.

23. Ibid.

24. Ibid.

25. Elton Miles, "Hell in the Oil Patch," unpublished manuscript in the possession of Russell Drake. Russell worked with Elton Miles of Sul

Ross University to get several of the stories about Graham published. Miles wrote up a shorter treatment that he expected to use as a chapter in a book he was doing on the Big Bend. In both cases the family denied permission to print the material after they had read it as they objected to the way Graham was portrayed. The stories of his fights in the bordello and in Boilermaker Bill's saloon rely on these earlier treatments. RDC.

26. Boog Barnett, interview by Russell Drake, RDC.

27. "Sheriff Fowler Makes Bond in Shooting of Graham Barnett," *San Angelo Standard,* December 8, 1931, 1.

28. Vern Davis, interview, RDC.

29. Montague. "Memoirs," 6. Brian Montague states that both men were suspected of being involved with bootleggers but provides no proof: "it was soon rumored that Harry [Odneal] was affording protection to many of the bootleggers," RDC.

30. Harris and Sadler (2004), 356-57. Carroll Bates was an unusual character. He had been city marshal and later police chief in San Angelo before going into the Rangers as a captain in 1917. When he was suspected of smuggling from his ranch at Santa Helena he was investigated by Gus Jones of the Bureau of Investigation. Jones and Bates were old friends from San Angelo where Jones had served as city marshal and later as a ranger and special ranger. Jones claimed Bates was working as an undercover informant. Further research shows that Bates continued to lead a remarkably weird career in and out of law enforcement. After being tried and convicted of bootlegging and serving an eighteen-month sentence he returned to San Angelo and went back to work for the police department as a finger print expert.

31. Montague, "Memoirs," 9, RDC.

32. Billy Rankin, interview by Russell Drake, RDC.

33. "Three Arrested," *San Angelo Standard,* July 27, 1925.

34. Harris and Sadler (2004), 565, Robert Sumrall (Nov. 28, 1894- Sept. 30 1944) was a career ranger having enlisted for the first time in December of 1919 and continuing with the Rangers until 1933.

35. "Three Arrested," *San Angelo Standard,* July 27, 1925.

36. "Ranger Gives Bail," *San Angelo Standard*, January 23, 1925.

37. Ibid.

38. *Terrell County Memorial Museum News,* November, 2012, "J. J. [Jack] Allen, Scholar, Soldier, Sheriff," 2.

39. Montague, "Memoirs," 5-6, RDC.

40. Interview with Annie Laura Barnett conducted by Russell Drake, RDC.

41. Montague, "Memoirs," 5, RDC.

42. Ibid., 5.

43. Ibid., 6.

44. Ibid., 6.

45. "Two Arrested for Robbery at Texon," *San Angelo Standard,* January 13, 1925.

46. Ibid.

47. J. T. Mace, "Statement of Facts," undated letter to Adjutant General, The James Ward Collection, Angelo State University.

48. Hickcox, interview, RDC.

49. Annie Laura Burnett, interview, RDC.

50. Montague, "Memoirs," 6, RDC.

51. "From the Bandera New Era," *Hondo Anvil Herald,* January 19, 1924.

52. Montague, "Memoirs," 6, RDC.

53. Ibid.

54. Ibid.

55. Ibid.

56. Ibid.

57. Montague, "Memoirs," 7, RDC.

58. Russell Drake Collection.

59. Kurt House, "Cold Steel and Warm Gold—Arms and Badges of Three Texas Ranger Captains," *The Texas Gun Collector*, Fall 2013, 26-30.

60. Robert M. Utley, *Lone Star Lawmen*, 156.

NOTES TO CHAPTER 9

1. *San Angelo Standard*, "Graham Barnett Admitted to Bail," August 9, 1925.

2. Ibid.

3. "Sumrall Guilty," *San Angelo Standard*, July 25, 1925.

4. "Examination for Barnett Tuesday," *San Angelo Standard*, July 27, 1925.

5. "Barnett Acquitted," *San Antonio Express*, July 27, 1927.

6. Ellison Carroll was one of the biggest names in competitive roping in the history of the game. He was known for beating Clay McGonagill in 1913 for the world's championship in steer roping. It should be noted that this was steer roping, not calf roping. A steer was 500-600 pounds and usually grumpy about taking part in the activity. Carroll and McGonagill were friends throughout their competition. In Carlsbad, New Mexico, McGonagill broke his rope during a five steer roping, and Carroll immediately rode out and gave McGonagill his own rope. For

more on Carroll see Mary Lou LeCompte, "CARROLL, JOHN ELLISON," Handbook of Texas Online.

7. John Holmes, interview. Russell's notes identify Holmes as a "land agent" in Rankin who had known Graham for a number of years. RDC.

8. J. O. Brooks remains something of a mystery man in the story. He was indicted on at least two occasions, once in 1921 for possession of liquor, again in 1925 in one of the large raids in the oil field area. Details on Brooks's style and organization are from notes made by Russell Drake.

9. Taylor Emerson, interview by Russell Drake. Russell's notes indicate that Emerson was the teller at the First State Bank of Big Lake. He and Graham knew each other well enough that Graham would spend the night in Emerson's hotel room.

10. The use of a backup weapon was a common practice at this time. Davis's comment that the gun had been modified, which makes it likely that the hammer spur was cut off and the front of the trigger guard removed to make access to the trigger easier. The modification was known as a Fitz Special after John Henry Fitzgerald, a Colt gunsmith and well-known marksman of the era. Similar guns were carried by Manual T. Gonzaullas of the Rangers, Charles Lindbergh, Bill Decker, Dallas County Sheriff, and any number of people who needed a serious back gun and had access to a good gunsmith or a hacksaw.

11. "Attorneys Seek Bail for Barnett," *San Angelo Standard,* July 29, 1925.

12. Ibid.

13. Ibid.

14. "Graham Barnett Admitted to Bail," *San Angelo Standard*, August 9, 1925.

15. "Attorneys Seek Bail for Barnett," *San Angelo Standard*, July 29, 1925.

16. Ibid.

17. Ibid.

18. Ibid.

19. "Graham Barnett Admitted to Bail," San Angelo Standard, August 9, 1925.

20. Ibid.

21. Ibid.

22. Ibid.

23. Ibid.

24. "Attorneys Seek Bail for Barnett," *San Angelo Standard,* July 29, 1925.

25. "Graham Barnett Admitted to Bail," *San Angelo Standard,* August 9, 1925.

26. "Attorneys Seek Bail for Barnett," *San Angelo Standard,* July 29, 1925.

27. Ibid.

28. Ibid.

29. Ibid.

30. *San Angelo Standard,* July 26, 1925.

31. "Examination for Barnett Tuesday," *San Angelo Standard,* July 27, 1925.

32. Ibid.

33. Montague, "Memoirs." 6, RDC.

34. Montague, "Memoirs," 13, RDC.

35. Graham was released on bail October 14, 1925. The four men who went on his bond were K. D. Harrison, L. M. Rankin, former sheriff, O. H. Graham, a cousin, and C. C. Lane. Bond was $5000.00.

Notes to Chapter 10

1. Montague, "Memoirs," 8, RDC.

2. Letter from Annie Laura Barnett to Levi Smith, August 24, 1925. Copies of letter archived by Jane Wilson, in the files of John Barnett.

3. Letter from Levi Smith to Annie Laura Barnett, September 17, 1925. Copies of letter archived by Jane Wilson, in the files of John Barnett.

4. James Weatherby Interview conducted by Russell Drake, June 3, 1995, Big Lake, Texas. RDC.

5. Ibid.

6. Ibid.

7. Ibid.

8. Annie Laura Barnett, interview, RDC.

9. District Court records, Jeff Davis County pertaining to the case *State of Texas No. 324 vs. Graham Barnett*, RDC.

10. Ibid.

11. Montague, "Memoirs," 8, RDC.

12. Ibid., 9.

13. Ibid., 9.

14. Ibid., 9.

15. Ibid. 9

16. Ibid., 9.

17. "Leave for Barnett Trial," *San Angelo Standard,* July 17, 1927. The brief news story includes the names of several other men who went along to the trial, including "Pecos Pete" Meador, a local gentleman who must have decided the ride would have been worth it.

18. Haynes, interview, RDC.

19. Sims, "Gun-Toters," 33.

20. Davis, interview, RDC.

21. Request for continuance, filed with District Court, Jeff Davis County, January 11, 1926, RDC.

22. Russell Drake Collection.

23. The Suspended Sentence Law of 1913 allowed the jury to avoid making any kind of punishment on a defendant until that defendant committed another offense. The judge did not have the authority to suspend a sentence without a recommendation from the jury. The law was a controversial one and repeal was sought in 1925 but it was not repealed until 1947. See http://caselaw.findlaw.com/tx-court-of-criminal-appeals/1379388.html, *Ivey vs. State of Texas.*

24. Request for Suspension of Sentence, Tom Green County, July 26, 1926, 1.

25. "Attorneys Seek Bail for Barnett," *San Angelo Standard,* July 29, 1925, 1.

26. "Graham Barnett Admitted to Bail," *San Angelo Standard,* August 9, 1925, 1.

27. "Noisy Watson Slain at Big Lake," *San Angelo Standard,* July 26, 1925, 1.

28. "Barnett Acquitted," *San Antonio Express,* July 27, 1927.

29. Judges charge to the jury, July 19, 1927, Pp 1479, Court Records.

30. Montague, "Memoirs," 7, RDC.

31. Russell Drake Collection.

32. Sims, "Gun-Toters," 1967, 33. Sims described Noisy Watson as an old friend, which may have colored his view of Graham somewhat.

33. Interview with a resident who wanted to remain anonymous, San Angelo, June 19, 2013, notes in possession of the author. It is interesting to note that members of her family had been involved in several feuding situations over time; however, none of them resulted in a reported shooting.

NOTES TO CHAPTER 11

1. Montague, "Memoir," 11, RDC.

2. Rick Smith, "Texas Morning," *San Angelo Standard Times*, October 10, 1976.

3. Glenn Williford, "The life and times of a Shootist: Graham Barnett, 1890-1931," *Quarterly of the Association for Outlaw and Lawman History* 23, no 1 (January-March 1999): 13-14.

4. L. J. Wardlaw, letter to Garrard, http://boards.ancestry.com/localities.northam.usa.states.texas.counties.upton/11.6/mb.ashx.

The letter is included in its entirety here to show the vehemence expressed by some people with regard to Graham.

Dear Mr. Garrard: I am in receipt of yours of the 16th. This is to advise you that I do know of the Sheriff at Rankin killing Graham Barnett, and that an indictment was returned and the case removed to Sonora for trial. I will be glad to join you and Judge Van Sickle in the defense, and will charge a fee of $500.00, with expenses. For your information, Cornell & Wardlaw, 20 years ago prosecuted Graham Barnett for the murder of Billy Babb at Langtry. I hardly think you need anyone to assist you in the defense of the sheriff, as that viper [Barnett] should have been killed a thousand times before he was. I was well and personally acquainted with Noisy Watson whom Graham Barnett killed some five or six years ago. In my opinion no more dastardly crime was ever committed than the murder of Noisy Watson. If rumors are correct as to the activities of Barnett in the Big Bend country, he killed enough Mexicans to build a dam sufficient to hold water 100 feet high at any place a dam might be built on the Rio Grande between El Paso and Del Rio. If I am to be employed in the defense of this case, I want such employment to be consummated at the earliest possible time, in order that I may get in communication with some people in Sutton County. Very truly yours, signed L. J. Wardlaw.

There was a tendency to overestimate deaths depending on if you were a Barnett supporter or not. Sim Weatherby also estimated the number of men killed by Graham as 600. He backed off of that exaggeration but the consensus on the border was that a large number of men were killed, although little hard evidence was ever produced. The reputation of a killer did much to create a mind-set with many people that this individual should be left alone because they had killed in the past and would do so again.

5. Williford, "Shootist: Graham Barnett," 14, RDC.

6. Zeb Decie, interview by Russell Drake, RDC.

7. Russell Drake, "Graham Barnett," unpublished manuscript, 25, RDC.

8. Lee Graham, interview by Jim Coffey, July 17, 2010, Mason, Texas.

9. Boog Barnett, interview, RDC.

10. Ibid.

11. Texas Ranger Records, letter from R. W. Aldrich to W. L. Wright, November 30, 1927. Material collected January 7, 1971, by Jim Ward. The Dr. James Ward Collection, Angelo State University, San Angelo, Texas.

12. Texas Ranger Records, letter from Captain W. L. Wright to Captain R. W. Aldrich, dated December 1, 1927. Material collected January 7, 1971, by Jim Ward. The Dr. James Ward Collection, Angelo State University, San Angelo, Texas.

13. Tom and Bobby Fowler, "Genealogy 2 Bill Fowler,"

http://mv.ancestry.com/
viewer/8cd51c71-6a81-4b61-9664-41763f315e7c/2797150/1275877194,
accessed July 18, 2016.

14. Ranger records do not show Fowler as a regular ranger. He did
have a special ranger commission, which he held from 1929-1930.

15. Starnes, interview, RDC.

16. "Highway Commission Ready to Prosecute 1926 License Users,"
El Paso Herald, February 27, 1927.

17. "Many Highway Allotments Marked Off," *The Eagle* (Bryan Texas),
March 5, 1927.

18. Untitled column, *El Paso Herald,* Tuesday March 1, 1927.

19. Ibid.

20. "Weight Inspector Named," *Dallas Morning News,* November 8, 1927.

21. "Car Hits horse; Man Hurt," *El Paso Evening Post,* January 12, 1928.

22. Highway Patrol records. Most of the records for the Highway
Patrol were destroyed in August of 1949. Russell was able to find one
record, a pay card, which indicated the beginning and ending dates of
his employment with the department. RDC.

23. Sim Weatherby, Vern Davis, and Brian Montague all commented
on Graham continuing to bootleg as an ongoing side job.

24. James Weatherby, interview, RDC.

25. Annie Laura Barnett, interview, RDC.

26. Virginai Noelke, *A History of the Cactus Hotel,* San Angelo Cultural
Affairs Council, San Angelo, 1996. The Cactus was San Angelo's premier
hotel and was noted for providing whatever the guest wanted. Noelke
describes how bellhops would buy liquor by the case, hide it in the
basement, and resell it to other bellhops who would then sell to hotel

guests. Women were provided by bellhops who acted as intermediaries between the guests and the ladies for a 40 percent cut of the profit.

27. Interview with Suzanne Campbell, Head Librarian West Texas Collection, Angelo State University, San Angelo, Texas. Campbell provided a number of stories concerning the gambling events. Mike Morris, former police officer, did a number of gambling raids in the Sharp End during a later era. He explained that the name of the area did not originally have anything to do with knives but rather referred to a boarding house named Sharp's Inn and over the years had taken on a more ominous tone with the people who tended to be a little more confrontational in their encounters.

28. Sadler and Harris (2004), 327. Bates was supposed to have a great deal of influence with the voters in Tom Green County. Sadler and Harris state that this was a primary reason for his appointment as a Ranger captain by Governor Ferguson.

29. Ibid. 360.

30. "Former Officer Denies Receiving Rum Ring Money," *Corsicana Daily Sun*, May 3, 1929, 1. Information concerning the Carroll Bates bootlegging situation was limited in the San Angelo newspaper but covered in depth in newspapers across the state.

31. "Government Plans to Rest in Trial of Former Officer," *Corsicana Semi-Weekly Light*, May 3, 1929, 1, Two local bankers testified that between May 1, 1926, and April 22, 1929, Bates had deposited $54,000.00, an amount equal to about $741,000.00 in 2015 dollars.

32. Ibid.

33. Montague, "Memoir," 11, RDC.

34. Weatherby, interview, RDC.

35. Russell Drake, "Graham Barnett," unpublished manuscript, 29, RDC.

36. Ibid.

37. Davis, interview, RDC.

38. Montague, "Memoir," 11, RDC.

39. Ibid.

40. James Cornell (1877-January 30, 1937) was a West Texas character. In 1921, when he was district judge for the 83rd judicial district, he had a dispute with rancher W. T. Holman. The incident occurred at the Sheep and Goat Raisers Association in Del Rio. The two met on a crowded Del Rio street and exchanged words and both drew their pistols. Holman had his under his shirt and it got hung up; Judge Cornell's did not. Cornell was tried for murder and found not guilty. Cornell commented to a number of people that the shooting nearly ruined his life and it is understandable that he tried to head off the Barnett-Bates encounter.

41. No one tells exactly the same story. One police officer (who was not there at the time of the incident) said Bates was in the Arc Light (Mike Morris). Brian Montague put it in front of the Landon Hotel, which was across the street from the Arc Light. In his articles in 1983, Rick Smith set the altercation in the Arc Light. Having it in the Arc Light makes more sense in light of what happened during the encounter.

42. "Texas Morning," *San Angelo Standard Times*, 1983.

43. Montague, "Memoir," 11, RDC.

44. Smith, "Texas Morning."

45. Davis, interview, RDC.

46. Montague, "Memoirs," 11, RDC.

47. Ibid.

48. Mike Morris, former policeman, interview by Jim Coffey, July 7, 2005, San Angelo, Texas.

49. "Couch Denies Wet Charge San Angelo," *Amarillo globe Times*, January 11, 1929.

50. Ibid.

51. "Twenty Given Fines and Terms in Angelo Trial," *Lubbock Morning Avalanche*, May 4, 1929.

52. "Denials Are Made of Charges Cited to Carroll Bates," *Lubbock Morning Avalanche,* May 3, 1929.

53. Ibid.

54. "Former Officer Denies Receiving Rum Ring Money," *Corsicana Daily Sun*, May 3, 1929.

55. Ibid.

56. Ibid.

57. "Twenty Given Fines and Terms in Angelo Trial," *Lubbock Morning Avalanche,* May 4, 1929.

58. "How Dry I Am Sends Men Off," *Lubbock Avalanche Journal*, May 5, 1929, col.1.

59. Ibid.

After serving his time, Bates returned to San Angelo and the police department, although not as chief. The city director shows that he was a fingerprint expert and also had a painting business on the side. He lived in San Angelo the rest of his life and died in 1946.

60. Most of the conjecture about Graham's involvement stems from working undercover in Big Lake in 1925 and in an unrelated incident later in 1930. Sim Weatherby hinted that Graham had worked undercover for a number of state and local agencies but proof is lacking. In 1930 Graham received a Special Ranger Commission at the request of Judge Sutton. The assumption was that he was gathering information but that he might need to carry a weapon or conduct an arrest; therefore, he needed some kind of legal means to do so. Several people have stated the long discussed but unsubstantiated idea that Graham continued the relationship he had with both Sutton and the Montague brothers over

an extended period of time and worked for them gathering information in a highly unofficial capacity.

NOTES TO CHAPTER 12

1. Billie Rankin, interview by Russell Drake, June 1990, RDC.

2. Ancestry.com, U.S. Social Security Death Index, 1935-2014 [database online], Provo, UT, USA: Ancestry.com Operations Inc, 2011.

3. Tony Hess and Russell Drake communicated by letter for several years. All of the information concerning Hess's life and adventures comes from these letters. Russell was able to interview Tony near the end of his life. The tapes provide more information but are very difficult to interpret. Tony still spoke with a strong Swiss-German accent and life on the border had given him something of a Spanish accent as well.

4. "Anton Hess" Ancestry.com, *Swiss Overseas Emigration, 1910-1953* [database on-line], Provo, UT, USA: Ancestry.com Operations Inc., 2008.

5. Tony Hess letter to Russell Drake, May 3, 1991, RDC.

6. Ibid. Tony Hess was one of those individuals who lived the American dream. He came to a new land, learned a new language and new skills and never stopped learning. He used the language of the day when he said he "made a hand." Quite a compliment for a cowboy.

7. Ibid.

8. Tony Hess letter to Russell Drake, January 14, 1991, RDC.

9. Texas Adjutant Generals Records 1836-1935 (https://tslarc.tsl.texas.gov/service/SR/f/fo/fow7146.pdf) accessed September 16, 2014. Some sources indicate that Fowler was police chief in McCamey but in his application for a Special Ranger Commission dated December 20, 1929, he lists his job as city marshal for two years. The town was not incorporated until 1926 and it is unlikely it had police force until much later. The marshal got the job done.

10. Tony Hess letter to Russell Drake, January 14, 1991, RD.C

11. H. Gordon Frost and John Jenkins, *I'm Frank Hamer* (Austin and New York: Pemberton Press, 1968), 151.

12. Clay Coppenger, *Forgotten Tales of Texas*, "The Dead Bank Robbery Bounty" (Mount Pleasant, South Carolina: The History Press, 2011), 105-106.

13. Bob Alexander, *Lawmen, Outlaws and S.O.Bs*, vol. 2 (Silver City, NM: High Lonesome Books, 2007), 148. Alexander makes a convincing argument that the shootings in Rankin were the result of good police work. He contends that Hamer had made up his mind concerning the illegalities of the shootings and then searched for evidence to support his position.

14. Robert M. Utley, *Lone Star Lawmen* (New York: Oxford University Press, 2007), 128.

15. Hamer had cause to suspect that something was wrong with what he called a "Murder Machine." In Stanton, two men, C. C. Baze and Lee Smith, were indicted for murder in connection with the shooting. See Alexander, *Lawmen, Outlaws and S.O.B.s*, 144.

16. Rankin, "Upton Officer Exonerated in Bandit Killing," *Upton County News*, April 5, 1928.

17. Ibid. The *Upton County News* listed, "Other rangers who testified in the case were Capt. Wright of McCamey, Light Townsend of Raymondville, Graves Peeler of Campbellton, Graham Barnett and Ranger Smith. Others who testified were H L Johnson, of Lubbock County, Sheriff Simpson of Lynn County, Sam Arnett president of the City National Bank of Lubbock. Deputy Sheriff Green of Big Spring, Otis Frances Sheriff of Midland, Sheriff Reeder Webb of Ector County, Joe Hogan inspector for the Texas and Southwestern Cattle Raisers Association, Operative Rogers of the Burns Detective Agency, W M Massie of Fort Worth, president of the Texas Bankers' Association, and several Rankin residents."

It is interesting that Graham was listed in the same group as current Rangers. As near as can be determined, Graham did not have a law enforcement position at the time that is part of the record. Why a civilian would be included in a group of pretty illustrious officers wasn't questioned by anyone. It does seem to indicate that perhaps he was working as a private investigator at the time although there is not printed proof to support that.

18. Ibid.

19. "Examining Trial for Dumas to be Held Wednesday," *Upton County News,* April 11, 1928.

20. Alexander, "Lawmen, Outlaws and S.O.Bs," 149-150. The three officers were indicted three years later in 1931. The three indictments were quashed based on motions filed by Brian Montague and James Cornell and brought before Judge Claude Sutton. It was an indicator of the lawlessness of West Texas at the time to determine how many gunmen the two lawyers defended and Judge Sutton sentenced. It must have been a very high number.

21. "Defeated Candidate Files Suit at Rankin," *Galveston Daily News,* August 21, 1928.

22. Billy Rankin interview with Russell Drake, June 1990, RDC.

23. Ibid.

24. Ibid.

25. Ibid.

26. Annie Laura Barnett, interview, RDC.

27. Davis, interview, RDC.

28. Ibid. During the interview Vern Davis made clear that Graham never gave Vern any trouble, even when he was drinking. Graham apparently had a lot of respect for some of the officers whom he couldn't intimidate and Vernon Davis was one of them.

29. Annie Laura Barnett, interview, RDC.

30. Ibid.

31. Texas Adjutant General's Service Records, call number 401-78, "William Clarence Fowler," https://tslarc.tsl.texas.gov/service/SR/f/fo/fow7146.pdf, accessed June, 2014.

32. Annie Laura Barnett, interview, RDC.

33. Montague, "Memoir," 12, RDC.

34. Sitton, "Texas High Sheriffs," 1988, 241.

35. Kevin Krause, "Unregistered Tommy Gun Triggers Queries at Agency," *Dallas Morning News*, December 4, 2006. Decker was known for carrying a Thompson in his car. His comment concerning carrying the Thompson was made by Vann "Ripp" Martin, sheriff of Kimble County, who knew Decker slightly and avidly followed his adventures as big city sheriff.

36. Traci Evans, "H. B. 'Butch' Purvis donation of a 1928 Thompson submachine gun from Ranger Captain Hardy B. Purvis," http://www.texasranger.org/artifacts/Purvis-Thompson.htm, accessed May 23, 2014.

37. Jim Coffey, "Will Wright: Rangers and Prohibition," *Texas Ranger Dispatch*, Summer 2006. http://www.texasranger.org/dispatch/MasterIndex/backissues.html

38. FBI records of "List of Thompson Submachine Guns sold in Texas from 1928 to January 6, 1936," RDC.

39. Montague, "Memoir," 12, RDC.

40. "Barnett Hunts Money for Gun," *El Paso Evening Post*, March 28, 1931.

41. Ibid.

42. Ibid.

43. Ibid.

44. "Posts $10,000 Slaying Bond," *El Paso Herald Post*, December 7, 1931. The article mentions the pawnbroker, also named Barnett, and the fact that Graham was well-known in El Paso but makes no mention of the resolution of the problem.

45. Joel Starnes, interview by Russell Drake, RDC.

46. In the handwritten notes for the Joel Starnes interview, Russell wrote, "Starnes wrote Barnett a check for the Thompson." There is no mention of when the check was written, possibly during one of the previous visits Graham made to Rankin earlier in the year. If Starnes wrote the check it must have been on a county account since it is unlikely he would have written a check on Bill Fowler's personal account, RDC

47. Tony Hess letter to Russell Drake, January 14, 1991, RDC.

48. "Courtroom Is Thronged for Fowler Trial," *San Angelo Standard*, March 14, 1932. The *San Angelo Standard* described Graham as watching for oil wells on the Elsinore, which implies some kind of guard to keep people from stealing either equipment or materials from some of the isolated sites.

49. "El Paso Funeral for Mack Adams Citizen of Marfa," *The Big Bend Sentinel*, October 10, 1947.

50. Boog Barnett, interview, Boog maintained that there was some kind of theft going on at the Elsinore during this period of time but that is difficult to confirm. RDC.

51. "Courtroom Is Thronged for Fowler Trial," *San Angelo Standard*, March 14, 1932.

52. Ibid.

53. The fight was memorable enough that the defense at the Fowler murder trial called Raymond McKay as a witness. McKay described the

fight and its aftermath as part of the defense's plan to show Graham as a man who made a threat and was capable of carrying it out.

54. "Fowler Case Goes to Jury," *Devil's River News,* March 25, 1932.

55. Montague, "Memoir," 13.

56. Bill Barnett, interview by John Barnett, December, 2006, John Barnett Papers.

57. Graham's first son was Talmadge Graham Barnett. Later in life he changed his name to Joe Graham Barnett Jr. to honor his father.

NOTES TO CHAPTER 13

1. Annie Laura Barnett, interview, RDC.

2. Anton Hess, interview by Russell Drake, 1990. Hess said that Graham lived on the Rosillos Ranch and drove over to Dripping Springs where they had a cow camp and picked Tony up there. The pair may have had a number of small camps set up where they could work some stock and move them later. RDC

3. Annie Laura Barnett, interview, RDC.

4. Montague, "Memoir," 14, RDC.

5. Juan Manuel Casas, *Federico Villabla's Texas* (Houston: Iron Mountain Press, 2008), 283-4.

6. Ibid.

7. Rick Smith, "Texas Morning," *San Angelo Standard Times*, October 22, 1976.

8. Ibid.

9. Anton Hess, interview by Russell Drake, RDC.

10. Elton Miles, "Graham Barnett, Big Bend Shootist," Unpublished manuscript, RDC.

11. Ibid.

12. Joel Starnes, interview, RDC.

13. Anton Hess, interview, RDC.

14. Anton Hess letter to Russell Drake, January 1, 1991, RDC.

15. Anton Hess letter to Russell Drake, January 26, 1991, RDC.

16. "Fowler Case Goes to Jury," *Devil's River News,* March 25, 1932.

17. Davis, interview, RDC.

18. Russell Drake Collection.

19. Montague, "Memoir," 11, RDC.

20. Montague, "Memoir," 11, RDC.

21. Ibid.

22. Ibid.

23. Annie Laura Barnett, interview by Russell Drake, 1958, RDC.

24. "Witnesses Give Details of Machine Gun Killing at Rankin," The *Devils River News* gives the name as Romo Chaves. The name was given as Shivers by the *Fredericksburg Standard,* December 11, 1931, "'Two Gun Barnett Shot to Death in Streets at Rankin." Tony Hess called him Shivley and disputed the allegation that he was a Hispanic named Chaves. What his name really was is still unknown.

25. Ibid.

26. Anton Hess letter to Russell Drake, January 1, 1991, RDC.

27. It is interesting that none of the people that Graham contacted on this trip admitted to giving him any money then or before except Bill Fowler. They all agreed that they were asked but in cross examination none would admit that they were involved in any way with Graham or his

fundraising project. It seemed as if all the old officers with whom he had worked either suddenly had a financial short fall or decided that whatever Graham had done for them in the past, needed to stay in the past.

28. Joel Starnes, interview by Russell Drake, RDC.

29. Ibid. Starnes was concerned when Graham showed up at the courthouse, probably because of Graham's previous visits. He was definitely a supporter of Fowler and, having seen Graham in Big Lake, was convinced he was up to no good. Starnes maintained in the interview that Fowler was not afraid of Graham, went so far as to comment that Fowler didn't seem to be afraid of anything, RDC.

30. Ibid.

31. "Fowler Case Goes to Jury," *Devils River News,* March 25, 1932.

32. Joel Starnes, interview with Russell Drake, RDC.

33. Ibid.

34. "Fowler Case Goes to Jury," *Devils River News,* March 25, 1932.

35. W. D. Riser was apparently a man of many skills. He was a lawyer, sold real estate, newspaper man and, in 1917, a county attorney in Rankin. He founded several newspapers and remained a prominent member of Upton County for years.

36. Joel Starnes interview by Russell Drake, RDC.

37. "Fowler Case Goes to Jury," *Devil's River News,* March 25, 1932. When he was asked about the money he said he gave it to Graham to avoid trouble. The exact nature of the trouble was not discussed in court, or if it was it was not reported.

38. Joel Starnes, interview, RDC.

39. Ibid.

40. Ibid.

41. Ibid.

42. "Fowler Case Goes to Jury," *Devil's River News*, March 25, 1932.

43. Ibid.

44. Ibid.

45. Ibid.

46. Ibid. All of the comments concerning the evening in McCamey were told and retold during the trial. Either Graham's drinking, or his slowly developing plan to possibly "take over the town," must have been responsible for his loud harangues. Fowler's plan to leave the situation alone and let Graham work himself up and out of his mood shows that Fowler did not bear Graham any ill will at this point. The public airing of their disagreement at the courthouse on Friday afternoon was the beginning of Fowler understanding that this problem was getting out of his control.

47. "Sheriff Freed in Slaying of Noted Figure," *Abilene Reporter News*, March 24, 1932. Tony Hess said in later testimony that Graham was "drunk on Friday night." People familiar with Graham probably recognized the old pattern of drinking and threatening.

48. "Sheriff Makes Bond of $10,000 in Shooting of Graham Barnett," *Devils River News*, December 11, 1931.

49. "Sheriff Fowler Makes Bond in Shooting of Graham Barnett," *San Angelo Standard*, December 8, 1931.

50. Ibid.

51. "Sheriff Makes Bond of $10,000 in Shooting of Graham Barnett," *Devils River News*, December 11, 1931.

52. "Sheriff Fowler Makes Bond in Shooting of Graham Barnett," *San Angelo Standard*, December 8, 1931. The news story states that "his companions finally persuaded him to leave." Hess probably had more

influence over Graham than Shivley had simply because they had been living and working together.

53. "Sheriff Fowler Makes Bond in Shooting of Graham Barnett," *San Angelo Standard*, December 8, 1931.

54. Anton Hess, interview by Russell Drake.

55. Blance Venion was the telephone operator. She recalled that Graham called the sheriff on Sunday morning but the exact time was not recorded in the news reports.

56. Rankin, interview, 1990.

57. Starnes, interview.

58. Ibid.

59. "Sheriff Fowler Wins Acquittal," *Devils River News*, March 24, 1932.

60. Ibid.

61. Ibid.

62. "Sheriff Fowler Wins Acquittal," *Devils River News*, March 24, 1932.

63. Ibid.

64. "Posts $10,000 Dollar Slaying Bond," *El Paso Herald Post*, December 7, 1931. Over time there have been a number of stories concerning the shooting with regard to where Graham was and whether Fowler got out of the car or not. The *Herald Post* was one of a number of newspapers that picked up the story and mentioned the distance and the conditions of the shooting. From this it would seem that Graham never saw the gun until Fowler began firing.

65. Starnes, interview. Starnes saw the body and stated that Fowler fired fifteen shots and Graham was hit nine times. He is the only one to make the claim of nine wounds. The *San Angelo Evening Standard* claims seven shots. All of the witnesses claim fifteen or sixteen shots fired.

66. "Sheriff Fowler wins Acquittal," *Devils River News,* March 24, 1932.

67. It is a minor point, but the Thompson ejects empty shells from the upper right side of the receiver. If Hess was on his knees he probably could not have seen the ejector of the Thompson, since it would have been blocked by the round drum magazine when viewed from the front. He may have seen Fowler struggling with the cocking knob on the top of the gun in an effort to clear the jam, or the gun may have been turned slightly as Fowler gestured at him. At any rate, the shooting had stopped prior to his being shot and that made all the difference in the world.

68. Anton Hess letter to Russell Drake, January 1, 1991, RDC.

69. "Two Gun Barnett Shot to Death in Streets at Rankin," *Fredericksburg Standard,* December 11, 1931.

70. Gene Echols, interview by Russell Drake, RDC.

71. "Fowler Case Goes to Jury," *Devil's River News,* March 25, 1932.

72. *San Angelo Evening Standard,* December 7, 1931.

73. Annie Laura Barnett, interview, RDC.

74. "Graham Barnett Is Buried with Simple Service," *San Angelo Morning Standard,* December 9, 1931.

75. *Western Folklore,* "The Ballad of Graham Barnett, Badman of the Big Bend in Texas," John Q. Anderson, vol. 24, no. 2 (April 1965): 77-85. The primary writer of the ballad was Gaynor Armstrong who cowboyed on the Bar N Ranch in the Big Bend.

76. Anderson, "Western Folklore," 85.

Notes to Chapter 14

1. Montague, "Memoir," 12, RDC.

2. "Sheriff Fowler wins Acquittal," *Devils River News,* March 24, 1932.

3. Montague, "Memoir," 11, RDC.

4. "Sheriff Fowler Wins Acquittal," *Devil's River News*, March 24, 1932.

5. "Courtroom is Thronged for Fowler Trial," *San Angelo Morning Times*, March 24, 1932.

6. Ibid. The San Angelo paper commented, "Tony Hess... sat in the witness chair clad in a bright red shirt."

7. Anton Hess letter to Russell Drake January 26, 1991, RDC.

8. Ibid.

9. Ibid.

10. "Courtroom Is Thronged for Fowler Trial," *San Angelo Morning Times,* March 24, 1932.

11. Ibid.

12. Ibid.

13. "Courtroom Is Thronged for Fowler Trial," *San Angelo Morning Times,* March 24, 1932. "There was some diversity of testimony as to whether the leather jacket that Barnett wore was buttoned all the way, the justice of the peace saying it was buttoned all the way up."

14. Ibid. "Some said it covered the Barnett gun. Others said two or more buttons were buttoned." The question was a serious one and needed to be pursued. It seems that the prosecution team did not understand that there was a difference between having a gun and being able to access it. Had Graham unbuttoned a couple of buttons on his jacket as he walked toward Fowler, the question would have been moot. Why none of Graham's family or friends who were familiar with his habitual carry technique made this point to the lawyers is unbelievable. It is a long chance but it is possible that everyone knew from the beginning what the outcome of the trial was going to be and they decided not to pursue some of the details.

15. Ibid.

16. Ibid.

17. Ibid.

18. Ibid.

19. Starnes, interview, RDC.

20. "Courtroom Is Thronged for Fowler Trial," *San Angelo Morning Times,* March 24, 1932.

21. "Fowler Declares He Killed Barnett 'to Save His Own Life,'" *Devil's River News,* Sonora, Texas, March 24, 1932.

22. Ibid.

23. Ibid.

24. "Sheriff Freed in Slaying of Noted Figure," *Abilene Reporter News,* March 24, 1932.

25. Starnes, interview, RDC

26. Ibid.

27. "Sheriff Fowler Wins acquittal," *San Angelo Morning Times,* March 24, 1932. While Weaver Baker's final charge to the jury "that justice be done" looked good in print, it was a pretty weak summary statement.

28. Starnes, interview.

29. "Sheriff Fowler Wins acquittal," *Devils River News,* March 25, 1932.

30. Montague, "Memoir," 15, RDC.

31. Ibid.

32. Ibid.

33. The note reads, "Mr. Lowery—Mr. Graham wants the guns and other exhibits that were introduced. He is entitled to them. [signed] Joe

Montague." The exact disposition of the firearms involved after they were returned to Joe Graham is unclear. At least one turned up in the collection of Sheriff Don Atkins of Runnels County.

34. Adams, interview, RDC.

35. Starnes, interview, RDC.

36. Starnes, interview, RDC.

37. "Corsicana Texas Man Wanted for robbery captured San Angelo today," *Corsicana Daily Sun*, March 7, 1935.

38. Bud Barnett, interview. The comment was made on several occasions by Annie and later by Bud and Conger (Bill). When it was mentioned it was quickly followed with a statement to the contrary, "I don't think they would have ever done it." RDC.

39. This information comes from an interview with Bud Barnett, Graham's son, and Joe Graham that was done shortly before Joe died. During the interview one of the two stated that the family had to go to court to collect the money from the insurance company who took the position that they never would have issued the policy if they had known who Graham was. It is more likely they meant that it wouldn't have been honored if they had known the business he was in. Again, one of the two stated that half of the money went to the lawyers, but the family did get about half of it. RDC.

40. Conger "Bill" Barnett, interview by John Barnett, December 23, 2010. The details concerning the family in California are based on this interview and a previous family history collected by John Barnett.

Notes to Post Script

1. Jim Harrison, "Larson's Holstein Bull," *In Search of Small Gods* (Port Townsend, WA: Copper Canyon Press, 2009).

2. Barnett, interview by Russell Drake.

3. Anderson, "Western Folklore," 81.

BIBLIOGRAPHY

This work relies heavily on research done by Russell Drake between 1955 and 2001. Russell became fascinated with the Graham Barnett legend and during the time he was a staff writer for the *San Angelo Standard Times* and the *Livestock Weekly,* he interviewed many people who knew Graham. After he moved on to other endeavors in writing he continued to collect and to search for people who might have information concerning Graham and the final encounter in Rankin with Bill Fowler. Russell kept all of his notes, some on envelopes, some on scraps of paper, just as he made them during the interviews. He met with Graham's widow and all of the children who were still alive when he began the work. He was so concentrated on the story and what the people were saying that he did not record other information such as dates of the interview and locations. Since much of the research he did was done before the easy availability of copy machines, he had to laboriously hand copy newspaper stories and legal documents that he found all over West Texas. Some of these sources have since been deleted from the sites he originally found them.

Additionally, he wrote letters to a number of people that he could not interview and he kept copies of both his letters and the responses. Tony Hess was one of these people and Hess's communication forms a large part of the chapter on the final days of Graham in the Big Bend and the trip to Rankin. He also interviewed Hess, who at the time was in his early 80s. Hess was almost deaf and spoke with a strong German/Swiss accent combined with some Spanish that characterized his long stay on the border. Russell was accompanied by Jeff Graham at this time and listening to the recording is an adventure in translation and interpretation.

Russell wrote at least three different treatments using his research. Each was about thirty pages long and was written with a sale in mind to some of the men's adventure magazines of the time. They were rejected. He also shared some of the research with Elton Miles of Sul Ross University, who wrote a treatment to be included in one of his folklore collections. Miles' treatment included stories from some fiction that had been written at the time. Miles was convinced that the stories were about Graham even though the character is identified as a border patrolman, and his activities do not match any of those that Russell had collected. That article contained some information that Miles had collected concerning Graham's later activities but were heavily colored by folklore. Miles' original title was "Hell in the Oil Patch" and was going to be included in a collection but apparently the family refused to provide permission to publish and it was not used.

All of Russell's work remained unused until John Barnett (Graham's grandson) and I published an article on Graham in the Chronicle of the Big Bend, published by Sul Ross. He contacted John and offered all of his material if we would write it. John was working on several projects at that point and was out of the country a great deal. He agreed to digitize all of the notes and collections Russell had put together, and provide them to me. I took Russell's research, combined it with mine, tried to find some kind of third party account such as newspapers or legal papers to supplement forty or fifty-year-old memories, and put it all together. I think we produced a pretty fair likeness of Graham and his time.

All of Russell's research is referred to as the Russell Drake Collection in the notes and in the bibliography.

Books

Abbott, E. C. *We Pointed Them North*. Norman: University of Oklahoma Press, 1939.

Adams, Mildred Babb. *From Darkness Into Light*. Seagraves, TX: Pioneer Book Publishers, 1978.

Alexander, Bob. *Lawmen, Outlaws and S.O.Bs: Gunfighters of the Old Southwest*. Silver City, NM: High Lonesome Books, 2007.

Aulbach, Louis F. *The Great Unknown of the Rio Grande.* Houston: privately published by Louis Aulbach, 2007.

Boatman, T. Nicole, Scott H. Belshaw, and Richard B. McCaslin. *Galveston's Maceo Family Empire.* Charleston SC: The History Press, 2014.

Casas, Juan Manual. *Francisco Villalba's Texas.* Houston: Iron Mountain Press, 2008.

Cranfill, Dr J. B. *Chronicle: A Story of Life in Texas.* New York: Fleming H. Revell and Company, 1916.

Coppenger, Clay. *Forgotten Tales of Texas.* Charleston, SC: The History Press, 2011.

Cox, Mike. *Wearing the Cinco Peso 1821-1900.* New York: Forge Press, 2008.

Frost, H. Gordon and John Jenkins. *I'm Frank Hamer.* Austin and New York: Pemberton Press, 1968.

Glasrud, Bruce A., and Harold J. Weiss. *Tracking the Texas Rangers: The Twentieth Century.* Denton: University of North Texas Press, 2013.

Harris III, Charles H., and Louis R. Sadler. *The Texas Rangers and the Mexican Revolution: The Bloodiest Decade.* Albuquerque: University of New Mexico Press, 2004.

———. *Texas Ranger Biographies: Those Who Served 1910-1921.* Albuquerque: University of New Mexico Press, 2009.

———. *Plan de San Diego: Tejano Rebellion, Mexican Intrigue.* Lincoln: University of Nebraska Press, 2013.

Harrison, Jim. *In Search of Small Gods.* Port Townsend: Copper Canyon Press, 2009.

Ivey, Darrell L. *The Texas Rangers: A Registry and History.* Jefferson, NC: MacFarland and Company, 2010

Jackson, H. Joaquin, and David Marion Wilkinson. *One Ranger.* Austin: University of Texas Press, 2005.

Massey, Sarah, ed. *Texas Women on the Cattle Trails.* College Station: Texas A&M University Press, 2006.

Means, Joyce. *Pancho Villa Days at Pilares*. Tucson: Privately Printed, 1988.

Richmond, Douglas R. and Sam W. Laynes, eds. *The Mexican Revolution-Conflict and Consolidation 1910-1940*. College Station: Texas A&M University Press, 2013.

Schreiner III, Charles, Audrey Schreiner, et al. *Pictorial History of the Texas Rangers*. Kerrville, TX: Y-O Press, 1969.

Sleeper, Gary. *I'll Do My Own Damn Killing*. Fort Lee, NJ: Barricade Books, 2006.

Sims, Orland. *Gun-Toters I Have Known*. Austin: The Encino Press, 1967.

Sitton, Thad. *Texas High Sheriffs*. Austin: Texas Monthly Press, 1988.

———. *Lord of the County Line*. Norman: University of Oklahoma Press, 2000.

Skelton, Skeeter. *Skeeter Skelton on Handguns*. Peoria: PJS Publication, 1980.

Skiles, Jack. *Judge Roy Bean Country*. Lubbock: Texas Tech University Press, 1996.

Spinks, M. E. *Law on the Last Frontier*. Lubbock: Texas Tech University Press, 2007

Tise, Sammy. *Texas County Sheriffs*. Albuquerque: Oakwood Printing, 1989.

Utley, Robert M. *Lone Star Lawmen*. New York: Oxford University Press, 2007.

Wilson, Jane. *Texon: Legacy of an Oil Town*. Mount Pleasant, SC: Arcadia Publishing, 2013.

UNPUBLISHED MATERIALS

Drake, Russell. "Graham Barnett." Unpublished manuscript in possession of the authors.

Graham, Joe. Autobiography of Joe Martin Graham. Manuscript online. Undated. https://familysearch.org/patron/v2/TH-303-43701-736-99/.

Miles, Elton. "Hell in the Oil Patch." Unpublished manuscript in the possession of Russell Drake.

Patterson, Pat. Pat Patterson Papers. Archives of the Big Bend. Bryan Wildenthal Memorial Library. Sul Ross University, Alpine, Texas.

Montague, Brian. Memoirs of Brian Montague-Graham Barnett. Russell Drake Collection.

———. Narrative on the Babbs. Russell Drake Collection.

LETTERS AND PERSONAL COMMUNICATION

Graham, Jeff. Letter to Russell Drake. February 24, 1986. Russell Drake Collection.

Hess, Tony. Letters. December 30, 1990-May 12, 1991. Russell Drake Collection.

ARTICLES

Anderson, John Q. "The Ballad of Graham Barnett, Badman of the Big Bend in Texas." *Western Folklore* 24, no. 2 (April 1965): 77-85.

Braudaway, Doug. "W. H. Dodd, Frontier Rancher, Businessman and Justice of the Peace." Val Verde County Historical Commission. http://vvchc.net/marker/Dodd%20narrative.html

Coffey, Jim. "Will Wright: Rangers and Prohibition. *Texas Ranger Dispatch.* (Summer 2006): http://www.texasranger.org/dispatch/MasterIndex/backissues.html

——— and John T. Barnett. "Graham Barnett: A Big Bend Shootist." *Journal of Big Bend Studies* 19 (2007).

Evans, Traci. "H. B. 'Butch' Purvis donation of a 1928 Thompson submachine gun from Ranger Captain Hardy B. Purvis." http://www.texasranger.org/artifacts/Purvis-Thompson.htm. Accessed May 23, 2014.

LeCompte, Mary Lou. "CARROLL, JOHN ELLISON," *Handbook of Texas Online* (http://www.tshaonline.org/handbook/online/articles/fcach), accessed September 29, 2015. Uploaded on June 12, 2010. Published by the Texas State Historical Association.

Humphrey, David C. "PROSTITUTION," *Handbook of Texas Online* (http://www.tshaonline.org/handbook/online/articles/jbp01), accessed August 13, 2015. Uploaded on June 15, 2010. Published by the Texas State Historical Association.

Justice, Glenn. "The Murder Trial and Killing of Hod Roberson." http://www.rimrockpress.com/blog/index.php?entry=entry080731-195204 Accessed July 21, 2008.

Schmal, John P. "Mexican Immigration in the Early Years." http://www.hispanicvista.com/hvc/Columnist/jschmal/020705jschmal.htm Accessed August 21 2013.

Waters, Monty. "More on 1917 Presidio Shootout," Glenn's Texas History Blog http://www.rimrockpress.com/blog/index.php?entry=entry090404-184548

———. "More on Nathan Fuller," Glenn's Texas History Blog. http://www.rimrockpress.com/blog/index.php?entry=entry081121-095548

Pilcher, Walter C. "CHICKEN RANCH," *Handbook of Texas Online.* (http://www.tshaonline.org/handbook/online/articles/ysc01), accessed August 13, 2015. Uploaded on June 12, 2010. Published by the Texas State Historical Association.

Smith, C. W. "J. J. 'Jack' Allen, Scholar, Soldier, Sheriff," Terrell County Memorial Museum News. November, 2012.

Smith, Rick. "Texas Morning," *San Angelo Standard Times*, October 3, 1976.

Williford, Glenn. "The Life and Times of a Shootist: Graham Barnett, 1890-1931." *Quarterly of the Association for Outlaw and Lawman History* 23, no. 1 (January-March 1999): 13-14.

Wilson, Jane Spraggins. "BEST, TX," *Handbook of Texas Online* (http://www.tshaonline.org/handbook/online/articles/hnb32), accessed June 09, 2015. Uploaded on June 12, 2010. Published by the Texas State Historical Association.

Yoder, Anne, comp. "Military Classifications for Draftees" http://www.swarthmore.edu/library/peace/conscientiousobjection/ MilitaryClassifications.htm Accessed March 2, 2015

Young, Sgt. Lee. "One arm Miller" Texas Ranger Dispatch. Issue Eight, Fall 2002. http://texasranger.org/dispatch/Backissues/Dispatch_Issue_0 8.pdf

GOVERNMENT PUBLICATIONS AND PUBLIC RECORDS

Texas Penal Code –Section 9.31 Self Defense. http://law.onecle.com/ texas/penal/9.31.00.html. Accessed March, 2014.

"Organization of the Texas Rangers 1911." Texas Ranger Hall of Fame http://www.texasranger.org/ReCenter/org1911.htm

Texas Adjutant General's Service Records 1836-1935. https://www.tsl. texas.gov/apps/arc/service/

National Prohibition Act, Title 2 Section 3. The Federal Judicial Center, http://www.fjc.gov/history/home.nsf/page/tu_olmstead_doc_5.html

District Court records, Jeff Davis County pertaining to the case State of Texas No. 324 vs. Graham Barnett.

U.S. Social Security Death Index, 1935-2014 [database on-line]. Provo, UT, USA: Ancestry.com Operations Inc, 2011.

County Court Records Sterling County, Sterling City, Texas

INDEX

Adams, Mack, manager of Elsinore Land and Cattle, 240

Adams, Mildred Babb (daughter of Will Babb), 48; different version of the shooting, 63-65

Arc Light Drug Store (or Saloon), site of the Graham-Bates encounter, 217

Armstrong, Gaynor (Cowboy) the last word on Graham, 294

Allen, J. J. (Jack): early experience in law enforcement, 165; conflict with Graham Barnett, 165-169; pursuit of horse thieves, 128; relates story of arrest, 166

Anderson, P. D., hired Graham as bodyguard, 235, 238

Babb, Bessie Mae (wife of Will Babb), notified of shooting, 61; at trial, 86; later life, 87

Babb, John, 38; and shooting of Will Babb, 58-60

Babb, William (Will)
background and personal history, 50-52
buys Aaron Billings place, 50
conflict with Barnett over grazing rights, 50
death of: circumstances leading to, 57-59
final confrontation, 59-60

Babb, William Isaac (Bill Ike)
as head of family, 43
children, 46
conflict with Victor Tippett, 48

Babb, William Isaac (Bill Ike) (continued)
indictment in Sonora, Texas, 45
move to Langtry area, 46

Babb, William M. (Cherokee Bill) head of family and early life, 44-45

Baker, Weaver (lawyer), prosecuted Fowler, 273, 280; court of inquiry, 268

Ballad of Graham Barnett, 270-271

Bandit Wars, intervention by Governor Ferguson, 91; origin of raids, 90; reaction from Texas, 90-91

Barfield, John (Sheriff), 227 involved in bank robbery shooting, 227-229; not indicted in conspiracy, 229

Bargasar, Tom, witness to threats against Fowler, 261

Barker, Dudley (Sheriff)
background as Texas Ranger and sheriff, 68
arrest of Will Ike Babb, 69-70
Downie Estate and other work, 211-212
hired Graham, 233
at Graham's funeral, 269

Barnett, Annie Laura Conger (wife)
borrows money from Levi Smith, 189-190
courtship, 82-83
family, 82
early married life, 83

Barnett, Annie Laura Conger (wife) (*continued*)
  impact of life in Upton County, 158-159
  later life, 285-287
  life on Buttrill Ranch, 121-128
  reaction to Graham's death, 269
  role at the ranch, 128-129
  moved to Sterling City, 172
  moved to California, 284
  parent attitudes toward Graham, 82
  physical appearance, 82
Barnett, Frank (father), leaves family, 17
Barnett, Chicora (mother), 14-18; role on ranch, 35
Barnett, Dewitt, Talmadge (Boog)
  birth, 14
  buys stock in Mexico, 72-73
  early cowboying, 22-26
  escorts Buck Billings to Mexico, 71
  final days, 287
  hunting with Graham, 19-20
  investigated by legislature, 117
  life with Joe Graham, 27-52
  relates horse theft and incursion into Mexico, 52-54
  makes deal on mule for Graham, 57-58
  provides information on Graham, 241, 270, 273, 274
Barnett, Harry, pawnbroker in El Paso, 238; scheme to acquire Thompson, 238-239
Barnett, Joseph Graham
  appearance in 1911, 37
  appearance in 1920, 128

Barnett, Joseph Graham (*continued*)
  arrests bootleggers and prostitutes in Upton County, 160-161
  attitude toward rustlers, 79-80
  attempt to re-join the Rangers, 1918, 124-126
  arrest of Ed Caulder, 136-139
  assisted Bob Sumrall with arrest, 164-165
  becomes enforcer for Joe Graham, 54-56
  birth, 14
  body guarding, 205-207
  borrowed money to feed family, 144
  bought part of Fisher and McDowell Cattle Company, 35
  buys ranch in Big Bend, 126
  bootlegging, 142-143, 242
  City Marshall in Presidio, 234-237
  comment to Annie about trip to Rankin, 254
  conflict with Babbs, 55-56
  confrontation with Harry Odneal, 174-175
  confrontation with Rangers, 133-135
  controversy over coat, 267-268
  courtship and marriage, 82-83
  death of, 267-269
  drinking and gambling, 36-37, 232
  dual personality, 161-162
  early cowboying, 23-25
  early experiences, 18-23
  Elsinore Land and Cattle Company, 240
  end of Ranger career, 117-119

Barnett, Joseph Graham (*continued*)
  explosive nature, 232-233
  fired from Big Lake Oil, 169-171
  false imprisonment trial,
    178-179
  funeral of, 269
  health problems, 232, 233
  hunting guide, 247
  interaction with family, 37-38
  indictment for false
    imprisonment, 175
  involvement with Spannell
    murder case, 112-117
  investigates the Kaw Boiler
    Works hold up, 168-169
  joins Texas Rangers (Company
    B), 98
  license inspector, 210-211
  method of carrying pistol, 40-41
  met with Joel Starnes in Rankin,
    256-257
  money problems, 232
  moved with family to work for
    Joe Graham, 26-43
  move to Buttrill Ranch, 121
  plan to kill Carroll Bates,
    216-217
  plans to develop a ranch in Big
    Bend, 248-249;
  plan to secure money from
    friends to fund ranch, 250
  plan to extort money from Bill
    Fowler, 250-252
  pledge not to drink or gamble,
    144
  pursuit of horse thieves into
    Mexico, 52-54
  raiding bootleggers and
    gamblers, 208-209
  reputation as an outlaw, 245

Barnett, Joseph Graham (*continued*)
  requests recommendation from
    Brian Montague for a job,
    144
  scout for outlaws in Chisos
    Mountains, 103-111
  fixing the Upton County
    election, 239-240
  shoot out with bootlegger at
    night, 159
  shoots and kills Will Babb, 57-60
  shooting of "Noisy" Watson,
    181-187
  special officer in Rankin and for
    Texon Oil, 143-177
  stock detective, 128
  special Ranger commission, 233
  strong arm tactics used in Upton
    County, 155-157
  testifies at trial for bank
    robbery, 229
  trial for Babb murder, 68-71
  World War I service, 124
  undercover work in Big Lake,
    172
  Thompson Sub-Machine gun,
    234-239
Barnett Legend
  ballad written about, 270-271
  growth of after Watson trial,
    205-207
  impact of on Graham Barnett,
    206-207
  fear of assassination, 253
  killing of Will Babb, 57-60
  origin of, 23-35
  Carroll Bates non-fight, 217-219
  legend fading, 231-232
  testimony about Graham,
    278-279

Barnett Legend (*continued*)
    Thompson Sub machine Gun,
      234-239, 257
    questions surrounding the
      shooting, 276-277
Barnett, Francis Marion (sister,
    Frankie, born 1892), 17
Barnett, Anna Lee (sister, Polly,
    born 1894), 17
Bates, Carroll (Texas Ranger)
    and bootlegging, 162, 220-223
    confrontation with Graham at
      the Arc Light, 217-219
    early career, 162
    moves to San Angelo and
      becomes police chief, 168,
      214-215
    partnership with Curley Shields,
      215
    problem with Graham Barnett,
      215-216
Barnett, Sidney (sister, born 1896),
    17
Belcher, C.C. (prosecutor), 68
Beard, A. G.
    joins Rangers, 99
    body guard for Gladys Johnson,
      111-112
    law enforcement career, 99
    scout in Chisos Mountains,
      103-111
Bender Hotel (McCamey), 260
Bergasser, Tom, testimony at trial,
    278
Best, Texas, oil field town, 144;
    development of, 153-154;
    reputation, 154
Blair, Bud (sheriff), 255
Big Lake, Texas, Santa Rita oil field
    near, 144; rodeo and roping in,
    179-180

Billings, Buck
    accusations against, 63
    hired Graham to work cattle, 57
    witness to shooting, 57-60
    disappeared in Mexico, 71
    testimony, 69
    cattle buying in Mexico, 72-73
    testimony and trial, 83, 85
Billings, Beulah, comments on the
    Babb killing, 62; view of Barnett
    acquittal, 86
Billings, Ike, Langtry City
    Constable, 61; arrest of Graham
    Barnett and transport to Del
    Rio, 61-62
Bishop, Leo (Texas Ranger), 155
Blann, Roger, witness at Watson
    shooting, 181-187
Brooks, J. O.
    appearance and reputation, 180
    conflict with Graham, 181
    description of social club/rec
      hall, 181-182
    owner of social club in Big Lake,
      163
    suspected bootlegger, 163
    connected with Noisy Watson,
      163
Brown, Jim (porter) at Brooks's
    recreation hall, 181; observed
    fight, 182-183, 186; testimony,
    197
Brown, R.P. stories about Graham
    Barnett, 20
Burke, Bill, (Boiler Maker Bill) fight
    with Graham, 160-161
Buttrill Ranch, characteristics
    of, 121-122; purchase by Joe
    Graham, 121
Carranza, Venustiano, president
    of Mexico, 93; connection to

Carranza, Venustiano, president of Mexico (*continued*), ; connection to border raids, 93-94

Carroll, Ellison, arrests Graham after shooting, 186; early life and history as a world champion roper, 180; met with Graham Barnett, 258-259; special officer in Big Lake, 180; testimony at Fowler trial, 277

Caulder, Ed, background, 136-137; relationship with the Sutton-Montague law firm, 136; suspected of murder of Bill Harris, 138; near lynching by Graham Barnett, 137-138

Christy, J. D. (sheriff) transported Graham to San Angelo after Watson shooting, 187 comment concerning undercover operation, 200

Ciudad Acuna (Las Vacas) Coahuila, 29

Colt Military Model 1902, 41

Conger, W. T., wedding gift to Annie Laura, 82

Conger, Joe (brother-in-law), lived in Rankin, 252; spent time with Graham Barnett, 269

Coots, George, cowboy, 39; experience with pistol, 39-40; suggestions for gunfighting, 40

Cornell, James (lawyer), prosecutor in Babb trial, 68; intervenes between Graham and Carroll Bates, 217-219; opinion that Graham had become a hired killer, 246

Davis, Vernon (Sheriff) alleges Graham bought off sheriffs, 252 arrested Graham four times, 139-142 early experiences with Graham, 20, 50, 69, 232 explosive nature of Graham Barnett, 232-233 impact of Will Babb shooting on Graham, 64 bootlegging, 161 comment on Graham's drinking, 140, 141, 171 guns, 182 speed with gun, 142 opinion of Carroll Bates, 216 opinion of Watson shooting, 196 Dead Horse Mountains, 71

Davidson, Ed, at funeral, 269

Denson, Cliff, witness to Watson shooting, 181-187

Dodds, W. H., 31; as witness to shooting, 59

Dodds Store, 56

Dripping Springs, horse camp in Big Bend, 245, 254

Elsinore Land and Cattle Company, 240

Eagles Nest (original site for Langtry), 30

Fairbanks, Albert, arrested by Graham, 164; lawsuit against Graham, 165

Files, Captain John (great-great-grandfather), 13

Ferguson, Governor Jim, plan to address bandit raids, 94; Rangers funding problems, 94

Files, David Sidney (great-grandfather), 13

Fowler, Clara (wife of Bill Fowler),
  meets Graham Barnett, 258
Fowler, William (Bill) (Sheriff), 3
  acquires Thompson from
    Graham, 239
  acquittal in murder case, 281
  alleges misconduct in election
    for sheriff, 230
  city marshal in McCamey, 227
  court of inquiry after Barnett
    shooting, 268
  early contacts with Graham
    Barnett, 161
  early life and career, 209
  fight with Barnett in Fort
    Stockton, 240-242
  final confrontation with Barnett,
    266-268
  later life, 283-284
  met with Graham Barnett,
    259-260
  successful run for sheriff of
    Upton County, 239-240
  special Ranger commission, 234
  threatened by Graham Barnett,
    242
  unsuccessful run for sheriff, 230
  promised Barnett position as
    deputy, 240
  testimony at murder trial, 279
Fox, Captain J. Monroe (Captain,
  Company B), past law
  enforcement experience, 97;
  problems supervising Rangers
  in Ysleta, 97-98
Franks, Albert, trustee and cook at
  jail, 260-263
French, Roy, arrested by Graham,
  164; lawsuit against Graham,
  165

Frontier mentality (philosophy),
  3-11
Fuller, Nathan, joins Rangers, 99;
  law enforcement career, 99; as
  railroad detective, 99; scout in
  Chisos Mountains, 103-111
Gambling: history of and attitudes
  toward, 151
Gerding, C.C., witness to threats,
  260
Gerrard, Tom (lawyer), 273
Gillis, Walter (lawyer), 68
Graham, Jeff, xii, 17, 19-20; opinion
  of Graham and Boog, 27-28;
  interaction between Grahams
  and Barnetts, 36
Graham, Joe M. (uncle), 3
  as risk-taker, 28
  as surrogate father, 23-40
  announces Graham's death, 269
  at Babb trial, 83-86
  buys Model T, 48
  drives out of Val Verde County,
    67-68
  drought, 127-128
  early life, 18-19
  move to Langtry, 28-29
  moved stock, 83
  owner of 33 Ranch, 47
  payments and profit sharing
    with Barnetts, 35
  requests Graham's guns, 282
  sells property in Langtry area,
    67-68
Graham, Joe S. (Texas A&M
  University), 270
Graham, Otto, 2
Grattis, E. A., witness to threats
  against Fowler, 260; testimony
  at trial, 278

Hayes, Sam, (Sheriff) opinion of Graham, 139; transported Graham to Fort Davis, 195

Hat Ranch (Crockett County), 19, 26

Hamer, Frank (Texas Ranger), endorsed Special Ranger commission for Graham, 233; investigation of bank robberies, 227-229; subpoenaed for Babb trial, 68; testifies in bank robbery-murder conspiracy, 229-230

Henderson, Tom, visit to Graham Barnett, 135-136

Hess, Anton (Tony), xii
accompanied Graham on last trip, 254-268
early life, 225-226
money-making schemes, 226
confidant of Graham Barnett, 240
observes Graham Barnett drinking, 249
later life, 284
plan to elect Fowler as sheriff, 227, 239-240
Fowler refuses to put Graham in sheriff's office, 240
plan to develop ranch, 227, 247-249
plan to extort money from Fowler, 250-252
no mention of machine gun, 257
witness to shooting, 266-268
witness at Fowler trial, 274-276

Hickcox, Charles N., comment on Graham and drinking, 139; on firing of Graham by Levi Smith, 171

Hill County Texas, 13

Hillsboro, Texas, 18

Henson, Davis, banker, 250

Hollis, John (Texas Ranger), 133-135

House, Reid, worked with Graham Barnett, 56; witness to Babb shooting, 59-61

Ingram, French, witness to Babb shooting, 61

Karnes, C. B., witness to Watson shooting, 181-187

Key Hotel (Rankin), 263

La ley de fuga (law of flight), 54

Lammey, J. W. arrested by Graham 164; lawsuit, 165

Lane, John (step grandfather), 14; family moved to Sterling City, 20

Lane, Omar, 20

Langtry, Texas, 29-31

Leach, T. M. "Stormy," employed Graham Barnett on ranch, 78-79

License Inspectors, 210-211

McCravey, W. R., witness to Watson shooting, 181-187

McLaughlin, Roy, arrested by Graham, 164; lawsuit against Graham, 165

McKay, Raymond, promoter and filling station operator, 240; fight with Graham Barnett, 240; testimony at Fowler trial, 278

Martin, Prosser, comments on Watson shooting, 193; confrontation with Graham Barnett, 193; problems with alleged witness to Watson shooting, 194

Martin, Vann (Ripp), 306, 347

Malone, Johnny, 166

Mexican Revolution, origins, 33-35;

Mexican Revolution, origins
(*continued*), ; cause of refugees
in Texas, 90-91
Miller, Arch, (Texas Ranger),
133-135
Montague, Brian, xii, 27
as collector of guns and stories,
130
asked to prosecute Graham, 188
asked to represent both sides at
the Fowler trial, 273-274
advises Graham on Ranger
confrontation, 133-135
on Bates and Barnett
bootlegging in San Angelo,
215
early life and career, 130-131
last meeting with Graham,
252-253
observes two sides of Graham
Barnett, 139
observations on the Fowler trial,
282
opinion of Joe Graham, 130
physical appearance, 130
loaned money to Graham, 144
opinion of the Babb family,
43-44
opinion on Barnett-Watson
trial, 201
recommended Graham for
special officer and deputy
job, 144
trades for Colt Single Action,
139
Montague, Joe
appointed district attorney, 172
chosen to prosecute Graham,
188
conflict with Harry Odneal and
Judge W. A. Wright, 173

Montague, Joe (*continued*)
conducted raids on bootleggers,
173
disruption in court room, 281
friendship with Barnett, 171
intervention by Barnett to end
threats, 174-175
judge at Fowler trial, 274
move to Fort Stockton, 171
observations on Fowler trial, 282
prosecuted Graham for shooting
of Watson, 196-201
threats against, 173
view of Watson case as "open
and shut," 187
Mosley, Jack (neighbor), 245
Neill, R. T. (attorney), 177
Northcutt, Beab, (justice of the
peace), 268, 276
Odneal, Harry (Texas Ranger)
deputy in Fort Stockton, 162
special investigator, 168
conflict with Joe Montague,
172-174
confrontation with Graham
Barnett, 174-175
Oil Industry, as instrument of
change, 152-153; history of in
West Texas, 152; impact on local
people, 152-153
Patterson, H. W. "Pat," on
reputation of Barnett after
killing of Babb, 64-65
Plan of San Diego, development,
93; goals, 92-93
Prohibition (Volstead Act),
attitudes toward, 149-150
Ranching Industry, effects
of economy and drought,
1918-1920, 127-128

Ramos, Basilio, charged with theft of several states, 93; connection to Plan of San Diego, 93

Rankin, L. M. (Sheriff), hired Graham, 143-144, 166-167, 335

Rankin, Texas, xii, 255-256, 264, 294

Ransom, Captain Harry, appointed by governor, 91; total war approach, 91

Rattle Snake Springs, 28

Rathbone, W. (rancher), 33

Riggs, Walter, possible witness to shooting, 78-79

Risner, W. D. justice of the peace in Big Lake, 187; witness to meeting between Graham and Fowler, 259

Roberson, H. L. (Hod), experience and reputation, 74-78; encounter with Federal Guerillas, 79

Robinson, Joe (Doc), witness to threats, 263; testimony, 276

Robertson, Forest, at funeral, 269

Rosillos Ranch, Graham Barnett managed, 245

San Angelo, Texas, 213-214; criminal activity in, 214-215

Santa Rita Oil Field, 144

Savage .32 Pistol, 41

Senter, Fred (Chief of Police McCamey), 260; testimony at trial, 278

Shannon, Clarence (Deputy Sheriff), confrontation with Graham Barnett, 230; involved in bank robbery shooting, 227

Sheriff, office of
attitudes toward law breaking, 14
role in the society, 145-146
concept of discretion, 145

Sheriff, office of (*continued*)
conduct of deputies, 146
impact of outside law enforcement on, 147-148

Sheffield, Bascom, drove Graham back to Fort Stockton, 219

Shields, Gerome (Rome), 214

Shields, J. A. (Curley), bootlegger in San Angelo, 214-215

Shivley, Romeo, 255; disappearance of, 270

Sims, Orland, ix; related story of juror, 196; view of Graham, 201

Smith, Levi (General Manager of Big Lake Oil), Christmas gifts, 158; developed Texon, 153

Smuggling, 150-151

Sonora, Texas, 45, 272, 274

Southern Pacific Railway, 30

Special Officers, role of, 154-157

Starnes, Joel, (Assistant County Clerk Upton County), 256-257; Graham's attitude, 258; reports to Fowler, 263-264; fear of Graham, 278; opinion about Graham's intentions, 279

Sterling City, Texas, 20-21, 25-26, 69, 81-87, 121, 140, 171, 179, 190-192, 215, 232, 270, 283-286

Stevenson, Bascom (lawyer), 273

Stull, John, death of, 44

Spannell, Harry (murderer), arrested in Marfa and moved to El Paso, 103; killed wife and Army major, 103; details of the murder case, 112-117

Sumrall, Bob (Texas Ranger), arrested men at county fair, 164-165; trial for false imprisonment, 175-176; found guilty and appealed, 179

Sutton County, 45, 51, 234, 274

Sutton, Claude (Judge), 137
 bail hearing, 189
 charge to jury, 200
 threats to Montague, 179
 heard Watson murder case, 195
 charge to the jury in Watson
  trial, 201
 requested special Ranger
  commission for Graham, 234

Sutton, John, attends trial, 195;
 life and career, 129, 130-131,
 137; comment on Carroll Bates
 and Graham Barnett, 211, 216,
 230, 233; partnership with
 Brian Montague, 130; physical
 appearance, 130

T.O. Ranch, (Riverside Ranch),
 background 74-76; Hod
 Roberson as manager, 76-78;
 Graham Barnett on, 76-78

Taylor, Creed, at funeral, 269

Texas Bankers Association, dead
 bank robbers reward, 227

Texas Rangers
 attempts at reform, 95-96
 changes brought about by
  reaction to border raids,
  91-93
 evolution from the Frontier
  Battalion, 94-95
 problems between Rangers,
  civilians, and minorities,
  95-96, 97-98
 training, 99-102
 warrantless searches, 100
 reputation of Rangers on border,
  101
 Company B: shooting incidents
  1916-1917, 102

Texas Rangers (continued)
 reforms and budget cuts after
  World War I, 122-125

Texon, Texas, oil field town,
 143-144, 153, 156, 159, 165, 168,
 170, 171, 174, 178, 195, 209, 259;
 development of, 153

Thompson Sub-machine gun, 1,
 235-239, 257, 267, 284, 295, 299

Thurmond, George (lawyer), 68

Tippett, Victor, conflict with Bill
 Ike Babb, 48; grazing sheep
 on free range, 48; witness to
 shooting of Will Babb, 57-60;
 notified Babb family of the
 shooting of Will Babb, 62

Tippett, Homer, eloped with Will
 Ike Babb's daughter, 48; grazing
 sheep, 49

Townsend, E.E. (Sheriff), hires
 Graham as deputy, 136;
 investigates murder of Ed
 Harris, 136-137; arrests Det
 Walker, 246; at funeral for
 Graham, 269

Vanderbilt, E. F., attorney for
 Graham in false imprisonment
 trial, 177; planned self-defense
 plea for Watson shooting,
 191-192

Val Verde County, 29

Vice in Texas, relationship of crime
 to law enforcement, 148-149;
 types of crimes, 148

Villalba, Francisco, feud with Det
 Walker, 246

Walker, Det, feud with Villalba
 family, 246; hired Graham as
 bodyguard, 24

Watson, Kirtley (Noisy)
 arrested for bootlegging, 163

Watson, Kirtley (Noisy) (*continued*)
character of as a factor in trial,
201
teamster and trucker, 163
fought with Graham Barnett,
163
confrontation and shooting of,
181-187
Watson murder trial: aspects of a
celebrity trial, 190-201; plans
for suspended sentence, 191;
requests for continuance, 191;
Prosser Martin inconsistencies,
193-194; witnesses disappearing,
194
Wade Ranch (Wade Place) Barnett
home in Big Bend, 128, 243;
family joins Graham in summer,
243
Walton, R. B. (witness to Watson
shooting), 184-185

Weatherby, James xi, 13; view of
Graham's drinking, 139; stated
father took Graham to Juno to
keep him out of sight, 190
Weatherby, Sim, friend of Graham,
190; handled Graham when he
was drunk, 190-191; smuggled
Graham to Sterling City after
trial, 216
Williams, John, arrested by
Graham, 164; joins lawsuit
against Graham, 165
Woodward, C. C. (witness at
Watson shooting), 181-187
Woodward, Walter (lawyer), 273
Yoacham, Jack (witness at Fowler
trial), 274
Yoacham Filling Station, 264-266
Ysleta, Texas, 97-98